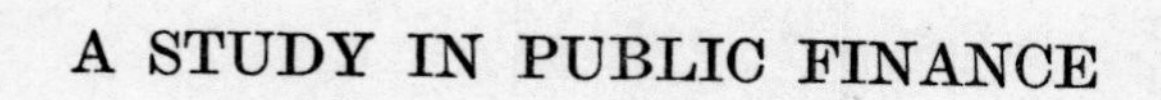

A STUDY IN PUBLIC FINANCE

A STUDY IN PUBLIC FINANCE

BY

A. C. PIGOU, M.A.

SOMETIME PROFESSOR OF POLITICAL ECONOMY IN THE UNIVERSITY OF CAMBRIDGE

AUTHOR OF

"THE ECONOMICS OF WELFARE", "EMPLOYMENT AND EQUILIBRIUM", ETC.

THIRD (REVISED) EDITION

LONDON

MACMILLAN & CO LTD

NEW YORK · ST MARTIN'S PRESS

1962

First Edition 1928
Second Edition 1929
Third Edition 1947
Reprinted 1949, 1951, 1952, 1956, 1960, 1962

MACMILLAN AND COMPANY LIMITED
London Bombay Calcutta Madras Melbourne

THE MACMILLAN COMPANY OF CANADA LIMITED
Toronto

ST MARTIN'S PRESS INC
New York

PRINTED IN GREAT BRITAIN

PREFACE

In 1921 I published a book entitled *The Political Economy of War*, containing several chapters on War Finance. In 1928 and 1929, when the first and second editions of the present work were in preparation, *The Political Economy of War* was out of print and it, therefore, seemed appropriate to include the substance of those chapters here. At the outbreak of the present war a revised version of *The Political Economy of War* was called for and those discussions had, of course, to go into it. For this reason I am not including them in the present new edition of *Public Finance*, and there is not, I think, now any important overlap between the two books.

The chapters on the Aftermath of Finance by Bank Credits and on War Debt and a Special Levy, which are out of date, are also omitted. The very thorough study, *The Taxation of War Wealth*, by Professor and Mrs. Hicks and Dr. Rostas, has removed any reason there might otherwise have been for re-writing the latter of these chapters.

Portions of Part I are rearranged and modified. In Part II on Tax Revenue three new Chapters (XIX-XXI), based on an article contributed to the *Economic Journal* of December 1932, have been added, while substantial alterations and, I hope, improvements have been made in some other chapters, particularly Chapters IX and (the present) XXII. The brief Part III on Public Finance in relation to unemployment policy is new. Professor D. H. Robertson has very kindly read through the typescript of it, though he has, of course, no responsibility for what is said.

A. C. P.

King's College,
Cambridge, *March* 1946

CONTENTS

PART I

GENERAL RELATIONS

CHAPTER I

CHAPTER II

CHAPTER III

PART I

GENERAL RELATIONS

CHAPTER I

PRELIMINARY

§ 1. In every developed society there is some form of government organisation, which may or may not represent the members of the society collectively, but certainly has coercive authority over them individually. As a rule the government organisation is broken up into a central government with large powers and a number of local government authorities with limited powers. The governing authority, whether central or local, is endowed with functions and duties, the detailed nature of which varies in different places. These duties involve the expenditure and, consequently, require also the raising of revenue.

§ 2. In modern conditions these processes are operated almost exclusively through the medium of money. It is true that on occasions governments make a levy of resources, of which they have need, in kind. Thus, in most European countries, even in peace-time, the services of soldiers are obtained by conscription ; and it has happened that civilian labour (*e.g.* in Bulgaria) has been called up in the same way. In war-time commandeering is apt to be extended over a much wider range. Buildings, motor-cars, horses, stocks of food and so on may be forcibly taken over. During the later years of the 1914–18 war the British Government commandeered the whole of the wool crop and the whole of the wheat crop of the country. During the recent world war women were conscripted for national service as well as men. Resort to methods of this kind is not, however, really alternative to the use of money. Conscripted persons are paid money wages and the owners of commandeered goods usually receive money compensation. What happens is not an abandonment of the money instrument, but a supplementing of it by compulsion on the public to sell services or goods, and authoritative fixing of the price at which sales are to be made. Thus we may lay it down, as a general rule for modern countries, that the spending and the raising of resources by government authorities are manifested in the form of spending and raising money.

§ 3. To this rule there is one exception that should be noted. A government may decide to take over and nationalise some large going concern — the Port of London, the railway system, the coal-mining industry or the liquor trade. In such a case it is certain not to raise the purchase price through taxes and very unlikely to raise it through the issue of a public loan. It will pay the sellers, not in money, but in interest-bearing government script. In so far as they retain this script the sellers will in effect, though not in form, have loaned the purchase price of their concern to the government; in so far as they sell the script on the market, the buyers of it will have done this. In neither case will the government itself actually disburse money; it will disburse new securities instead.

§ 4. Though, apart from special cases of this kind, money is practically always the medium of public finance, it is not the thing in which it really deals. The money is merely a ticket embodying command over services and goods. It is these, not the money that represents them, which constitute the real object of all transactions. This is, of course, a truism. But it is a truism the detailed implications of which are complex. Apart from the special cases referred to in the last paragraph and apart from creations of new money, every completed act of public finance is alike in form. £100 million are obtained by the government from the public and are paid over to certain other persons. This money is purchasing power. When it is taken away, those persons from whom it is taken are constrained to give up other things (including perhaps some leisure) which they would have had if it had not been taken away. The government then pays out the £100 million. It is evident that there are a great number of different ways in which the providers of taxes or fees or loans can modify their purchases and activities in order to furnish the £100 million: and a great number of different ways in which the £100 million can be paid out and in which the output of different sorts of goods and services can accordingly be effected. Thus important divergences of substance underlie the similarities in money form.

CHAPTER II

PRINCIPLES OF COMPENSATION

§ 1. In the second section of the preceding chapter it was shown that, though, when a government authority assumes possession of a thing or service, it usually makes in return a payment of money, this circumstance is not incompatible with commandeering, in the sense of compulsion upon owners to sell at a price not fixed by them. It is, indeed, only rarely that there is need for this. The quantity of any particular sort of thing or service that a government requires is as a rule fairly small compared with the producing power of the country in respect of that sort of thing or service ; and, therefore, if there is no great urgency, its demand can be satisfied at a price which does not yield any abnormal profit to anybody. There would be no point, for instance, in a government's commandeering the motor lorries or the clerical labour that it needs in the ordinary course, because it could not well pay less for the commandeered things than the market price, and, for the market price, it could get them without commandeering. There are, however, two cases to which these considerations do not apply.

§ 2. First, a government may decide to take over certain *existing pieces of property* the reproduction of which would be, if not impossible, at all events extremely wasteful, either because it wishes henceforward to operate these itself or because expropriation of the existing owners is essential to the successful conduct of some large scheme. Thus it wishes to nationalise, either permanently or temporarily, the railway system or the telephones or public-houses and, to this end, needs to buy out, or to obtain a lease from, existing owners of these things. Here it is confronted with a seller possessing monopoly power, and, unless it can override him by law, may be forced to pay a sum that will yield him a much larger income than he has been deriving, or has hoped to derive, from his property, so that he, in effect, levies a ransom on the public. Again, a government, in order to facilitate the building of a railway or the establishment of small holdings or some other social end, has need of certain *particular pieces* of land. Once more it is confronted by monopoly, and, unless it can exercise legal compulsion, is liable either to have a socially useful enterprise estopped or to be mulcted of outrageous sums. In such conditions compulsory purchase at an officially fixed price is the obvious and only solution. Closely similar considerations arise if a government decides to nationalise permanently or temporarily *all* property rights in coal mines or land rents or mining royalties. Since the government needs *all* of them, it is not in a position to bargain in the market, and some of the sellers, unless there is compulsion, may, therefore, be expected to stand out successfully, just as a monopolist might do, for an unreasonable price.

§ 3. Secondly, a government may require suddenly very large quantities of articles which are normally reproducible, but the production of which takes a considerable time, so that it wishes to draw on already existing stocks. Sudden and very large government demands of this kind greatly exceeding present capacity for new output are only likely to occur in time of war. Horses, motor-cars, stocks of certain sorts of food or particular classes of foreign securities may be needed in the largest procurable quantities all at once. To offer the market price or even something a good deal better would not call out *at once* offers to sell from *all* even from those persons who might be expected to make offers eventually; and some owners would not sell at all for any reasonable price. In essence there is not very much difference between this situation and that discussed in the preceding section. Once more potential sellers of what the government needs are in an exceptionally strong position, and could, in the absence of compulsion, extort terms and cause delay highly injurious to the public interest.

§ 4. We have then, in the various conditions contemplated above, to consider on what principles the amount, if any, of the purchase price, or compensation money, paid for things and services purchased compulsorily may properly be determined. On this matter there are large differences of opinion, and several distinctions will need to be drawn. One general observation should, however, be made first. There is a widespread tendency to describe failure to compensate for the withdrawal of particular property rights in terms, such as robbery, which imply that something *illegal* is being done. But property rights are the child of law, which is itself the creation of the public political authority. It is evident, therefore, that, except where there is an overriding written constitution, there can be no question of *illegality*, whatever a sovereign public authority may choose to do in respect of property rights hitherto enjoyed by its citizens. A statute passed in due form by the British Parliament taking away all property rights, or some particular property right, from all red-haired men, or from some particular red-haired man, might be objectionable, but could not possibly be illegal. The use of such a term as robbery, therefore, when applied to acts of sovereign public authorities, is inappropriate. That term signifies the taking away by force or fraud of something to which the robbed person has a legal right. When a public authority acts in due form it never does this : it withdraws a right which it has itself created ; and, from the point of view of legality, nobody can have any ground of complaint. The expropriation by a private person of something to which another private person has a legal right and the withdrawal by the public authority of that legal right are acts of entirely different kinds. Any use of words that tends to confuse them should be avoided.

§ 5. Fundamental to the problem of compensation is the principle of equity. This principle in its barest form asserts that *similar persons should be treated similarly*—by the public powers as by anybody else. Sidgwick held that knowledge of it is given in direct intuition. This view implies that, if there is a given aggregate of private good — not of good things — available for distribution among two or more exactly similar men, a further element of public good is created when this private good is divided among them equally. Now, it is held by certain ethical philosophers that the only elements of good are states of consciousness. If this is so, equity, which is a relation between states of consciousness, clearly cannot be an element of good, or, apart from its effects, have any ethical value. The issue thus raised is an important one. For our present purpose, however, it is not necessary to enlarge upon it. For, even if Sidgwick's view that equity is itself a good be rejected, there are available other considerations adequate to establish the principle of equity in its economic applications. First, if £1000 has to be taken from two people of equal wealth and similar temperament, the law of diminishing utility shows that less hurt will be caused by taking it in equal parts from each of them than by taking it in any other proportion. Secondly, if it is taken in any other proportion, a sense of being unfairly treated will be created in the person who pays the larger amount; and this is in itself an evil. Thirdly, unequal treatment of different people, where no good cause can be shown for it, breeds a sense of insecurity all round; for everyone feels that he may be the next victim. This discourages people from working and saving to obtain possession of durable things, and so indirectly strikes a blow at the accumulation of capital much heavier than would be struck by the collection of an equal sum of money on some intelligible non-arbitrary plan. It will be generally agreed that these considerations taken together establish the principle of equity, for the purpose of the present inquiry, on a firm basis.

§ 6. Unfortunately, however, the principle in its barest form, as sketched above, cannot be applied to practice, because in real life no two persons ever are exactly similar. Hence the principle must be expanded, so that it declares: "different persons should be treated similarly unless they are dissimilar in some *relevant* respect". In the abstract nobody is likely to quarrel with this. But the importation of relevance, none the less, raises difficult issues: for we have to decide what dissimilarities are, and what are not, relevant. In the last resort this can only be done by direct judgement applied to the detailed circumstances of particular cases. But the task of direct judgement can be made easier by a preliminary survey of a more general kind. To this end it is convenient to distinguish between the commandeering of a few individual items within a class of similar things and the commandeering of the whole of a class of things — under which latter head will be included the commandeering of a single thing if it is the sole member of a class. I shall consider first the commandeering of particular items within a class, and shall begin with commandeering which takes place at a time when general conditions are stable.

§ 7. In stable conditions the notion of membership of a class presents no serious difficulty. It may, no doubt, be pointed out, for example, that there are a number of different types of motor-car; and it may be asked whether a particular car is to be regarded as a member of the class "cars in general" or of the class "cars of its own type". But, since general conditions are supposed to be stable, so that the relations between the owners of different types of car are constant, it does not matter whether this question is answered in the one way or in the other; and there is no need to cavil at any classification with which common sense and general usage present us. Without, therefore, pressing this matter further, we may proceed to illustrate the sort of commandeering that has now to be studied. Examples are afforded by the expropriation of particular pieces of land which happen to lie on the road of a proposed railway, or which are specially fitted for small holdings (whether they are taken over completely by the public authority or are subjected to compulsory leasing); or of particular horses or stores of hay, or of particular buildings that happen to be suitable for billeting troops. The principle of equity clearly requires that the owners of those particular items should not be hit harder by government action than similar owners of other similar items. They should be paid such amount of compensation as is required to prevent this.

§ 8. It may perhaps be suggested that this way of looking at the matter is too simple, and that true equity requires us to take into account the wealth and family estate and, perhaps, the age of the several persons affected. This, however, is not so. These things are, indeed, highly relevant to the amount of taxation that the several owners should be made to bear. They are also relevant when what is contemplated is a compassionate allowance to deal, of grace, with hard cases to which the principle of compensation is held to be inapplicable. But they are not relevant to the question whether, in fact, that principle is applicable, whether, for instance, compensation should be paid for the commandeering of certain people's motor-cars or land. It would be "unfair" to pay such compensation to married men but not to bachelors, or to poor men but not to rich men; for, as we must presume, differences in these respects have already been taken into account in the assessment of general taxation. To regulate compensation payments in the light of them would be to count the same thing twice over — to punish a man a second time for one offence. In like manner, when we have to do with the expropriation of particular items of property within a general class, considerations connected with the character of that class as a whole are not relevant. If it is held that the class is one on which special burdens ought to be assessed, this should be done by taxes affecting the whole class, not by arbitrary blows at particular items within the class. When particular items are expropriated, it may, indeed, be held, on grounds connected with the nature of the class, *e.g.* liquor licences, that no compensation should be paid out of *general* funds. This is, however, in no way incompatible with the payment of compensation to the owners of the particular items; for this can be done out of funds raised from the owners of all the items in the class affected, including the owners of the expropriated items.

§ 9. There still, however, remains a difficulty. The principle of compensation — for the kind of case contemplated so far — is established, but the amount of compensation that will put a man whose field or motor-car has been commandeered in the same position as one whose similar field or car has not been commandeered is not yet defined. If the thing commandeered were seven sacks of No. 1 red winter wheat, the payment required would obviously be the market value of this number of sacks; for that payment would enable the expropriated proprietor to replace exactly what had been taken from him, so that, except for his share in the taxes needed to provide the compensation money, in respect of which he stands on the same footing as everybody else, he would not be affected at all. But a particular piece of land or a house, or possibly even a motor-car, may have a special value to the owner greater than its market value. To part with it may involve a loss to him of what *he* values at £10,000, though the market only values it at £2000. In these circumstances what value ought to be taken as the basis of compensation? The principle of equity suggests: the monetary representative of the special value of the property right to its owner. For, if the market value is taken, he is really hit harder than other people because he happens to own this particular piece of property. This conclusion must, however, be qualified before it can be applied to practice. When the particular piece of land or house has a special value to its owner because, when associated with him, it carries goodwill — *e.g.* a shop in the place where the owner is known — this goodwill can without great difficulty be valued and reckoned in the compensation money. But when it has a special value due to sentiment and so on, no such objective valuation is feasible, and account cannot, therefore, be taken of it. We must content ourselves with such rough justice as is afforded by the payment of something, say 10 per cent, in excess of market value as compensation for disturbance.

§ 10. When general conditions are no longer supposed to be stable, more awkward issues have to be faced. Let us suppose that we are dealing with something to which the difficulty discussed in the preceding section does not apply, so that in normal times the market value, a perfectly definite thing, would be proper compensation to an expropriated person. In normal times this market value would correspond roughly to cost of production, and the payment of it would, therefore, maintain the expropriated person's position at once as against other persons with similar bits of property, as against other persons with dissimilar bits of property, and as against himself previously. In times of disturbance, however, this is no longer true. There are three things for equity to choose from: equivalence to other owners of similar property, equivalence to other owners of dissimilar property, and equivalence to the expropriated person's self in the past. An illustration of the difficulty is afforded by the action of the British Government in commandeering some ships, but not all ships, from private owners during the 1914–18 war. The owners of non-commandeered ships were making enormous profits, as compared both with themselves previously and with the owners of most other sorts of property. Would it have been proper to compensate the owners of commandeered ships upon terms that enabled them also to do this? The government in fact paid pre-war Blue Book rates, which were designed to put the commandeered owners into their pre-war position, but which, in fact, since no allowance was made for the fall in the purchasing power of money, put them in a rather worse position than this. To the plain man — apart from the failure to take account of the change in the value of money — this arrangement would probably commend itself

as fair. Why, he would ask, should a particular ship-owner be compensated for not being allowed to get an unexpected and unworked-for windfall, merely because another ship-owner has had that piece of fortune? If, however, instead of a boom, there had been a great slump in the value of ships, the plain man would not have thought it reasonable for the government to pay for commandeered ships at pre-war rates, which then would have stood much above the rates currently received by other ship-owners. The plain man's thought seems in fact to be: arrange your compensation terms in times of disturbance in such wise that the owner of commandeered goods is prevented from enjoying windfalls that he would have got apart from the commandeering, but is not saved from suffering anti-windfalls which he would have suffered apart from it. This view lacks logical symmetry; but it is, none the less, the one which most students — the present writer among them — will be inclined to adopt.

§ 11. There remains for consideration one peculiar case also associated with times of disturbance. Suppose that an insurrection breaks out in a particular part of the country, and that, in order to deal with it, the government has to commandeer motor-cars and houses there; or, more strongly still, that it has to do this because the district has been invaded by a foreign enemy. This commandeering is merely an incident in a larger whole; and the question whether compensation should be paid for it must turn on whether or not compensation is being paid for the damage that the insurrection or invasion has inflicted on other property owners in the district. If the government is unable or unwilling to make good that damage, it would be unreasonable to expect it to make good the damage caused by its own commandeering. The same class of consideration applies to commandeering, *e.g.* of surviving houses, required to meet the distress caused by an earthquake in a town where most of the houses have been destroyed. Apart from these special cases we may lay it down that, for the expropriation of particular items within a general class, compensation should always be paid in such wise that the owners of the expropriated items are not subject to damage through expropriation from which the owners of other items in the class are exempted.

§ 12. We now turn to the problem of compensation in its

application to classes of items instead of to particular items within a class. This problem in one aspect is equivalent to the problem whether, or in what circumstances, the compensation to be paid to an expropriated individual inside a class should be provided by taxes spread over the whole community rather than by taxes confined to members of that class. Under the former plan the class, some of whose members have been expropriated, is compensated for the damage thus done to the class as a whole : under the latter plan it is not. An instance of the former plan is afforded by the 1914–18 arrangements for the commandeering of ships that have just been discussed : an instance of the latter by Balfour's Liquor Licences Act, in which a compensation fund for expropriated licensees was obtained by a levy on licensees who were not expropriated. We have to consider in what conditions the one, and in what the other, of these rival policies is called for.

§ 13. First, in so far as the act of expropriation of particular items within a class either itself causes, or is bound up with a policy that causes, an increase in the value of other items within that class, there is a clear case for levying the compensation money from the owners of those benefited items. Thus, if the State commandeers a piece of land to enable a tramway to be built to the outskirts of a town, with the result that the surrounding land is made more valuable, the owners of this surrounding land ought plainly to pay. The same argument holds if neighbouring licensed houses are benefited by the compulsory closing-down of rivals. This is the principle of betterment. In the abstract its equity is beyond debate ; though in some circumstances we may be debarred from applying it in practice by inability to determine with any exactitude *who* have enjoyed the betterment and *how much* betterment they have enjoyed.

§ 14. Secondly, when a class, some among whose members are being expropriated, is enjoying as a whole exceptional good fortune, there is much to be said for taking the compensation money from the class, even though its good fortune is not due to the expropriation policy. Thus it would seem that the money to pay for commandeered ships during 1914–18 might well have been obtained by a special levy on ships that were not commandeered. An arrangement of this kind, if it could be worked in practice, would almost certainly commend itself to the plain man's sense of equity ; the commandeering of some ships at pre-war rates being regarded as a partial set-off to a windfall to ship-owners as a class, which, even so, would have remained very large.

§ 15. Apart from these special cases there is not in principle any reason for throwing the burden of compensating particular expropriated members within a class upon the members of that class, except when it can be shown that the class as a whole ought to be subjected to a burden larger than it is at the time bearing under the existing system of national and local taxes. This issue is most conveniently discussed in connection with the expropriation of classes as wholes — whether classes of one member or of many members ; — with the expropriation, for example, of private railway companies, telephone companies, royalty owners, land-owners in general, slave-owners, owners of feudal rights, owners of rotten boroughs, and so on. We need not consider again here the difficulties that arise in periods of disturbance or those connected with the fact that certain things have a special value to their present owners. Apart from these difficulties we have to ask : Ought compensation to be paid in any or all of the above cases in such wise as to put the owners of the expropriated class of things in the same position as other owners, or are there relevant peculiarities about the expropriated class that warrant a refusal to pay full compensation, or even to pay any compensation at all ?

§ 16. Certain property rights have a defective legal status. Thus the holders of licences for the sale of alcoholic drinks have no legal title to a renewal of their licences, so that to refuse to renew is not to remove any legal right. On this ground it may be argued that here there is no case for compensation. Against this I answer that *reasonable expectation* is a more fundamental thing than legal right. Thus, if from the beginning of the world every licence had always been renewed, the absence of legal right would clearly be a mere technicality. It does not, of course, follow that the compensation paid should be equal to what it would have been if there had been a legal right ; for generally, if there is only custom, the reasonable expectation of renewal will be *pro tanto* less. This, however, will be reflected in the market value of the "right"; and, apart from the considerations to be set out in § 18, compensation up to this value will, therefore, be proper.

§ 17. Arguments for refusing compensation are sometimes based on the manner in which certain rights have originated. Such arguments have been used in regard to proposals for the nationalisation of land and of mineral royalties. These things, it is said, ought never to have become subject to private property rights. Whereas other property is the fruit of man's labour and waiting, mineral deposits and land are a free gift. *Therefore*, so runs the argument, they may properly be expropriated without compensation; they should be put back into the same legal position that unfound gold and silver in this country hold. Now, the question whether land and mineral deposits ought to have been allowed to come into private hands is much disputed. But in fact they have so come, and their present owners have bought or inherited them in exactly the same way as other people have bought or inherited other sorts of property. To expropriate them without compensation and not so to expropriate other sorts would involve grave inequities. For suppose that, shortly before the new law was passed, one man A had exchanged with another man B £100,000 worth of land against £100,000 worth of War Loan. Expropriation of land alone would leave A untouched, while taking the whole fortune of B; though, until a moment previously, A was, and B was not, an owner of land. The unfairness is gross and palpable. The argument for compensation implied in it derives its main force, of course, from the circumstance that land is a marketable commodity. The mere fact that a man has enjoyed an unwarranted right in the past is not, if his right is inherently indefensible, a good ground for continuing it. But things that have lasted a long time are in actual life frequently transferred by sale. *In general*, therefore, I conclude that the origin of particular classes of property rights in the distant past is not relevant to the compensation issue.

§ 18. A more difficult question arises when it is claimed that the activities associated with certain classes of property rights, although hitherto permitted by law, are anti-social. This plea is not applicable when the State is proposing to buy up particular property rights in order to exercise them itself on the lines on which they are being exercised now; for this intention on the part of the State *implies* that the activities in question are not, in its view, anti-social.[1] Examples are the State purchase of privately owned railways and telephones. When, however, the State seeks, not to transfer to itself, but to destroy, a particular class of property right, the presumption is that it does consider the activities associated with that right anti-social. In cases of this kind advocates of compensation lay stress upon the fact that the activity attacked has hitherto been legal: that people have invested money in it, trusting to the law; and that it is unfair to hit them in a way that other investors in equally legal enterprises have escaped. Opponents of compensation, on the other hand, point out that, if compensation is paid for the abolition of this class of right, an expectation of compensation, should anti-social but legal activities afterwards be prohibited, is created. Therefore people are encouraged to make anti-social investments more than they would be either if it were certain that there would be no compensation or if compensation were doubtful. It may, perhaps, be thought that, with compensation at *market value*, this effect would not follow, because market value will allow for any uncertainty there may be. But this is a fallacy. For to announce beforehand that, should expropriation take place, market value compensation will be paid would remove the uncertainty, and, consequently, cause market value to be on the basis of certainty, not uncertainty. Though, therefore, in an isolated case, when expropriation is decided on for a thing in respect of which the prospects of compensation have been uncertain, market value may be the *immediately* appropriate basis, it may not be the *ultimately* appropriate basis, when account is taken of the effect on the market values of other anti-social concerns. It should be noted that this argument does not apply with full force to the expropriation of rights, which either (1) have become anti-social

[1] It is sometimes suggested that, when the State takes over something in order to operate it itself, the case for compensation is strengthened by the fact that there will be a fund out of which compensation can be paid. There does not seem, however, to be very much in this, except from the relatively unimportant point of view of budget technique; for, presumably, if the State decides to abolish a thing rather than run it, this means that it expects a larger final "fund" of welfare to be furnished in that way.

for the moment through an external act, *e.g.* the right to publish meteorological reports, rendered anti-social by the outbreak of war, or (2) have only recently come to be thought anti-social by a significant number of people. In actual practice the conflict between the opposing arguments has worked out variously on different occasions. Thus, in the United Kingdom, when the abolition of rotten boroughs was first mooted, it was proposed to pay compensation: when it was carried out in 1932, no compensation was paid. When slavery was abolished in the West Indies, twenty millions were voted by the Imperial Parliament in compensation to the owners; but, when slavery was abolished in the United States after the Civil War, there was no compensation. In like manner no compensation was paid in the United States to persons engaged in the liquor industry when the country "went dry". An intermediate arrangement would be to alleviate somewhat the burden on expropriated persons, but not to put them in as good a position as they would have been in if not expropriated. To this end the government might make a compensation payment reckoned to yield some fraction, say one-half, of the income which the expropriated persons would have had otherwise. Alternatively it might give substantial notice of expropriation. With the rate of interest standing at 5 per cent a notice of fifteen years is roughly equivalent to halving the burden.

§ 19. In the whole of the foregoing discussion we have been concerned with the compensation to be paid when government authorities take forcible possession of pieces of property hitherto in private ownership. But provision is also often made for compensating loss and damage arising in other ways. Thus there are regulations in this and other countries for workmen's compensation in respect of accidents; and during the second world war provision was made for compensating owners of property who had suffered damage from air attack. The problems associated with these sorts of compensation are outside the scope of this book. It is evident, however, that many of the considerations set out above are relevant. The question, for example, whether compensation for bomb damage should be provided out of general revenue or out of a special levy on house-owners is closely analogous to that distinguished in § 12.

§ 20. A word may be added about another type of compensation, where the need for compensation — if need is admitted — arises out of government action, though not out of government commandeering. After a currency catastrophe, such as took place in Germany and elsewhere in the aftermath of the 1914–18 war, after the rush of a galloping inflation has been stopped, the country affected is bound to find itself with its original monetary unit worth a great deal less in terms of commodities than it used to be worth before the catastrophe. It is open to the government to retain this old monetary unit, as the French did with the franc; to create a new monetary unit with the same name as the old, decreeing that all the old money in existence shall be convertible into it at much less than face value, as the Germans did with the mark; or to create a new monetary unit with a new name, such as the Austrian schilling, exchangeable against such-and-such a quantity of the old money. In all these cases holders of physical units of the old money are in the same position. But, *prima facie*, contracts that were entered into before or during the process of the catastrophe are affected differently under the German from what they are under the French or Austrian arrangements. For, whereas under those two arrangements all values embodied in contracts are reduced in real terms in the measure in which the value of the old money is reduced, under the German plan, unless a law is passed to the contrary, these values will only be reduced to the extent, if any, to which the real value of the new money unit is less than the value which the old unit of the same name had when the contract was made. In fact, however, in the most important case of this type of devaluation, namely that of Germany, the old marks and contracts in terms of these marks were put by the law on a common footing in relation to the new stabilised mark. Thus, in all the post-war devaluations, whatever their detailed form, contracts in terms of the old money have in fact been devalued along with the money itself.

§ 21. Now, where one person has lent money to another at a time when the real value of that money was high, but receives interest or a return of the principal of his debt in a depreciated form, he has clearly suffered a grievance. Exactly how serious his grievance is cannot be determined unless we know how far the monetary collapse was anticipated, and so discounted in the terms of his contract. But, with catastrophic collapses, it is certain that, before the crisis began and in its earlier stages, the event will scarcely have been discounted at all, and even in the later stages it is very unlikely to have been discounted adequately. Therefore, it would seem proper, if the practical difficulties could be overcome, to provide for a writing-up of contract debts adjusted in some degree to what the value of money was at the time when they were made. It has to be remembered, however, that, after a currency crisis, there will be outstanding, not only a large mass of contracts between individuals, but also a large mass of debts owing to individuals by the government. Since it may well be that the government would be greatly embarrassed in balancing its budget if these debts — or the interest upon them — were to be paid in money of the value that ruled when they were incurred, it is not to be expected that any law for revising contracts will write-up debts from the government in a ratio equivalent to the depreciation which has occurred: and it is difficult to defend a policy which would write-up debts due from private persons much further than debts due from the government. Hence a partial writing-up of debts to mitigate, and not to remove, the injury suffered by creditors is the utmost that anybody can hope for. In Germany after the mark had been stabilised a law was passed granting to creditors for private debts, *e.g.* bond-holders of companies, who bought their bonds prior to July 1, 1920, a valorisation up to 25 per cent of the original gold value at the time of purchase, and to holders, who bought after July 1, 1920, and who, therefore, it is presumed, bought speculatively, up to 15 per cent. In view of the difficult position of the State finances, creditors of the government who bought government bonds prior to July 1920 were granted a valorisation of only 12½ per cent, new bond-holders apparently being granted nothing. Moreover, certain classes of contracts, which had already been settled in depreciated money, were reopened in the interest of the creditors. Thus, mortgages which had been paid off between January 1, 1922, and the introduction of the new law, were revised and revalued up to 25 per cent of their original gold value. Plainly, however, a policy of this kind cannot be carried far. To reopen on a large scale transactions which have been closed, and on the strength of whose closing new contracts, it may well be, have been made, would throw industry into chaos, and could not be attempted with any prospect of success.[1]

[1] Cf. Hargreaves, *Restoring Currency Standards*, pp. 97-8.

CHAPTER III

NON-TRANSFER AND TRANSFER EXPENDITURES BY GOVERNMENT AUTHORITIES

§ 1. EXPENDITURES of money by government authorities may be conveniently separated under two heads, expenditures that purchase current services of productive resources for the use of those authorities and expenditures which consist in payments made either gratuitously or in purchase of existing property rights to private persons. The former group include expenditures on the maintenance and building-up of the army, navy, air force, civil service, educational service, judiciary, Post Office, municipal tramway service and so on. The latter include expenditures on the payment of interest on government debt, pensions, sickness benefit (as paid in money) and unemployment benefit ; also subsidies on the production of particular kinds of commodities, sugar, milk, meat or houses ; also payments made in the redemption of government debt, *i.e.* the repurchase of government securities. The former type of expenditure I called, in my first edition, exhaustive, in the second, real expenditure. It is perhaps better to call them, simply, non-transfer expenditures. The latter type must in that case be called transfer expenditures.[1] The fundamental distinction between them is that non-transfer expenditures do, but transfer expenditures do not, give rise to what economists are accustomed to call social (money) income, *i.e.* the money value of current output. For precision of thought, however, certain loose ends need to be gathered up.

§ 2. Thus, while no difficulty arises when government authorities purchase the services of labour, capital or land directly, there is an awkwardness when they purchase commodities that these factors of production are engaged in making. For the commodities which they buy are already

[1] In her book, *The Finance of British Governments, 1920–36*, Mrs. Hicks uses the term transfer expenditure in a sense quite different from mine, namely one intended to indicate the extent to which real income is redistributed through government action in favour of the poorer classes. Thus for her the main part of the cost of the educational services is transfer expenditure, but that of the service of the National Debt is not.

existing pieces of property and it *might* happen that the dealers from whom the government authorities bought did not replace them. In this case the government expenditures would not be engaged in purchasing current services of productive resources and so would not generate any social income. This sort of difficulty is, however, not quantitatively important. In general the purchase by government authorities of ordinary commodities — income goods — may be taken to entail and in effect to constitute an equivalent purchase of the services of productive resources that make them.

§ 3. A more serious awkwardness arises out of the fact that some transfer expenditures made by government authorities consist in payments to foreigners ; directly in respect of interest and sinking fund on foreign-held debt and indirectly in respect of the subsidies on such part of subsidised home-produced goods as happens to be exported. This external transfer expenditure differs in important respects from internal transfer expenditure. Its implications are more like those of non-transfer expenditure. Were government authorities to make these foreign payments in kind by purchasing home produce and sending it abroad to meet foreign interest claims, the government payment would actually *be* non-transfer expenditure. There is, therefore, much to be said for calling these government expenditures non-transfer, or at all events for classing them along with internal non-transfer and not with internal transfer expenditures. I shall regard them as a special type of non-transfer expenditure.

§ 4. In the light of the above, it is natural to suppose, subject to minor qualifications, that non-transfer expenditures, since they entail a using-up of productive resources in government service, impose a corresponding restriction on the use of productive resources by the citizens of the country in private service, but that transfer expenditures, while altering the distribution of resources for private service, leave the sum-total of them intact. This, however, is not correct.

§ 5. It would not be correct even if the collection and expenditure of moneys by government authorities had no effect on the extent to which productive resources find employment. The reason is that a substantial part of non-transfer government expenditure is devoted to providing services such as protection against robbery and personal violence, educational facilities, public health services and so on, which, if government authorities did not provide them, private persons would be forced in a measure to provide for themselves. Thus, if non-transfer government expenditures were reduced, by no means all the productive resources set free from government service would be available to provide services to private persons *additional* to those they actually enjoy. A substantial part would be absorbed in replacing through private enterprise services which public enterprise had hitherto provided. Thus there is an important offset to the gain which the public in their capacity as individual consumers would derive from reductions in non-transfer government expenditure. Indeed it may well be that they would achieve *no* net gain, but, on the contrary, suffer a net loss.

§ 6. But this is not all. It is not the fact that operations of public finance have no effect on the extent to which productive resources find employment. On the contrary, on occasions certain sorts of government expenditure call into activity productive power which, apart from them, would have lain dormant. When this happens an expansion in the use of productive resources for government service does not imply an equivalent contraction in their use for private service. It is thus important to understand how far it is likely to happen.

§ 7. A completed act of public finance in respect of any sum of money includes both the raising and the spending of that sum. *Prima facie*, when revenue is collected by direct taxes and devoted by government authorities either to non-transfer (income-generating) expenditure or to transfer expenditure, aggregate money income is the same as it would have been if this two-sided act of public finance had not taken place. For the money passed to government in these taxes and subsequently expended, whether by it or by the transferees, would, it might seem, have been expended with an equal effect in generating income had it been left to " fructify in the pockets of the people " ; and, *prima facie*, the same thing is true when the money required by government authorities is raised by loans from the public. But the scale of money income depends in part on the income-velocity of money, or, if we will, on the proportion of the total stock of money that people choose to hold in active, as distinguished from savings, deposits ; and this in turn depends in part on a balancing at the margin of the convenience and so on obtained by holding resources liquid and the advantage of engaging them in income-generating activities. If, therefore, the community as a whole, including the government, becomes keener on any sort of investment or consumption, the income velocity of money and so, other things being equal, aggregate money income will be higher than it would be otherwise. Large government non-transfer expenditures in time of war, for example, are likely for this reason to be associated with an enlarged income velocity of money and, therefore, even though the stock of money is not different from what it was in peace-time, with larger money income. Even straight transfers of purchasing power via the government from ordinary taxpayers to pensioners or holders of government stock may affect the income velocity of money, and so aggregate money income, because the proportions in which different categories of persons hold their money in active and in savings deposits may be different. Thus, even when there are no complications connected with the creation of credits by banks, there is no warrant for holding that the operations of public finance are irrelevant to the size of aggregate money income. On the contrary, they are always likely to be relevant in some degree.

§ 8. For our present purpose, however, the significant thing is not money income but real income — output as a whole resulting from the activity of productive resources. It does not follow that, because public finance is in all circumstances liable to affect aggregate money income, it is also in all circumstances liable to affect this. Broadly, we may lay it down that, when arrangements in public finance affect the scale of aggregate money income, rates of money wages *tend* so to adjust themselves that the employment percentage for factors of production is not affected. But these adjustments are only made slowly. It follows that, if any given set of public finance arrangements is kept in being continuously, industrial activity will be much the same as it would be with any other set of arrangements. But, if the arrangements vary from time to time, the level of industrial activity on occasions, and even on the average, may be considerably affected. It should be noted that a system of unemployment insurance, since more money is paid out in benefits in bad times than in good, embodies *varying* public finance arrangements even though the system itself is established once for all.

§ 9. The parts played by non-transfer and transfer expenditures in finance by government authorities vary, of course, from place to place and from time to time. For the central government of Great Britain it appears that, the Post Office and grants to local authorities being left out of account, the service of the internal debt and pensions, which constitute a dominant part, though not the whole, of transfer expenditure, amounted in 1913 to some 21 per cent and in 1923 to some 53 per cent of aggregate government expenditure.[1] According to the (1943) White Paper transfer payments accounted for 41 per cent of the expenditure of the central government in 1938 and for 11 per cent in 1943 ; while for all government expenditures, including those from extra-budgetary funds and by local authorities, the corresponding percentages were 36 and 10.[2]

[1] Cf. *Report for Commission on the National Debt*, p. 235.

[2] Cmd. 6520, p. 25.

CHAPTER IV

THE FINANCE OF BUSINESS UNDERTAKINGS OPERATED BY PUBLIC AUTHORITIES

§ 1. It is not the purpose of this volume to enter upon controversial issues as to how far public authorities should undertake forms of activity which might be undertaken by private concerns in the ordinary way of business. It is well known that in some countries the railways are run by joint-stock companies ; in others they are operated by the government ; in yet others they are worked as semi-public concerns. Again, in the United Kingdom, it has often been urged that the coal mines and the service of supplying intoxicating drinks should be "nationalised", and various ingenious forms of public administration, designed to eliminate the dangers, on the one hand of political management and on the other of bureaucracy, have been advocated for them. Yet again, such "public utility services" as gas supply, water supply, tramways and electricity are sometimes in the hands of private companies and sometimes in those of local authorities : and the comparative advantages of the two arrangements are hotly debated. It is important that the right choice should be made between these rival arrangements, and it is evident that this choice must turn in the main on the questions (1) which of the two, in the existing economic and political conditions of the country we are studying, is likely to prove technically the more efficient, and (2) whether and how far it would be practicable under private enterprise to prevent the operators from making monopolistic exactions from the public.[1] These are not problems of Public Finance, as I understand that term. I do not propose, therefore, to discuss at all the question over what classes of enterprise it is desirable that public operation should be extended, but to proceed on the assumption that this is already determined. Our interest in the matter is thus limited to the question in what way the products of publicly operated enterprises should be paid for.

[1] Cf. *The Economics of Welfare*, Part ii, chap. xxii ; also *Capitalism versus Socialism*, *passim*.

§ 2. The enterprises with which we have here to do, since, *ex hypothesi*, they might be undertaken by private concerns in the ordinary way of business, are necessarily of a sort which it is *practicable* to finance by fees charged to those persons who make use of the goods or services supplied by them. They do not include undertakings such as the upkeep of the army, navy and civil services, but only undertakings which are specifically "beneficial" to particular individuals. Thus a nationalised Post Office, telegraph system, telephone system, railway system, road system, or educational system, and a municipalised tram, gas, water or milk supply belong to our subject-matter. For the services rendered by some of these enterprises, *e.g.* the Post Office, railways and gas supply, fees are invariably charged; for those rendered by others, *e.g.* roads and education, fees have sometimes been resorted to, but more frequently no charge is made, the expense being borne by the general body of taxpayers. The purpose of the present chapter is to inquire, given that public authorities have decided to perform certain functions which it is technically possible to finance by fees, in what conditions that method of finance is desirable.

§ 3. It is plainly in the general interest that the resources of the community should be so distributed among different services that the last unit devoted to any one of them yields the same satisfaction as the last devoted to any other. Aggregate resources being limited, this implies a certain restriction in the supply of every service, as against the amount of it which people would use if they were allowed to have at no cost as much as, at no cost, they desired. If no restriction is imposed, there is a social waste, the extent of which depends on the nature of people's demand for the service. If that demand is highly inelastic, in such wise that they would take much the same amount of the service if it were given away for nothing as they would do if a cost-price fee were attached to it, the waste will be small: if the demand is highly elastic, it will be large. Where the conditions are such that the waste resulting from gratis supply in unlimited quantities would be large, that method is ruled out of court. Where, however, the waste would be small, it needs further study.

§ 4. The most important services falling into this category are elementary education, medical attendance and water supply. Elementary education has an inelastic demand because people who want it want it badly and will purchase it whatever, within reasonable limits, it costs: whereas people who do not want it will not be induced to take it, except under compulsion, even if it is offered to them for nothing. Medical attendance has a highly inelastic demand because, when people are well, they do not want doctoring at any price, and, when they are ill, they want it very much. Water has a highly inelastic demand in ordinary conditions because it is, in any event, so cheap that to most people variations in its price do not seem to matter. Moreover, all these three things, education, medical attendance and water, are things that carry indirect benefits not obvious at first sight to the purchasers, so that, from a social point of view, it is desirable that they should have more of them than they would be likely to buy at cost price if left to their own devices. Thus, in regard to these services, a good part of any apparent waste that might come about in consequence of gratis supply in unlimited quantities would not be real waste. So strongly is this realised in the case of elementary education that in Great Britain the government, not content with gratis supply, has framed legislation to ensure compulsory use.

§ 5. Arguments about waste are plainly inapplicable when it is a question of substituting gratis supply in unlimited quantities, not for individual purchases at an aggregate price varying with the *actual* quantity of purchase, but for individual purchases at an aggregate price varying with an *estimated* quantity of purchase. Thus, when the water-rate which a man has to pay is based, not on his actual use of water as determined by meter, but on his assumed use as determined by the size of his house, the existence of the rate will make no difference to the amount of his consumption. In like manner, where people are accustomed to pay for the services of a doctor by subscriptions to a sick-club, the amount of which is independent of the extent to which they individually call in a doctor during a year, no difference would be made to the amount of doctoring they ask for if doctors' services were provided free at the public expense. Arrangements of this kind, it will be noticed, could not in practice exist unless the service in question were, in its own nature, one of fairly inelastic demand. Thus the fundamental condition that makes gratis supply in unlimited quantities feasible is always inelasticity of demand.

§ 6. When this condition is not satisfied, gratis supply in unlimited quantities is, as was said in § 3, *not* a feasible arrangement. But this does not necessarily rule out gratis supply altogether. Whether it does so in fact depends on whether the conditions are such that public authorities can so limit supply as to prevent a large waste of resources without creating for themselves other intractable problems. The most important service in connection with which conditions of this kind prevail is that of roads. Public authorities are free to decide of their own motion how many roads to make and in what state of repair to maintain them ; and there is not, in general, any danger of such overcrowding as to render necessary the forcible exclusion of any would-be users. The case of roads is, however, peculiar. As a rule we have to do, not with services furnished by a passive instrument in which very little prime cost is involved, but with consumable commodities or such services as the actual carriage of goods or passengers on a railway. Here to make no charge for the commodity or service and yet to restrict the supply of it below what people would wish to take at a nil price must lead to serious difficulties in distribution. The quantity demanded exceeding the quantity forthcoming, the sharing-out of what supplies there are will be determined by luck, physical force, the possession of private influence with the distributing agents, and so on. The only way in which public authorities can obviate this is by some system of rationing the available supplies among would-be consumers, such as was in fact employed for certain commodities during the two wars. Since it is administratively impossible to construct any such system otherwise than upon broad and simple lines, allowance cannot be made for detailed variations of circumstance as between particular individuals. Even in war-time, with commodities so simple as staple foods, the difficulties and anomalies were very great. It is certain that any attempt, in time of peace, to ration, say, railway travel would collapse in exasperation and ridicule. In all cases of this kind, if gratis supply without limitation of quantity is ruled out on grounds of waste, gratis supply in any form is ruled out.

§ 7. Considerations concerning waste thus enable us to say,

with regard to several classes of goods and services, that, if the government decides to provide them, it should finance their provision by fees. For certain goods and services not included in this class the same conclusion can be reached on other grounds. *Prima facie* it is fair that the users of ordinary services should pay for them in proportion to their use, and should not receive a subsidy at the expense of other people. No doubt, in some circumstances social welfare can be promoted by taxing relatively rich people for the benefit of relatively poor people, and, although it will not often be desirable for such transfers as are made to the poor at the expense of the rich to be distributed among them in proportion to their consumption of a particular commodity, this may be desirable sometimes. In that event the fee due from poor people should be partly or wholly remitted, the loss being made good out of the general revenue.[1] Elementary education is a service which, it is generally agreed, may properly be treated in this way. It is felt that, when, as in this country, government compels a man to accept that service at its hands, whether he wishes to or not, it would be unfair to ask him to pay for it. This, however, is a rare case. For most kinds of goods and services supplied specifically to individuals, even when gratis provision would be technically practicable, it is deemed fair to charge fees on an equal scale to all consumers.

§ 8. In certain conditions, however, the adoption of this system would cause great inconvenience and involve heavy expenses of collection. M. Colson argues forcibly that this consideration, though of comparatively small weight as regards the use of canals and rivers by large vessels, which usually make long voyages and can be visited at stopping-places at considerable distances apart, is of immense weight as regards roads. "Là, les transports sont fractionnés indéfiniment ; les piétons, les petits véhicules sont innombrables ; beaucoup de transports, presque tous dans les campagnes, sont effectués

[1] It is sometimes held that funds for the subsidy should be raised, not out of the general revenue, but by charging fees in excess of costs to richer classes of consumers — that, for example, cheap workmen's tram and rail tickets should be financed in this way. Unless, however, we have decided on general grounds that rich purchasers of these particular services ought to be taxed *for general purposes* through a tax assessed upon them, this contention is, I think, unsound : for there is no reason to single out, to bear the cost of the subsidy, those particular rich men who happen to ride frequently in trams or trains.

par les intéressés avec leurs propres moyens, sans qu'aucun contrat, aucune écriture les constate. Les trajets sont extrêmement courts, de sorte qu'il faudrait une armée d'employés, répartis de kilomètre en kilomètre sur un réseau immense, pour les relever tous — sans d'ailleurs qu'on puisse y suppléer par des abonnements, car l'utilisation des véhicules et la proportion représentée par les transports, dans le travail fourni par les chevaux de culture, sont trop inégales. La perception de péages sur les routes était encore possible, quand le roulage à grande distance représentait l'élément principal de leur fréquentation ; depuis que le développement des chemins de fer n'y a plus laissé subsister qu'un trafic local, cette perception entraînerait des frais et une gêne intolérables, si on voulait la généraliser ; elle n'est plus admissible qu'au passage des rares ouvrages d'art ayant entraîné des dépenses exceptionnelles, et c'est pourquoi, en fait, on y a renoncé partout ailleurs, dans tous les pays civilisés."[1] In short, a little "unfairness" as between individuals must in this matter be accepted in order to avoid a greater evil.

§ 9. As a result of this discussion it appears that, when public authorities provide commodities and services for the specific use of particular individuals, gratis supply to the users is but rarely desirable. The broad general rule should be to finance these public enterprises by charging fees to users of the commodities and services concerned proportioned to the amount of their use, and adequate in the aggregate to cover all costs. This conclusion, of course, leaves open the further question whether or not taxation should be levied *through* these commodities and services. If a particular commodity or service, which happens to be provided by a public authority, is adjudged a suitable object on which to assess a tax, all that is necessary is to embody the tax in the fee charged, thus raising the fee above what is required to cover normal costs of production by the amount of the tax to be imposed.

[1] *Cours d'économie politique*, vol. vi, pp. 52-3.

CHAPTER V

THE RANGE OF GOVERNMENT EXPENDITURE

§ 1. In so far as government departments engage in the manufacture of goods and services to be sold for fees so arranged as to cover cost of production, the amount of resources which will be devoted to these purposes is automatically determined by the public demand. The main part of a modern government's activity is not, however, of this class. The bulk of its non-transfer expenditure is devoted to services of a general sort — defence, civil administration and so on — which cannot practicably be sold against fees to individuals; while the whole of its transfer expenditure is outside the range of fees altogether. Hence there is no automatic machinery to determine how far expenditure shall be carried; and some other method has to be employed.

§ 2. At any given moment it is probable that large parts of current transfer expenditure will be regulated by practically irrevocable contracts. In Great Britain at the present time expenditure on the services of the debt, war pensions and old age pensions clearly belongs to this class. On the other hand, expenditure on subsidies to particular industries or particular classes of persons and expenditure on Poor Relief are optional, in the sense that the government is free, within fairly wide limits, to determine their amount by present policy. With the exception of government payments in interest and sinking fund on foreign-held debt, practically all non-transfer expenditure is optional in this sense, so far as legal considerations go: but, as regards a great deal of it, economies could not be carried very far except at the cost of breaking away from deeply rooted traditions. The optional parts of expenditure — the only parts which are practically subject to control — ought plainly to be regulated with some reference to the burden involved in raising funds to finance them. This aspect of Public Finance is an important one. But it is not a main theme of my present study, and can only be touched upon briefly.

§ 3. As regards the distribution, as distinct from the

aggregate cost, of optional government expenditure, it is clear that, just as an individual will get more satisfaction out of his income by maintaining a certain balance between different sorts of expenditure, so also will a community through its government. The principle of balance in both cases is provided by the postulate that resources should be so distributed among different uses that the marginal return of satisfaction is the same for all of them. Evidently this is true of the non-transfer expenditure of governments, so far as this is not already determined by past contracts. Among various forms of optional transfer expenditure the same principle evidently holds ; and — though here the matter is more difficult to envisage clearly — it also holds between optional non-transfer expenditure in general and optional transfer expenditure in general. Expenditure should be distributed between battleships and Poor Relief in such wise that the last shilling devoted to each of them yields the same return of satisfaction. We have here, so far as theory goes, a test by means of which the distribution of expenditure along different lines can be settled.[1]

§ 4. This method of approach suggests an analogous test for determining how large government expenditure in the aggregate ought to be. If a community were literally a unitary being, with the government as its brain, expenditure should be pushed in all directions up to the point at which the satisfaction obtained from the last shilling expended is equal to the satisfaction lost in respect of the last shilling called up on government service. This last, or "marginal" shilling is, of course, to be regarded as made up of parts contributed by all of the separate contributors to government funds in proportion to their respective contributions, not as the last shilling taken from the poorest contributor. So interpreted, the above conception, though, as will be shown in a moment, it is not adequate to the conditions of real life, nevertheless enables some useful, if fairly obvious, deductions to be drawn.

§ 5. First, it enables us to see that the *optimum* amount of government expenditure, whether for actual using-up or for transfer from relatively rich to relatively poor persons, is

[1] For a criticism of the view that the concept of sacrifice can properly be used in this way and for a reply cf. *post*, Part II, Chap. I, § 3.

likely to be larger, the greater — the numbers of the population being given — is the aggregate income of the community. For, other things being equal, the marginal sacrifice involved in raising n shillings (assumed to represent a given real value) from any group will be smaller, the larger is the number of shillings constituting the public income. Immediately after a war, in which capital equipment has been allowed to run down and the organisation of markets has become dislocated, real income will, in general, be diminished, and, with it, capacity to provide resources for government. Therefore, certain government expenditures, which it used to be worth while to undertake, a country may no longer be able to " afford ". Secondly, other things being equal, if and when new opportunities for expenditure by government that would yield large benefits or obviate large evils, are opened up, and no corresponding opportunities for expenditure by private persons are opened up at the same time,[1] the balance between the marginal benefit and the marginal damage of raising revenue will be struck at a higher point; *i.e.* more revenue ought to be raised. Thirdly, when aggregate income and population are given, if a large part of the income is concentrated in the hands of a few rich persons, it is possible to frame a tax-scheme that will raise a given revenue with less *immediate* marginal sacrifice than would be imposed under any scheme if the income was spread evenly over the whole community.[2] Lastly, other things, including income-distribution, being equal, the *immediate* marginal sacrifice involved in the raising of a given revenue will be smaller the more progressive is the revenue-raising scheme. Thus, subject to what will be said in Part II, Chapter IV on the relation between *immediate* sacrifice and *total* sacrifice, a government may properly engage

[1] The purpose of this qualification is to exclude such things as the invention of new uses for capital (*e.g.* in railway building). These do not necessarily give ground for raising more revenue, even though government is fully competent to build railways ; for private capitalists are also competent to do this.

[2] When we speak of the distribution of income as a relevant factor in this connection, we assume that the main part of an ordinary man's income (other than the part absorbed in taxation) is used for his own consumption and investment. Obviously, if all rich men were accustomed to give away income to such an extent that, after their gifts, everybody had equal amounts for consumption and saving, we should have a state of things equivalent for practical purposes to one in which all incomes are initially equal.

in larger expenditures (1) the less even is the distribution of income among its citizens and (2) the more progressive is the revenue-raising scheme that it decides to employ.

§ 6. The foundation of the foregoing analysis was the assumption, set out in § 4, that the community is a unitary being for which the government acts as brain. In fact, of course, this is not so. If battleships were goods that people need for individual personal use, that would not, indeed, matter. There could still be the same sort of balancing at the margin between clothes purchased individually and battleships purchased through the government as there is between clothes purchased individually and coal purchased through a co-operative buying agency. But battleships are a collective good, to be used in the general interest by the government. Consequently, any taxpayer's desire to contribute towards buying them is dependent, not only on his desire that the country shall possess them, but also on the number of them which are being made available by the contributions of other people. The government is not, therefore, simply an agent for carrying out on behalf of its citizens their several separate instructions ; it cannot simply balance at the margin each man's desire to buy battleships against his desire to buy clothes, in the way that an individual balances his desire for clothes against his desire for coal. As the agent of its citizens collectively, it must exercise coercion upon them individually, securing the funds it needs either by a contemporary tax or by a loan associated with a subsequent tax to provide for interest and sinking fund. Where, however, coercion intrudes there are introduced two new elements, of which the method of analysis so far described takes no account. The first of these is the cost of administration. This includes, not merely the costs of the government departments which have to collect and distribute the funds raised from the public, but also the costs thrown on the public themselves in the form of accountants' and solicitors' fees, together with the trouble to which taxpayers are individually put in filling up income tax forms and so on. The second element is less obvious but not less important. The raising of an additional £ of revenue necessitates increasing the rates at which taxation is imposed, either now or (if resort has been had to loans) subsequently. With some sorts of taxes this inflicts indirect damage on the taxpayers as a body over and above the loss they suffer in actual money payment. Where there is indirect damage, it ought to be added to the direct loss of satisfaction involved in the withdrawal of the marginal unit of resources by taxation, before this is balanced against the satisfaction yielded by the marginal expenditure. It follows that, in general, expenditure ought not to be carried so far as to make the real yield of the last unit of resources expended by the government equal to the real yield of the last unit left in the hands of the representative citizen. It follows, further, that the extent of the gap which ought to be allowed varies according to the methods available for raising extra funds; being greater where it is necessary to resort to methods that involve large indirect damage than where there is opportunity for comparatively harmless expedients.

CHAPTER VI

THE PLACE OF LOANS OTHER THAN WAR LOANS IN PUBLIC FINANCE

§ 1. In normal times the main part of a government's revenue is required to meet running expenses that occur more or less regularly year after year. There can be no question that in a well-ordered State all such expenditure, apart from that met by fees, will be provided for out of taxation, and not by borrowing. To meet it by borrowing, whether from foreign or domestic lenders, would involve an ever-growing government debt and a correspondingly ever-growing obligation of interest. In the end more would have to be spent in providing the interest every year than would have been required if the government had paid its way out of taxes from the beginning. The national credit would suffer heavy damage ; and ultimately the annual obligations of the government might come to exceed the maximum sum that it had the power to raise in tax revenue, even for the purpose of transfer expenditure.[1] This thesis is universally accepted. Nobody would suggest that government expenditure of a regular nature, such as expenditure on the army, navy and civil service, should normally be met otherwise than out of taxation. This does not mean, indeed, that this class of expenditure should never, in any circumstances whatever, be financed out of loans. Other things being equal, it is plainly desirable, since changes in taxation always involve disturbance, to keep the rates of taxation as nearly as possible constant from year to year. In so far then as running expenses fluctuate, it may be desirable, when practicable, to arrange a budget so that good and bad years make up for one another, a deficit in one balancing a surplus in another. It may also be desirable, where a part of these expenses consists in a sinking fund for

[1] Under the English system, in which interest on government debt is counted as income assessable to tax, it would never, of course, be possible for interest on internal debt actually to exceed the national income so conceived, though it might approach asymptotically towards it. But the interest might easily come to exceed the maximum sum that it was practicable for any government to raise by taxation.

debt, to use this as a buffer to keep annual taxation constant. By these devices the *rates of taxation* may be kept steady where the income of the people is steady, in the face of moderate fluctuations in the current expenses of government. The same line of thought suggests that, where the income of a country fluctuates, it may similarly be legitimate to meet *fixed* running expenses by a succession of budgets with surpluses and deficits that cancel. For, with different incomes, to maintain the same budget revenue would necessitate tax rates varying inversely with prosperity. From this point of view we should hesitate to condemn the government of a country, which had been subject to a sudden disaster, for meeting ordinary expenditure, even for several years on end, out of loans, while attempting to set its house in order. Moreover, as will be shown in Part III, in some circumstances a case may be made out for using budget deficits in bad times offset by surpluses in good times as a means of steadying and improving employment. But, subject to short-period adjustments, there is a very general agreement that ordinary running expenses should be met out of current taxes. Even short-period adjustments may be opposed on the ground that, if once that policy is admitted, governments will in practice incur deficits and raid sinking funds in bad times, but will neglect to budget for compensating surpluses in good times.

§ 2. Next, consider government expenditure devoted to producing capital equipment — a national electricity plant, municipal gas works or tramways and so on — the fruits of which will subsequently be sold to purchasers for fees. Here it is generally agreed that the required funds ought to be raised by loans. If this is done, violent and sudden changes in tax rates are avoided: the people who benefit from the service which the new capital equipment renders pay for it in proportion to their use; and, provided, of course, that the fees charged are sufficient to wipe out the principal of the loan during the lifetime of the capital equipment, no additional taxation has ever to be raised on account of it. Upon this matter, as upon that of the proper method of finance for normal recurrent expenditure, there is no room for controversy.

§ 3. Let us turn then to expenditures of a sort that have to be met only on special occasions, but are not "remunerative" in the sense that they yield fruits to be sold for fees. Here purely fiscal considerations suggest that such expenditures, *if financed by loans*, ought, in general, to be financed in such a way that the loans are paid off out of taxes before the need for further similar expenditures is likely to recur. For, if this is not done, there must result an ever-growing debt and, eventually, the need for ever-growing taxes to provide interest upon it, much as would happen if ordinary running expenses were financed out of loans. Further, at the time a loan is raised evidence should be given of ability and intention to provide adequately for the service of it by imposing new taxation sufficient to cover interest and a reasonable sinking fund.[1] Failing this, confidence in the financial stability of the State is liable to be damaged at the time, while later on, when the exceptional expenditure has been completed, the country will be confronted with an unlooked for and *prima facie* unwarranted increase of taxation; and this may well cause discontent. But, though it is clear that resort to loans ought not to be had in any fuller measure than these limits allow, it is not clear that resort ought to be had to them up to these limits.

§ 4. It is sometimes thought that whether and how far an enterprise or enterprises ought to be financed out of loans depends on whether and how far future generations will benefit

[1] The view that loans of the kind we have been considering should be paid off in a not over-long period is often given concrete form in the establishment of a sinking fund. This is not, of course, a necessary condition of repayment. There is nothing to prevent a government from paying off a loan to which no sinking fund is attached by buying it up in the market or, if provision is made for redemption at a fixed price, by redeeming it. Nor is the establishment of a sinking fund a guarantee that the principal of a loan will in fact be paid off as originally intended, even if the sinking fund is in no sense raided: for there is nothing to prevent a government from effecting new borrowings *pari passu* with paying off the old loan. None the less, the legal establishment of a sinking fund at the time loans are floated is of real effect in promoting repayment; for it is politically much more difficult for a government in difficulties to raid an established fund, or to fill it by borrowing, than it is for it simply to refrain from setting aside money, not specifically called for by a previous undertaking, for discharging debt. It may be added that, when a sinking fund is decided upon, it may take the form either of a fixed annual sum to be devoted towards providing interest and repayment of principal throughout the period of the loan, or of a fixed annual sum for repayment of principal *plus*, each year, the sum required in that year for interest. This latter plan involves a less violent change than the other in the year following the completion of repayment, and is also somewhat less likely to be abandoned in the later years of the loan. (Cf. Pierson, *Principles of Economics*, vol. ii, pp. 629 *et seq.*)

from it. This conception rests on the idea that the cost of anything paid for out of loans falls on future generations while costs met out of taxes are borne by the present generation. Though twenty-five years ago this idea could claim some respectable support, it is now everywhere acknowledged to be fallacious. It is true that loans *raised from foreigners* entail a burden represented in interest and sinking fund on future generations in the borrowing country. But interest and sinking fund on *internal* loans are merely transfers from one set of people in the country to another set, so that the two sets together — future generations as a whole — are not burdened at all. There are, indeed, certain minor qualifications that should be made to this general statement.[1] But in the broad it is true — and obvious. The choice between finance by taxes and finance by loans cannot be made on this basis. On either plan, except with foreign loans, it is the present generation that pays.

§ 5. The issue thus is not one of justice between generations, but rather of what is technically convenient and politically feasible. So understanding it, some authorities hold roundly that for enterprises that are not expected to yield a money return loans should not be resorted to at all. Thus Bastable once wrote: "Non-economic (*i.e.* non-remunerative) expenditure is primarily to be met out of income, and, unless it can be so dealt with, ought not to be incurred. National culture, education, the promotion of social progress are all most desirable; but their promotion is not so pressing an object as to need the use of borrowing by the public powers. It is, indeed, true that much of State expenditure may be regarded as indirectly productive, and as likely to add to the national income in the future. A loan for the purpose of extending education, or for improving the housing of the workers, though it does not directly provide the interest needed, may yet so increase the income of the community as to make the tax receipts greater, without any increase either in rates or in rigour of collection. Regarded in the abstract, such a proceeding seems defensible: the real objections to it arise from the difficulty of application. The results of expenditure of the kind are hard to trace or measure, and any statement respecting them must rest in a great degree

[1] Cf. my *Political Economy of War*, 2nd edition, chap. vii.

on conjecture. The cost of the loan is definite and precise, and it constitutes a real burden on the resources of the society. Prudence seems accordingly to suggest that borrowing should hardly ever be adopted except for strictly economic expenditure, and then only when the extension of the State domain is clearly advisable."[1] This strict rule points, I think, the right path in ordinary circumstances — subject to the very important exception, to be examined at length in Part III, that on occasions public works, if financed by loan but not if financed by taxes, may constitute a valuable means of combating unemployment. It is plain, however, that Bastable's rule cannot be extended to conditions in which non-remunerative government expenditures on a wholly abnormal scale have to be undertaken, as in combating the consequences of an earthquake or to meet an imminent threat of war. To collect what is required, and required at very short notice in these conditions, through the machinery of taxation is politically and administratively impracticable. The Chancellor of the Exchequer should, indeed, wield the weapon of taxation strenuously ; but that by itself will not suffice.

[1] Bastable, *Public Finance*, Book v, chap. v, pp. 621-2.

PART II

TAX REVENUE

CHAPTER I

PRINCIPLES OF TAXATION

§ 1. In this Part the quantity of government expenditure, both non-transfer and transfer, is taken as given. Such part of it as is met out of fees is ruled out of account, and the device of borrowing, whether from the public or from the banks, is ignored. Moreover, except in Chapter IX, we are concerned solely with the problem of *raising* revenue, not with the wider problem of *raising and spending* it. In this first preliminary chapter our task is to seek for fundamental principles of policy.

§ 2. Under any tax system the actual provision of the taxes, the expenditure of the proceeds being left out of account, involves a certain burden of sacrifice upon each taxpayer, and the burdens upon different taxpayers bear certain relations to one another. For a comparison between different tax systems yielding equal revenues from a given community there are thus suggested *prima facie* two criteria of merit: first, the size of the aggregate sacrifice imposed: secondly, the nature of the relations between the several items that make up this aggregate. It must, indeed, be admitted that no test which is centred in sacrifice, in the sense of loss of satisfaction, goes quite to the root of things. For, of equal satisfactions, one may embody more *good* than another: as between a greater and a less sacrifice of satisfaction, the greater may carry the smaller amount of evil. When this happens, it is, of course, the aggregate of good and evil, not the aggregate of satisfaction and dissatisfaction, to which a wise government will look. On this ground defence is sometimes made of special taxation upon the consumption of alcoholic drink. This consideration has not, however, a wide range of importance. In seeking to construct a standard for comparing the merits of different tax systems I shall ignore it, assume that the standard must be built somehow upon sacrifice and canvass only the part to be played in this standard by the amount of aggregate sacrifice and the manner in which this aggregate is distributed among the taxpayers.

§ 3. Here at the outset we are confronted with a fundamental difficulty. To speak of aggregate sacrifice or satisfaction and the distribution of these things implies that satisfactions are, at least in principle, capable of being summed. If they are not, neither least aggregate sacrifice nor equal sacrifice can possibly be used as principles of taxation. It has been argued that they cannot in fact be summed, sometimes on one, sometimes on another, of two grounds; first, that, as being states of mind, they are in their nature non-quantitative; secondly, that, whatever be the case with different mental states of the same person, every mind is eternally separate from every other, so that there is no way in which the mental states of different people can be compared or combined. It is necessary to consider both these contentions.

The first of them need not, I think, detain us long. It is too patently contrary to experience. We all know that we are happier — enjoying more satisfaction — at one time than at another and that some events inflict on us greater sacrifice than others. Whether we can properly claim to feel, say, "twice" as happy or suffer "twice" as large a sacrifice of satisfaction on some occasions as on others is more doubtful; but that is not required. Different satisfactions and sacrifices to the same person *are* quantitatively comparable.

The second contention is more persuasive. For certainly nobody can lay his mind alongside that of another person, and we cannot *disprove* the suggestion that, of two apparently similar persons in exactly equivalent situations, the satisfaction enjoyed by A is enormously greater than that enjoyed by B. Thus, while direct measurement is unattainable, indirect measurement by objective tests is unreliable. But, after all, we cannot *disprove* the suggestion that other people do not exist at all! In the ordinary affairs of life, while recognising the existence of individual idiosyncrasies, racial differences, differences due to habits and training and so on, we always assume that groups of *prima facie* similar men will be mentally affected by similar situations in much the same way; that they will get roughly equal enjoyment from a dish of ham and eggs and will suffer a roughly similar sacrifice from surrendering their seat in a railway carriage. We *expect* similar situations to produce similar mental effects, and it is only when they seem not to do so that in normal non-philosophic moods we think there is something to explain. If so much as this be granted, we are free, with proper caution, to use, as our fathers did, the classical concepts of aggregate sacrifice and the distribution of sacrifice.

§ 4. Some authorities hold that to make the aggregate sacrifice associated with the raising of revenue as small as possible is an ultimate principle: others that to make the sacrifice borne by all the several members of the community equal is an ultimate principle: others that both these principles are ultimate, so that, when they conflict, we are faced with a dilemma irreducible in theory, and in practice to be met only by rough compromise. The business of the present chapter is to investigate these views.

§ 5. Before that task is attacked, the meaning to be attached to our central concept must be made clear. By the sacrifice which a tax system imposes upon any individual I mean the difference between the net satisfaction he would have enjoyed had there been no tax system — it will be understood that benefits arising out of the government's expenditure of tax proceeds are here left out of account — and the net satisfaction which, under the aegis of this tax system, he does enjoy. Even under a system so constructed that the taxation of A has no effect whatever on the satisfaction enjoyed by B, this is not, in general, equivalent to the satisfaction which is, so to speak, carried to or away from him by the money he actually pays in taxation. The reason is that tax systems may cause taxpayers to work more or less hard, and so to have a larger or smaller income (apart from taxation), than they would otherwise have done: and that the effect of this upon their net satisfaction is not represented in the money paid over in taxation.[1] If we were concerned only with taxes assessed upon the consumption of particular commodities, the point I am making would be more obvious: for it is now a

[1] Thus suppose, for simplicity, that each unit of a given taxpayer's work yields £1. Let a be the number of units of work performed annually before taxation is imposed, $\phi(a)$ the aggregate satisfaction involved in the resulting consumption, and $F(a)$ the aggregate dissatisfaction involved in the work that provides it. Then the taxpayer's net satisfaction $= \phi(a) - F(a)$.

After the imposition of taxation suppose that this taxpayer pays in

familiar idea that the amount of consumers' surplus (expressed in terms of money) destroyed by taxation may differ widely from the amount of the taxation raised. But a moment's reflection shows that the point is valid over a wider range than this.

§ 6. In my view there can be no question that, subject to the qualifications set out in § 2, least aggregate sacrifice is an ultimate principle of taxation. The levying of taxes is a part of the functions of government. Apart from the possible effects of the action of one government upon the subjects of other governments, which, for the present, I ignore, there is general agreement that all of a government's activity should be regulated with a view to promoting, in the highest possible degree, the welfare of its citizens. This is the touchstone by which the whole of its legal system — and its tax laws are, of course, a part of its legal system — must be judged. The day in which the welfare of one category of citizens could plausibly be ranked above that of another is past. Nobody would venture to claim now that a smaller amount of welfare accruing, say, to a nobleman should be preferred to a larger amount that might be made to accrue to a peasant. So far as political theory is concerned, maximum aggregate welfare is everywhere accepted as the right goal of government; and when, as of course often happens, actual governments pursue a different goal, their practice may be more or less plausibly explained away, but is never openly defended. In the special field of taxation this general principle is identical with the principle of *least sacrifice*. Its validity appears to me to be given directly in intuition.

§ 7. The claim that *equal sacrifice* is an ultimate principle of taxation is more controversial. In Chapter II of Part I reference was made to Sidgwick's principle of equity — the principle, namely, that similar and similarly situated persons ought to be treated similarly. In Sidgwick's view this principle

taxes £k, does $(a+h)$ units of work and has a net income (after paying the tax) of $(a+h-k)$ £. Then his sacrifice, as I have defined it,

$$=\{\phi(a)-\mathrm{F}(a)\}-\{\phi(a+h-k)-\mathrm{F}(a+h)\}. \qquad (1)$$

The amount of satisfaction carried by the money he actually pays over in taxes

$$=\phi(a+h)-\phi(a+h-k). \qquad (2)$$

This expression is only equal to expression (1) in the special case in which $h=0$

is an ultimate one. If that be so, the proposition that equal sacrifices ought to be imposed upon similar and similarly situated persons must be an ultimate principle of taxation. I am not prepared to deny that this is so — that equality in this sense and in this degree is a good in itself. But equal sacrifice among similar and similarly situated persons is an entirely different thing from equal sacrifice among all persons. Is equal sacrifice in this wider sense an ultimate principle of taxation? Anyone who maintains that it is is faced with a serious difficulty. It is possible, no doubt, to wring from the principle of equity the proposition that taxation ought to inflict equal sacrifices upon everybody: but it is also possible to wring from it the proposition that the legal system as a whole, including laws of taxation, ought to be impartial between persons, in the sense of securing to all of them equal net satisfactions. On the basis of Sidgwick's intuition, to say nothing of the claims of equi-proportional sacrifice, there is at least as good a case for taxation that makes net satisfactions equal as for taxation that makes sacrifices equal. Indeed there is a better case. For people's economic well-being depends on the whole system of law, including the laws of property, contract and bequest, and not merely upon the law about taxes. To hold that the law about taxes ought to affect different people's satisfactions equally, while allowing that the rest of the legal system may properly affect them very unequally, seems not a little arbitrary. These considerations do not, it must be conceded, demonstrate anything. They should, however, shake seriously the confidence of anyone who is inclined to assert that a generalised principle of equal sacrifice in taxation is given in intuition. For my own part

I hold that intuition makes no deliverance on this matter, and that in fact equal sacrifice, otherwise than as between similar and similarly situated persons, is not an ultimate principle of taxation.

§ 8. If this be granted, we have one ultimate principle, namely, least sacrifice, whose claim is undisputed: and a second ultimate principle, equal sacrifice among similar and similarly situated persons, but not among others, whose authenticity is somewhat less secure. If the second of these principles is recognised as well as the first, there is, for analysis, a conflict of ideals. Both the "ultimate" principles must be brought before the tribunal of something more ultimate still, *i.e.* the principle of maximum good, and weights must be assigned to them so proportioned that good as a whole, including the good of equality, shall be made as large as possible. In practice, however, as will appear presently, tax arrangements that conform to the principle of least sacrifice always and necessarily conform also to the principle of equal sacrifice among similar and similarly situated persons. Hence, even if the principle of equal sacrifice between similar and similarly situated persons is a true ultimate principle, since it can be deduced from the principle of least sacrifice, it is not a *necessary* one. Though, therefore, for academic persons there may be a more complex esoteric doctrine, for politicians and men of affairs we may properly assert that least aggregate sacrifice is the one ultimate principle of taxation.

CHAPTER II

TAX SCHEMES AND TAX FORMULAE

§ 1. A TAX scheme addressed to any taxpayer is a list of statements relating quantities of payments required from him to selected objective conditions. Thus a payment may be required if he satisfies the condition of existing; a payment if he satisfies the condition of having red hair; a payment if he satisfies the condition of possessing £*x* of income; a payment if he satisfies the condition of expending £*y* of income upon beer; a payment if he satisfies the condition of receiving £*z* of income from land; a payment if he satisfies the condition of owning *w* acres of land; and so on. The several statements in the above sense embodied in any tax scheme I call tax formulae; every tax formula being made up of two elements, an object of assessment and a function — the tax function as I shall call it — relating together quantities of this object in the hands of individual taxpayers and quantities of revenue to be raised from them by assessment on it.

§ 2. Theoretically the object of assessment embodied in a tax formula may be anything whatever. In practice, for a great many tax formulae, it is some sum of money; the income that a man derives from work, or from property, or from true rents, or from windfalls, or from the exercise of monopoly power; the income that a man expends upon beer, betting, motor-cars, tea, or any other object; the fortune that a man leaves at death or that another man inherits; and so on. For some tax formulae it is a quantity of stuff, as with specific taxes upon commodities and with taxes per acre on land, whether in general or as employed in particular occupations. In the special case of a poll-tax the object of assessment is not a variable quantity, and, therefore, this tax may at first sight seem difficult to class along with the others. The difficulty can be got over, however, in a way to be explained immediately.

§ 3. In any tax formula the tax function which relates quantity of revenue to be raised from individual taxpayers to quantity of assessable object in their hands, might, so far as *a priori* considerations go, be anything we please. For practical purposes, however, the range of possibility is limited in important ways. This is true of all tax formulae, whatever the object of assessment embodied in them. It can be best illustrated, however, in the special case of a formula in which the object of assessment is income. In this case the following limitations are, practically speaking, sure to be present. First, no government would accept a tax formula under which the tax levy on a nil income is other than nil. Secondly, no government would accept one in which the *amount* of taxation assessed on a smaller income is greater than the amount assessed on a larger income. These two conditions in combination rule out, it will be noticed, negative levies. Thirdly, no government would accept a tax formula under which the *average rate* of taxation increased for some increases in the amount of income and decreased for other increases, *i.e.* was progressive for some scales of income and regressive for others. Fourthly, no government would accept a formula which imposed on any income a levy greater than the amount of that income. If we write the tax formula $R = \psi(x)$, where R is the revenue required from a taxpayer, and x the amount of his income, these conditions will be expressed thus :

(1) $\psi(o) = 0$.

(2) $\psi'(x)$ is positive (or zero) for all values of x.

(3) If $\left\{\dfrac{d\frac{\psi(x)}{x}}{dx}\right\}$ is positive for some values of x, it cannot be negative for any values of x ; and *vice versa*.

(4) $\psi(x) <= x$ for all values of x.

Among the functions which these rules allow a very important one is the proportionate tax, in which $\psi'(x)$ is constant, so that $\psi(x)$ can be written kx. Another important form is that in which the *average* rate of tax per unit of assessable object increases as the quantity of this object grows, but at a rate of increase, which, after a point, approaches to or reaches 0.

That is to say, $\left\{\dfrac{d^2\frac{\psi x}{x}}{dx^2}\right\}$ is positive for all values of x up to a point, thereafter approximating to zero. The problem of classifying a poll-tax also finds a solution. This tax may be described, with a certain straining of our meaning, as a limiting type of income-tax. The formula $R=\psi(x)$ correctly describes it when ψ is such that $\psi(x)$ is constant for all values of x greater than A (the minimum income) and is less than A.

§ 4. All tax formulae, the excluded no less than the included group, can be classed, so to speak, into families. Thus, consider two formulae, $R=\psi(x)$ and $R=\phi(x)$. These formulae may be said to belong to the same family if, when m is any constant, $\psi(x)=m\phi(x)$ for all values of x. In other words, two formulae belong to the same family when the revenue raised under one of them is some (the same) multiple of that raised under the other for all scales of income. Thus all proportionate taxes, whatever their rate, belong to the same family; all poll-taxes, whatever their amount, belong to the same family; all taxes represented by the equation $R=a\left\{\frac{x^2}{5000}-20\right\}$, $R=b\left\{\frac{x^2}{5000}-20\right\}$ and so on belong to the same family. On the other hand, all proportionate taxes belong to different families from all progressive and from all regressive taxes; and, in general, any tax represented by the equation $R=\psi(x)$ belongs to a different family from one represented by $R=\phi(x)$, except, as indicated above, when $\psi(x)$ is equal to $\phi(x)$ multiplied by some (the same) constant for all values of x.[1]

[1] Some readers may find it convenient to develop this classification of tax formulae further. We describe the members of one family by equations $R=a\psi_1(x)$, $R=b\psi_1(x)$ and so on; and members of another family by $R=a\psi_2(x)$, $R=b\psi_2(x)$ and so on; and we arrange our notation in such wise that, for some one value of x, $\psi_1(x)$, $\psi_2(x)$ and so on are all equal. The choice of the value of x for which this equality shall prevail and of the values which $\psi_1(x)$ and so on shall then have is, of course, quite arbitrary. Let us postulate, therefore, that, when $x=1000$, $\psi_1(x)$ and so on shall all be equal to 10. This is convenient because it implies that, given this value of x, $\frac{\psi_1(x)}{x}$, $\frac{\psi_2(x)}{x}$ and so on $=\frac{1}{100}$: in other words, that the *rate of tax* is one per cent. On this basis every possible tax formula can be expressed by an equation of the form $R=m\psi(x)$, provided only that the formula imposes *some* levy on incomes of £1000: and for every possible tax formula *the rate of tax per cent* imposed on incomes of £1000 is equal to m. If we name m the tax constant and $\psi(x)$ the tax function, all members of one family will have the same tax function but different tax constants. To illustrate this method of classification, let us write t for the rate per cent of any tax, so that the formula $R=m\psi(x)$ is equivalent to $\frac{t}{100}=\frac{m\psi(x)}{x}$ or $t=100\frac{m\psi(x)}{x}$. Then, for all taxes under which the levy made is *proportionate* to income, $\frac{\psi(x)}{x}=$ a constant $=\frac{1}{100}$, so that $t=m$; that is to say, the *percentage rate* of

§ 5. No comment is required at this stage upon the families of poll-taxes and of proportionate taxes. But of the others something further may conveniently be said here. Consider the tax formula $R = a\psi(x)$. The *average rate of tax* imposed on an income x is measured by $\frac{a\psi(x)}{x}$: and the *marginal tax* imposed on an income x (*i.e.* the rate at which the aggregate tax levy increases as x increases) is measured by $a\psi'(x)$. When a tax formula is said to be *progressive*, the meaning may be *either* that $\frac{a\psi(x)}{x}$ increases as x increases *or* that $a\psi'(x)$ increases as x increases. The former meaning signifies that $\frac{d\frac{a\psi(x)}{x}}{dx}$ is positive, the latter that $a\psi''(x)$ is positive. If we were including in our purview tax formulae in which the average rate of tax increased for some increases of x and decreased for others, we should find that some of them, in respect of certain values of x, were progressive in one of the two senses distinguished above, but not in the other. When, however, formulae of this mixed type are excluded, it can be shown, third and later differentials being ignored, that all of those remaining, if progressive in the one sense, must be progressive in the other also. For

$$\frac{d\frac{a\psi(x)}{x}}{dx} = a\left\{\frac{1}{x}\psi'(x) - \frac{1}{x^2}\psi(x)\right\}.$$

This is positive for all values of x, if $x\psi'(x) > \psi(x)$ for all values of x, *i.e.* if $\psi''(x)$ is positive for all values of x: which proves the above proposition.

tax is equal to the tax constant, as I have defined it. Again, for lump-sum taxes, *i.e.* a poll-tax, $m\psi(x)$ is a constant, and, therefore, since, when $x = 1000$, $\frac{\psi(x)}{x} = \frac{1}{100}$, $\psi(x) = 10$ for all values of x. The formula, therefore, becomes $R = 10m$; and the *amount* of the tax is equal to ten times the tax constant. Yet again, suppose that the tax formula embodies a particular sort of progression, in such wise that the revenue is always equal to $\frac{1}{5000}$th part of the square of the income (up to the point at which it becomes equal to the income). In my notation the tax constant in this formula is 20, and the tax function $\frac{x^2}{100000}$. If the formula of the tax had been $R = \frac{1}{10000}x^2$, the tax constant would have been 10 and the tax function the same as before. I do not suppose, however, that many persons will find this elaboration worth while.

§ 6. The preceding analysis shows further, that, for all formulae included in our review, if one member of any tax family is progressive, all must be progressive; and, if one is regressive, all must be regressive. Thus every tax family can be described unambiguously as progressive, proportionate or regressive. When, however, we come to consider *degrees* of progression or regression, the matter is not so simple. These degrees may be taken to refer to progression or regression either in average rates of tax or in marginal rates. In the former sense the degree of progression, in respect of income x, of the tax formula $R = a\psi(x)$ is measured by $a\frac{d\frac{\psi(x)}{x}}{dx} = a\left\{\frac{1}{x}\psi'(x) - \frac{1}{x^2}\psi(x)\right\}$; in the latter sense by $a\psi''(x)$. These two expressions only bear a constant relation to one another in the special case in which the degree of progression or regression in the second sense is the same for all values of x.[1] It is, therefore, necessary to choose one or other of the two forms. I choose the second and shall measure the degree of progression or regression of a tax formula in respect of an income x by $a\psi''(x)$.

§ 7. It is possible to imagine an arrangement under which different members of a community are subjected by one and the same taxing authority to taxes containing different tax formulae. Thus to A, who is, perhaps, now earning £1000, it might be announced that, if he earns £900, he shall be taxed 9 per cent, if he earns £1000, 10 per cent, if he earns £1100, 11 per cent; while to B, now earning £1100, it is announced that, if he earns £900 he shall be taxed 20 per cent, if £1000, 21 per cent, if £1100, 22 per cent, and so on. In like manner A might be assessed at a poll-tax of £1000 and B at one of £100, A at a tax of 20 per cent of his expenditure upon beer, B at one of 40 per cent. In the modern world, however, to operate such an arrangement would be extremely difficult. Except in very special circumstances the opportunities which it would offer for tyranny, vindictiveness, personal favouritism and, as regards commodity taxes, evasion through resales, rule it out of court. To obviate abuses taxes must be assessed under

[1] In that case, since (from § 3) we know that $\psi(0)$ and $\psi'(0)$ both $=0$, the expression $a\left\{\frac{1}{x}\psi'(x) - \frac{1}{x^2}\psi(x)\right\}$ is easily shown to be equal to $\frac{1}{2}a\psi''(x)$.

some machinery of general rules based on *objective* standards. Hence, every tax formula in a general tax scheme must embody one and the same announcement to every taxpayer. It must say to each, for example: "If you *or anybody else* are a married man with one child and have such-and-such an income, you must pay so much". If one man A is told that he will be taxed 11 per cent, 10 per cent or 9 per cent, according as he earns £1100, £1000 or £900, everybody else in a similar position must be told the same. If a poll-tax is imposed, conditional on existence, of, say, £100, *everybody* must pay that sum, whatever his wealth. If a tax of £5 per acre is imposed on land, *every* holder of 100 acres must pay £500, though one holder may be a millionaire, another relatively poor. If a 10 per cent tax on tea is imposed, two men of equal income, one of whom drinks tea while the other dislikes it, must pay different amounts of tax. This obligation, under which governments lie, to subject all members of the community to the same tax scheme,[1] has an important consequence. Since some people are of different tastes and sensibility as regards income from other people, if governments were not tied by this condition, any given revenue could be raised with a smaller aggregate sacrifice than the smallest which can be inflicted now. The ideal of least sacrifice has, in short, to be pursued subject to a handicap. We seek least sacrifice, not in an absolute sense, but relative to the condition that a single (the same) tax scheme shall be presented to every citizen.

[1] When England and Ireland were united under the same taxing authority it was strongly argued that, owing to the divergent tastes of Englishmen and Irishmen, it was improper to subject them to the same tax formulae in respect of beer and whisky, but the same formulae were in fact applied to both. Cf. *post*, Chapter VII, § 2.

CHAPTER III

THE INTERACTION OF DIFFERENT TAX FORMULAE

§ 1. WHEN a tax scheme consists of more than one tax formula, the revenue yielded by it is not, in general, equal to the sum of the revenues which would have been yielded by each tax formula, had it been imposed by itself. The relations involved being somewhat complex, I propose in the following paragraphs to analyse them briefly.

§ 2. First, when a given revenue is being collected and used up by the government — not merely retransferred, *e.g.* in interest, to the public [1] — the fact that this quantity of revenue is being raised, irrespective of the manner of its raising and so of its announcement effects, is liable to modify the yield of further taxes, if such are imposed. *Some* sorts of further taxes are, indeed, unaffected. Thus a poll-tax, or a tax of so much per acre on all land, or a tax proportionate to true rents, will yield the same revenue whether much or little revenue is being raised contemporaneously in other ways. Again, the yield of taxes on earned income will not be affected at all events directly — indirect effects are considered in § 3; — for they are normally assessed on income reckoned prior to any payments made out of it to meet other taxes, so that these payments do not affect the magnitude of the assessed object. On the other hand, any ordinary commodity tax will yield less revenue when the taxpayers are than when they are not impoverished by other taxation. So will taxes on investment income and death duties, because impoverishment will lessen capital accumulations. Hence, the raising of money by one set of taxes — always presuming that the money is employed for non-transfer purposes — commits ravages of greater or less extent upon the yield of certain other taxes. Yet again, in a very poor country, a tax on bread may yield *more* if there are than if there are not heavy other taxes, because people may be forced down to bread in substitution for more expensive foods.

[1] Even if the money is retransferred to the public, we are not secure against consequences of the type discussed in this paragraph, unless it is retransferred to different taxpayers in proportion to their tax payments.

§ 3. Secondly, the extent to which the yield of new taxes is affected by the existing tax system depends, not only on the amount of the revenue that is being raised under that system, but also on the way in which the levies made under it are distributed among different income groups. Thus, if the existing tax system is made up of taxes which strike predominantly rich people — if, for example, its main constituent is a steeply graduated income tax — there will be left over less money in their hands, and more in the hands of poor people, than would have been so left if the existing tax system had consisted mainly of duties upon staple articles of general consumption. It follows that a new tax at a given rate on commodities mainly consumed by the rich will yield less additional revenue in the former case than in the latter; while, *per contra*, a new tax at a given rate on commodities bought chiefly by the poor will yield more additional revenue. Thus, to put the same point from another angle, when the amount of additional revenue required is given, in case (1) a champagne tax would have to be at a higher rate and a death duty formula of given steepness would have to be on a higher scale [1] than in case (2); and, *per contra*, a tax on beer would have to be at a lower rate.

§ 4. Thirdly, when the amount of revenue being raised and the distribution of the burden under it are both given, the yield of further taxes is liable to be modified by the *nature* of the existing taxes, and to be modified in different ways according to what the further taxes are. Thus, if the main body of the revenue — *of given amount* — is being raised by a poll-tax, an income tax conforming to a given formula will yield more revenue than it would do if the given amount of revenue were being raised through a number of commodity taxes. For the poll-tax, while causing the marginal utility of money to persons mulcted under it to rise in the same way that commodity taxes yielding equal revenue would do, differs from these taxes in that it threatens no additional levy on these persons, if, to compensate themselves, they do more work, and so obtain and spend more income.[2] Consequently,

[1] In the language of Chapter II, § 4, footnote, the tax constant would have to be larger.

[2] This argument, it will be noticed, assumes that the monetary and banking system is of a normal kind; not such that money income is held constant irrespective of what happens to real income.

where the rest of the tax system consists of a poll-tax, there will be more income available for assessment under income tax, and so a bigger yield from any given scheme of income tax, than there would be if the rest of the system consisted of commodity taxes. Again, if there exists in the rest of the tax system a heavy tax on one of two rival commodities (say beef), so that people rely for their meat supplies chiefly upon mutton, a new moderate tax on the other rival (say mutton) will yield much more revenue than if the revenue actually being collected from beef were being raised in some other way. *Per contra*, if there exists in the rest of the tax system a heavy tax on one of two complements (say tea or malt), a new moderate tax on the other complement (sugar or hops) will yield much less revenue than it would have yielded otherwise. The matter is still further complicated by the mutual character of some of these reactions. Thus, if a tax on beef already exists, the imposition of a new tax on mutton will cause the yield of that tax to increase; while the imposition of a new tax on sugar or hops will cause the yield of an existing tax on tea or malt to decrease. Therefore the addition to aggregate revenue due to the new tax is not equal to the yield of the new tax; and the relation between these two things may differ for different new taxes in different ways depending on the structure of the other parts of the tax system.

§ 5. In the light of these considerations it is obvious that, when a given amount of additional revenue is required, we shall often be unable to tell what member of any given family of tax formulae — or, to take a simple special case, what rate of one or another sort of tax — would yield that revenue, until we know both what amount of revenue is already being raised and also what tax formulae are being employed to raise it.

CHAPTER IV

THE PRINCIPLE OF LEAST SACRIFICE AND THE DISTRIBUTIONAL ASPECT OF TAXATION

§ 1. WHEN revenue is raised in any country, the total of it is always made up of parts taken from a number of different individuals in varying economic situations. There are, therefore, two factors upon which, when the amount of the revenue to be raised is settled, the aggregate sacrifice involved in raising it depends. These are, on the one hand, the way in which the several parts of the total money impost are *distributed* among people in different economic situations, *i.e.* different degrees of wealth, and so on; and, on the other hand, the scheme of formulae in which their own particular liability is *announced* to each several taxpayer. In a subsequent chapter the complicated interrelations between these two aspects of taxation will be examined. In this chapter I shall inquire to what distribution of tax levies the principle of least sacrifice would lead if we were free to ignore altogether announcement aspects.

§ 2. Before we set out on our task, however, it is necessary to be clear as to what precisely we understand by the announcement aspects of taxation and what we mean by ignoring them. The announcement of a tax as a rule causes people to modify their conduct with a view, in some measure, to avoiding the pressure of the tax. Thus, if beer is subjected to a duty, they are likely to buy less beer. Hence, it is natural to say in a loose way that, when we rule out the announcement aspects of taxation, we are supposing that it does not cause people to modify their conduct. That, however, would be an absurd supposition. If a man, who, apart from taxation, would have an income of £2000, is compelled to pay £500 to the government, and the government does not return it, that man *must* modify his conduct. When I rule out the announcement aspects of taxation, I assume that this £2000 man, mulcted of £500, acts in the same way, not as he would have acted if he had not been mulcted, but as he would act if the £500 was taken from him in a lump-sum levy not alterable in amount by anything that he chooses to do. In the circumstances after the levy he would now (1) do the same amount of work that he would have done if untaxed, (2) have a net income of £1500, and (3) distribute it over different sorts of purchases, not in the proportions in which he would have distributed his original £2000 had it remained intact — he would certainly have spent a bigger fraction of this on luxuries and a less fraction on such things as food and house-room — but in the proportions in which an untaxed £1500 man of the same temperament as himself would distribute his income. It is this precisely, and nothing other than this, that we have to suppose if we wish to rule out of consideration the announcement aspects of taxation, while including all the distributional aspects.

§ 3. The problem of tax distribution has not, of course, to do with particular taxes viewed in isolation. The principle of least sacrifice requires that the *whole body* of tax levies shall be distributed in a certain way, and, failing *optimum* distribution, it informs us that one kind of distribution inferior to the *optimum* is, nevertheless, superior to another kind. If the rest of the tax system is settled and we have to decide by what means to raise a given amount of additional revenue, our choice must depend, not on how the burden of the new tax will be distributed, but on how that of the new tax and the old taxes together will be distributed. This depends on the nature of the old taxes as well as on the nature of the new one. New tax A will conform better to the principle of least sacrifice than new B if these old taxes are of one sort, but new tax B will conform better if they are of another sort. For example, if X and Y are persons in all respects similar, a particular tax ought to strike them both equally if the rest of the tax system strikes them equally ; but, if the rest of the tax system strikes X more severely than Y, the particular tax, to redress the balance, ought to strike Y more severely than X. As Marshall writes : " Onerous taxes, imperial and local, must be treated as a whole. Almost every onerous tax taken by itself presses with undue weight on some class or other ; but this is of no moment if the inequalities of each are compensated by those of others, and variations in the several parts synchronise. If that difficult condition is satisfied, the system may be equitable, though any one part of it regarded alone would be inequitable." [1]

§ 4. So much being understood, we may conveniently begin our discussion by assuming that all the sacrifice due to taxation is direct immediate sacrifice to the taxpayers concerned, and that there are no indirect sacrifices arising in the future to be taken into account. This assumption being held in mind for later reference, we may note that Mill, in his discussion of tax distribution, fell, or at least gave the appearance of falling, into a serious error. He wrote : " Whatever sacrifices it (a government) requires from them (classes of persons) should be made to bear as nearly as possible with the same pressure upon all ; *which, it must be observed, is the mode by which least sacrifice is occasioned to the whole* ".[2] It is possible that in this passage Mill was taking into account something more than distributional consequences ; though I do not think that this is so. In any event, whatever interpretation we may give to his pronouncement, the truth is that, when distributional aspects are alone in question, least aggregate sacrifice will *not* be promoted by a system inflicting equal sacrifice all round. This is very easily seen. For, if the abstraction of £1000 from an income of £10,000 inflicts the same sacrifice as the abstraction of £100 from an income of £1000, then the abstraction of £1100 from a £10,000 income *must* inflict less aggregate sacrifice than the abstraction of £1000 from that income *plus* the abstraction of £100 from the £1000 income. In order to secure least aggregate sacrifice taxes should be so distributed that the marginal utility of the money paid in taxation is equal to all the payers. If the utility of the last penny paid by A were less than that of the last paid by B, a reduction of sacrifice could be secured by transferring a part of B's assessment to the shoulders of A. Thus the distribution of taxation required to conform to the principle of least aggregate sacrifice is that which makes the *marginal* — not the total — *sacrifices* borne by all the members of the community equal.

§ 5. If we push further towards the concrete, it appears that a system of equimarginal sacrifice fully carried out would involve lopping off the tops of all incomes above the minimum income and leaving everybody, after taxation, with

[1] Marshall, *Memorandum on Imperial and Local Taxes* [C.—9528], p. 113.
[2] *Political Economy*, Book v, ch. ii, § 2, par. 1. The italics are mine.

equal incomes. If the amount of revenue required is not enough to absorb the whole of the surpluses above the minimum — if, in Edgeworth's words, there is not enough taxation to go round — the logical procedure would be first to take for the government's needs the tops of the highest incomes, and then to continue taxing middle grade incomes and giving bounties from the proceeds to the smallest incomes till a dead level of equality is attained. If this latter procedure is ruled out and we are only allowed to impose taxes up to the amount of the revenue required for the government's needs, this revenue should be collected exclusively from the highest incomes, these being all reduced in the process to the level of the highest untaxed income. Of course, in so far as tastes and temperaments differ, allowance ought, in strictness, to be made for this fact; if, for instance, A is so sensitive that he could obtain from the 5000th £ of a £5000 income as much satisfaction as B could obtain from the 1000th £ of a £1000 one, there would be no ground for taking money from A rather than from B. But, since it is impossible in practice to take account of variations between different people's capacity for enjoyment, this consideration must be ignored, and the assumption made, for want of a better, that temperamentally all taxpayers are alike. On that assumption, the procedure sketched out above is what the canon of equimarginal sacrifice dictates.

§ 6. The result thus attained appears at first sight to be complete and conclusive, so long as attention is restricted to the distributional aspects of taxation and announcement aspects are ruled out of account. It is, however, in fact, subject to a very important qualification. For the assumption set out at the beginning of § 4, to the effect that the only sacrifices which result from taxation, and have, therefore, to be reckoned with, are contemporary sacrifices, is invalid. Sacrifices may also occur which are of an indirect sort and impinge upon the future, maybe upon persons who were not yet born at the time the taxes were levied. It would, no doubt, be possible, by artifices of definition, to bring these future sacrifices into account without modifying the formula of equimarginal sacrifice as set out above. It is, however, more convenient to say that, when there are no relevant future sacrifices, the principle of least sacrifice requires equimarginal *contemporary* sacrifice, and that, when there are relevant future sacrifices, some modifications in that arrangement are required. Let us examine these in detail.

§ 7. The chief of them may be set out as follows. There is reason to believe that the proportion of their incomes which very poor people devote to saving, as against consumption, is, as indeed it must be, very small, and that, as we advance up the scale of incomes, the proportion saved becomes larger.[1] It follows that, even though people, when taxed, distributed the money left to them among different uses in the same proportions as before, the collection of a given revenue would cut down savings more, the more largely the taxes levied to produce that revenue were concentrated upon the upper strata of incomes. Moreover, as was observed in § 1, as a matter of fact people, when taxed, do not distribute their cuts in equal proportions among all ways of employing money. The income-elasticity of their demand for some things is larger than for others. For savings it is probably very large. They save what is left over after their normal standard of life, a fairly rigid thing, has been satisfied. It follows that, when taxation is concentrated upon the higher strata of incomes, the cut in savings will be even larger than a calculation based on the comparative proportions in which different classes save suggests.[2] This means that taxation can only be distributed in accordance with the formula of equimarginal contemporary sacrifice at the cost of contracting the annual volume of new savings, and thus, in so far as individual savers invest and do not hoard or allow other people to consume their savings,[3]

[1] Cf. my *Employment and Equilibrium*, part ii, ch. vi.

[2] In applying these general considerations to the special case of Great Britain it is essential to bear in mind that a very large part of the country's annual savings is provided through additions made by joint-stock companies to their reserves out of undistributed profits, which are subject to the standard rate of income tax, but not to sur-tax. The White Paper (Cmd. 6520), 1944, estimates that in 1938 net personal savings amounted to £158 million and net impersonal savings — somewhat wider than undistributed profits — to £170 million (pp. 11 and 29).

[3] It would be wrong to infer that this qualification is unnecessary on the ground that, with the definitions ordinarily employed (cf. *Employment and Equilibrium*, part i, ch. iii), aggregate savings and aggregate investment are necessarily equal, so that it is impossible for any net savings to be hoarded. This is so. But it is only so because, when one man saves more than he invests and thus — apart from transferring the balance to be invested by somebody else — hoards it, somebody else's income and, therefore, somebody else's excess of income over consumption, *i.e.* saving, is reduced to a corre-

the annual accumulation of new capital instruments.

§ 8. When the annual creation of new capital is checked, those who in the future will work in conjunction with capital instruments will, their numbers being given, obtain less real earnings than they otherwise would have done, and so will suffer a sacrifice. If we suppose that their numbers are going to increase in a given measure, the check imposed on capital accumulation may force them to accept lower real rates of pay, whereas, had there been no check, their earnings rate might have been sustained in spite of growing numbers. This class of effect does not enter into the consideration of a person whose income is contracted by taxation. The cut that he makes in his savings, unlike that which he makes in his purchase of consumption goods, thus involves a by-product of extra sacrifice to other people, unconsidered but obviously not irrelevant to aggregate sacrifice conceived in the widest sense. Apart, therefore, from accompanying State action designed to counteract the effects which a concentration of taxation upon rich people must have upon capital accumulation, it appears that the principle of least sacrifice points to a system somewhat more merciful to these people than the canon of equimarginal *contemporary* sacrifice would commend.[1]

§ 9. Alongside of this consideration must be set another, which analytically is of like character. Up to a point every £'s worth of any man's purchases of certain sorts of commodities, besides yielding directly satisfaction commensurate with his desire for it, also yields a by-product. This by-

sponding extent. Thus individuals *can* make savings in the form of money hoardings. Taxation which discourages them from this does not hinder the accumulation of new capital instruments. On the contrary, it causes money income, and so probably both real investment and real consumption, to be larger than it would otherwise have been.

[1] The essence of the foregoing argument can be brought out in an abstract illustration. Suppose that a community consists of two persons, one normally earning a small income and the other a large income, that the latter is responsible for all capital accumulations, and that both live for ever. Then the aggregate satisfaction of the poor man, looked at *sub specie aeternitatis*, is a function, not only of the money income left, after taxation, to himself, but also of that left to the rich man. Therefore, to maximise satisfaction in the aggregate, we do not require a tax distribution such that the last £ taken from the poor man imposes on him a sacrifice equal to that which the last £ taken from the rich man imposes upon the rich man. It must impose a sacrifice equal to that which the last £ taken from the rich man imposes on the rich man *plus* that which the last £ taken from the rich man imposes indirectly on the poor man.

product is his own, and perhaps his children's, increased productive efficiency, and the satisfaction which the increased output due to this increased efficiency will yield later on. If, in consequence of taxation, his consumption is cut down in such wise that his or his children's efficiency is reduced, the loss of satisfaction to him and them, *i.e.* the ultimate and total sacrifice imposed, is larger than the immediate sacrifice. Moreover, it should be noted, the mere fact of a man spending part of his income on things that do not promote efficiency — "conventional necessaries", and so on — is no proof that cuts in his income, if such are forced upon him, will be made in ways innocuous to efficiency. There will be *room* for making them in these ways, but a man may easily prefer to hold on to conventional necessaries even at the expense of doing without real necessaries. It should be noted further that the quantity of consumption, cuts below which damage efficiency, is not the same for persons in all walks of life. It may well be that a navvy's efficiency will be as large with an expenditure of £300 a year as with any larger expenditure, while that of a philosopher, who needs quiet and mental stimulus, would be reduced if his expenditure had to be cut down from £1000 to £900. These, however, are secondary matters. The main point is that, when taxation cuts down net incomes, and so net expenditures, among people with small incomes, but not when it cuts down the expenditures of moderately well-to-do or rich persons, there is involved an indirect element of sacrifice additional to the direct sacrifice with which alone §§ 4-5 were concerned.

§ 10. This result and that attained in § 8 in some measure cancel one another. The discussion of §§ 4-5 neglected, on the one side an important element of sacrifice associated with the taxation of large incomes, on the other an important element associated with the taxation of small incomes. Plainly in any final judgement both these neglected elements ought to be taken into account. When they are combined, the net result is that both poor people and rich people are less satisfactory subjects of taxation than they appear to be at first sight. The scale is tipped against the unfortunate intermediate class of moderately well-to-do persons.[1]

[1] What has been said here does not, and is not intended to, throw light on the way in which the volume of saving is affected by the collection *together*

with the expenditure of revenue. Our argument, as was premised in Chapter I, § 1, has assumed the expenditure and has been concerned with comparing different ways of raising the money required. Obviously the effects of the government raising *and* spending money are different according to the way in which it spends it. With non-transfer expenditure what is devoted to building houses does, while what is devoted to the maintenance of the army and civil service does not, constitute saving. With transfer expenditure what happens depends on the power and will to save of those to whom the transfers are made. Of transfers to war pensioners and old-age pensioners it is improbable that any substantial part is devoted to saving. Of transfers in payment of interest to domestic holders of war loan a considerable amount is likely to be saved. In view of the fact that a large part of war loan is held by banks, insurance companies, joint-stock companies, and so on, while the holders of the bulk of the remainder are well-to-do persons, it may well be that the savings made out of the money transferred by the recipients actually exceed the savings which would have been made out of it by the original holders, had it been left in their hands. (Cf. *The Report of the Committee on National Debt and Taxation*, p. 99.) Transfers in repayment of the principal of their debt to domestic holders of war loan are practically certain to involve a net increase of savings: for, while substantially the whole of the repaid principal will be reinvested by the recipients, some of the money raised in order to provide for the repayment is sure to have been taken from consumption.

CHAPTER V

THE PRINCIPLE OF LEAST SACRIFICE AND TAX ANNOUNCEMENTS TO EQUAL-INCOME GROUPS

§ 1. In this chapter I propose to ignore distributional considerations in the same way that in the preceding chapter I ignored the varying effects of announcing their liability to taxpayers through different tax formulae. To this end it is necessary to make the highly unreal assumption that we have to do with an income group the whole of whose income is earned by work and all of whose members are exactly alike, not only in temperament, family estate and so on, but also in the amounts of income which they respectively enjoy. On this basis we have to study the different amounts of sacrifice which are involved when a given revenue is raised by one or another form of tax announcement. I shall leave on one side commodity taxes and shall assume that the whole revenue is to be collected under a single tax formula in which the object of assessment is income, a poll-tax being included, as explained in Chapter II, § 3, as a limiting type of income tax. I assume further in accordance with what was said in that place, that formulae under which aggregate revenue raised *decreases* as income increases (*i.e.* under which $\psi'(x)$ is negative for relevant values of x) are excluded.

§ 2. When in these conditions a given revenue is being raised and when the functions relating quantity of income to the satisfaction derived from and to the dissatisfaction involved in obtaining it are given, the aggregate sacrifice involved will be smaller the more the tax formula employed causes the volume of work and so of income to increase, or the less it causes it to diminish. To show this, let us suppose that a definite amount of income, R, is taken from a representative taxpayer by the government, of which R_1 is used up and $(R - R_1)$ retransferred to the taxpayers. Let $\phi(x - R_1)$ be the aggregate quantity of satisfaction received by the taxpayer from the $(x - R_1)$ income that is left available to him ; and let $F(x)$ be the aggregate quantity of dissatisfaction that he undergoes in producing income x. Then clearly the net satisfaction enjoyed by him will be as large as possible, *i.e.* the sacrifice imposed on him will be a minimum, if the tax formula employed in collecting revenue R allows x to be such that the marginal utility to him of $(x - R_1)$ income is equal to the marginal disutility to him of producing x income; *i.e.* to be such that $\frac{d\phi(x - R_1)}{dx} = F'(x)$. Now, since we have excluded tax formulae under which the aggregate levy made is smaller for a larger than for a smaller income, it is evident that no *included* formula can cause x to have a larger value than that yielded by the above equation. Call this value X. It is further evident that, as between any two formulae yielding the same revenue R, one of which causes x to have a value falling further below X than the other, the aggregate satisfaction enjoyed by the taxpayer must be greater, *i.e.* his aggregate sacrifice must be less, under the first formula than under the second. Thus the merit from the standpoint of least sacrifice of various tax formulae yielding a given revenue, a given amount of which is used up by the government, can be ranged in an order corresponding to the amount of work that is done, and so income created, under them. This result is perfectly general and includes the case in which none of the revenue from the representative taxpayer is used up but the whole is transferred back in a lump sum to the taxpayer. In that case, distributional effects being ignored, R_1 in our equation has simply to be written equal to 0.

§ 3. It has not been necessary to our argument to say anything about the relation between the amount of work done when some revenue is being raised by taxation and when none is being raised. Nevertheless, it may be worth while to add a word about that.

§ 4. When revenue raised by taxation is used, up by government it is plain that, with some tax formulae (*e.g.* a poll-tax), the taxpayers will do more work than they would do were no revenue being raised. For with a poll-tax, if they only do the same amount of work, the marginal utility of the income left to them will be larger than the disutility of the work done in producing the marginal unit of it.[1] But with all other

[1] In so far as tax revenue is used up by a government in providing people with things, *e.g.* elementary education, on which or on substitutes for which they would otherwise have spent the money now handed over in taxes, the

(included) tax formulae the amount of work done when a given revenue is being raised and used up by the government will be less — apart from the case of an absolutely inelastic supply of work — than with the poll-tax formula ; and it is easy to see that in certain conditions with certain formulae it will be less than it would be if no revenue were being raised at all.

When revenue raised by taxation from the representative taxpayer is not used up by the government but transferred back to him (*e.g.* as interest on holdings of government securities), this combined process cannot with any tax formula — even with the poll-tax — cause the quantity of work done to be larger than it would have been had no revenue been raised ; for, since what is taken from the representative man is simultaneously returned to him, the imposition of a poll-tax will leave the marginal utility of the income available to him when he does any given amount of work the same as it would have been had no revenue been raised.

Thus the relation between the quantity of work done when some revenue is being raised and the quantity when none is being raised is not the same if the revenue is used for transfer purposes as if it is used for non-transfer purposes. This, however, is a digression outside the field of our present investigation.

§ 5. When the revenue that is required is the maximum that it is possible to raise from a given group (all of whose members are similar and enjoy equal incomes) through any member of a given family of tax formulae, it is unlikely that there will be more than one member of the family capable of yielding that revenue. For the family of lump-sum or poll-taxes it is impossible that there should be more than one member — in this case more than one rate of tax — which is thus capable. For the family of proportionate taxes the same thing is true ; and it is also true of many other families of tax formulae. There will, indeed, in a complete theoretical inventory, be some families of which it is not true. This, however, is a refinement. Practically speaking, we may say that

marginal utility of money to them is, of course, not raised. But, as will have been gathered from Part I, Chapter V, the main part of a government's non-transfer expenditure out of tax revenue is likely to be devoted to things — national defence and so on — which, if it had not provided them, would not have been provided at all.

the maximum revenue possible of attainment by any member of a family of tax formulae is attainable by only one member of that family. When the revenue that is required is less than the maximum which it is possible to raise through any member of a tax family, this is no longer true. For the family of poll-taxes there is still only one member that will yield this revenue. But for the family of proportionate taxes there are always two members. Any revenue, other than the highest revenue obtainable through any proportionate tax, can be secured either by a rate of tax lower than the maximum-revenue rate or by a rate of tax higher than this. There is a choice, in fact, between a relatively low rate of tax collected from a relatively large income — which comes into being just because the rate is low — and a relatively high rate collected from a relatively small income. For other families of tax formulae the same thing is true in general. Thus let us describe the members of a family by equations in which R, the revenue collected, is equal respectively to $a_1\psi(x)$, $a_2\psi(x)$ . . . $a_m\psi(x)$, $a_{m+1}\psi(x)$ and so on, where an a with a larger suffix is always greater than one with a smaller suffix, and, where $R = a_m\psi(x)$, is the equation of that member of the family which yields maximum revenue. Then any revenue other than the maximum will, in general, be yielded both by some member which precedes the maximum-revenue member in the order set out above and by some member which succeeds that member. For some families of tax formulae certain revenues other than the maximum will be yielded by more than two members. It is easy to see that, when a given revenue can be obtained from two or more members of a given family of tax formulae, work will be diminished less and, therefore, in accordance with the preceding argument, a smaller aggregate sacrifice will be suffered, if, so to speak, the *lowest in rank* of these members is chosen. For the family of proportionate taxes this, of course, means that the lower rate of tax capable of yielding a given revenue should be chosen in preference to the higher rate. For other families it means that, their members being arranged in an order of the kind illustrated above, a member in which the suffix of a is smaller should be chosen in preference to one in which it is larger. In what follows, therefore, when I speak of the tax formula belonging to any family that will yield a given revenue, I shall always mean, where two or more members will do this, the lowest in rank among them.

§ 6. When any given revenue has to be raised, our main problem then lies, not within different tax families, but between the appropriate representatives, or strongest candidates, from different families. This being so, it is important to observe that candidates from all families will not always be available. When the revenue required is very small, relatively to the income which the community would have in the absence of taxation, few families will be without a potential representative. But, as the revenue required becomes larger, more and more families are forced to withdraw, because the revenue which their strongest representative could raise is less than what is needed. It is possible in theory to arrange the different families in an order according to the maximum revenue which the strongest member of each can yield. Thus, in a community *all of whose members have equal incomes*, if the revenue required exceeds a certain size, no formula other than a member of the poll-tax family will avail to raise it. When the revenue required falls, certain families of regressive formulae are able to provide members adequate to the task. For smaller revenues the family of proportionate taxes is able to do this ; and for still smaller revenues families of progressive formulae become available. As between formulae for which the *rate* of regression or progression is constant for all values of x, those which are more regressive or less progressive, in the sense defined in Chapter II, § 6, are competent to provide larger revenues than less regressive or more progressive formulae. There is one type of formula, that represented by the equation $R = (x - \kappa)$, when κ is a constant, which deserves more particular mention. This is the type that would be required, in a community of persons with *dissimilar* incomes, to satisfy the canon of equimarginal contemporary sacrifice. Obviously, however, under it nobody would have any interest in securing an income in excess of κ. Hence, apart, of course, from coercion to work, no revenue whatever would be forthcoming. In other words, this type of formula is only available in respect of a nil revenue !

§ 7. As between available formulae, in the sense explained in the preceding section, certain comparisons can be made in a general way irrespective of the quantity of revenue that is being raised. It is easy to see that, for *any* quantity of revenue, a system of levying it which involves a lower marginal rate of tax will always check work (or prevent work from expanding) less than a system which involves a higher marginal rate. By marginal rate, of course, is meant the additional increment of taxation, which, under the scheme, would be imposed on an additional increment of income in excess of the income that actually stands subject to tax. Now, under a poll-tax this marginal rate of tax is plainly nil. Since we have excluded from view all formulae under which it might be less than nil, this proves that in a community, all of whose members are similar and enjoy equal incomes, a poll-tax is, from the announcement point of view, the *optimum* method of raising a given revenue. Remembering that we have ruled out of account tax formulae which are progressive for some and regressive for other values of x, we observe further that, for a given revenue, the marginal rate of tax must be smaller under any regressive tax than under a proportionate tax; and under a proportionate tax than under any progressive tax. Hence, in accordance with the argument of § 2, from the standpoint of least sacrifice regressive tax formulae are superior to proportionate formulae; and proportionate formulae are superior to progressive formulae. In like manner, as between formulae in which the rates of regression or of progression, as defined in Chapter II, § 6, are constant for all values of x, more regressive formulae are superior to less regressive formulae, and less progressive formulae to more progressive formulae.

§ 8. When our view is extended to cover formulae in which rates of regression and progression are not constant, it is no longer possible to draw up an order of merit in an absolute sense, *i.e.* irrespective of the quantity of revenue which has to be raised. This is to be expected because, for different amounts of revenue, different members of the several families are needed. Let John of family A and Johann of family B be the appropriate members to raise revenue R_1: while Henry of family A and Heinrich of family B are the appropriate members for revenue R_2. There is, then, nothing to prevent John winning against Johann, while at the same time Henry loses to Heinrich. In our symbols John and Johann are represented respectively by $R_k = a_k\psi_1(x)$ and

$R_k = b_k\psi_2(x)$, and Henry and Heinrich by $R_r = a_r\psi_1(x)$ and $R_r = b_r\psi_2(x)$. Then John will be superior to Johann, provided that $a_k\psi_1'(x) < b_k\psi_2'(x)$ in the neighbourhood of revenue R_k, and Henry will be superior to Heinrich provided that $a_r\psi(x)_1' < b_r\psi_2'(x)$ in the neighbourhood of revenue R_r. It is obvious that these two inequalities do not imply one another. Comparisons between the merits of different families of formulae cannot, therefore, in general, be made except with reference to given quantities of revenue. We are only able to lay down universally, in respect of *any* revenue, that, on the assumptions here taken, the appropriate member of the family of proportionate taxes is inferior to the appropriate member of any regressive family and is superior to the appropriate member of any progressive family.

§ 9. In what has been said so far we have been concerned to discover *whether* arrangement A is better or worse than arrangement B, and nothing has been said about *how much* better or worse it is. From any group of similar persons with equal incomes a given revenue can be raised with less sacrifice by a poll-tax than by a tax proportioned to income derived from work, and by a tax proportioned to income derived from work than by a progressive tax ; but we do not know whether the difference made to aggregate sacrifice by the choice of one or other tax formula will be trifling, considerable or large. Now, whatever the amount of revenue to be raised from any group of similar persons with equal incomes, it is easy to see that, if the quantity of work that taxpayers chose to do only varied to a very slight extent with the prospect of reward — if, that is to say, the elasticity of supply was extremely small — the difference made to work done and, therefore, to aggregate sacrifice, by choosing a poll-tax, a proportionate tax, or a highly progressive tax would be trifling. Hence, in order to determine practically how important it is to choose a good tax formula for any income group rather than a bad one, we have to consider whether the elasticity of the supply of work by taxpayers in that group is likely to be large or small. With the great majority of people, once their occupation is decided upon, the quantity of work which they do is only to a very limited extent within their own control. Their hours are fixed by rule ; the intensity of their efforts in many cases by custom and tradition; their age of retirement by pension arrangements. It is only a comparatively small number of persons for whom the question often arises: "Is it worth my while to do this extra piece of work, in view of the fact that, if I do, a part of the proceeds will be taken away in taxation?" The Minority of the Committee on National Debt and Taxation write: "In the large and growing field of salaried enterprise [as contrasted with the medical, legal and such other professions as are usually remunerated by fees] both work and remuneration (and frequently also the age of retirement) are fixed, and the taxpayer cannot earn more by working harder or longer to compensate for his increased taxation; nor can he reduce his liability to pay taxes by diminishing his output of work, unless he gives up his employment altogether. With the growth of joint-stock enterprise it appears to us that the case of the taxpayer who can and does adjust his output of work in accordance with his liability for taxation is so exceptional that it cannot now have any serious effect upon the total national output of productive work."[1] Moreover, in the higher walks of industry wealthy men in control of large concerns are often much more interested in the success of their concerns as an index of capacity and a means to power than in variations in the amount of their net private incomes, which are in any event ample. The Colwyn Committee, with the assistance of the Board of Trade, attempted to compare, from this point of view, the effects of the comparatively low pre-1914 taxation with the high taxation of 1922–3, and concluded "that the comparison lends no support to the view that the weight of post-war taxation tends to deter the wealthy man from continuing in business after reaching the age at which he might well retire".[2] It must, indeed, be conceded that, from a long-period, as distinguished from a short-period point of view, the extreme rigidity of work supply, to which the above considerations point, is somewhat relaxed. A man considering whether to undertake the effort and expense necessary to fit himself for a difficult type of work will, in large part, determine his choice by reference to the prospect of reward. If the prize of success, should it be won, is subject to heavy taxation, enterprise is likely to be discouraged to a significant extent. Nevertheless, on a general view of the

[1] *Report*, p. 380. [2] *Report*, p. 162.

whole matter, it will, I think, be agreed that, in all income groups, for the great bulk of income receivers the supply of work is markedly inelastic. It follows that, whatever group of persons of like incomes we are considering, the difference made to aggregate sacrifice by choosing one or another announcement formula with income as object of assessment from among those that are practically open to us [1] is likely, so far as the argument has gone hitherto, to be small.

§ 10. This, however, is not the end of the matter. So far we have tacitly supposed that all sorts of income tax are non-differential as between various types of work in which people may choose to engage. In fact this is only true of one type — proportionate income tax. With progressive income tax there may be very heavy differentiation against enterprises in which there is a chance of large gain to be set against the chance of large loss, as compared with safe enterprises of equal actuarial promise. For, if ten men between them invest £100,000 in a safe enterprise yielding 5 per cent, there result ten incomes of £500 each ; but, if the ten invest in ten hazardous enterprises of equal aggregate promise and nine of them lose their money, the successful one must receive in compensation an income of £5000, the aggregate tax on which is much larger than on ten incomes of £500 each.[2] Stamp pointed out that this differentiation is eliminated so far as risks are covered by insurance, the premiums for which enter as (untaxed) expenses of the business. Many risks in industry are in fact covered in this way — ships, for example, are regularly insured against loss at sea — but others, such as the risk of failure in new ventures, cannot be so covered.[3] There is a strong presumption that the consequent differentiation must unduly check daring in industry, thus indirectly damaging production and, through it, aggregate satisfaction. *Pro tanto*, therefore, the disadvantage on the announcement side of steeply progressive, as compared with proportionate income tax, is more serious than the consideration set out in the last section suggests.

[1] Under cover of this phrase I rule out formulae of the type described at the end of § 6, under which all incomes in excess of a defined sum are taxed 20s. in the £.

[2] Cf. Hawtrey, *The Economic Problem*, p. 371.

[3] Cf. " Taxation, Risk-bearing and the Price Level ", *Economic Journal*, June 1928, pp. 208-9.

CHAPTER VI

DISTRIBUTIONAL AND ANNOUNCEMENT CONSIDERATIONS IN COMBINATION

§ 1. THE analysis of the preceding chapters has dealt separately with the effects on aggregate sacrifice of the way in which the taxation required to yield a given revenue is distributed and, for cases where all income is earned and revenue is raised through a single tax formula based on income, with the effect of the way in which it is announced. It is now necessary to attempt a synthesis. When a given revenue has to be raised — the effects of spending the revenue being ignored — from a community, the amount and distribution of whose income is given, there must be some definite tax scheme which, when account being taken both of announcement effects on aggregate satisfaction and of effects via distribution will involve less sacrifice than any other scheme would do.[1] From Chapter IV we know that the scheme which minimises sacrifice from a distributional point of view is one conforming to the canon of equi-marginal immediate sacrifice modified by regard for the indirect consequences of high taxation upon the rich in checking capital accumulation and on the poor in diminishing productive efficiency. In like manner we know from Chapter V that the scheme which minimises sacrifice from an announcement point of view is one under which the levy on each taxpayer is independent of the amount of work he does. If, therefore, levies conforming in *amounts* to the distributional ideal could be made in a *manner* conforming to the announcement ideal, we should have, from the standpoint of least sacrifice, the optimum means of raising tax revenue. As was argued in Chapter II, however, a government, in constructing tax schemes, is obliged to act by general rules, and cannot make separate and independent arrangements with individual taxpayers. Its practical task, therefore, is to devise a system of general rules approaching as nearly as may be to that absolute *optimum* which would be attainable if individual

[1] It is, of course, theoretically possible that there might be three or four " best " schemes all involving the same amount of aggregate sacrifice; but this point we may safely neglect.

dealing were permissible. How well it is possible to perform that task, in other words, how nearly it is possible, in the raising of a given revenue, to bring aggregate sacrifice down to what it would be ideally, in yet other words, how close a relative maximum conditioned by the obligation to impose general rules can be brought to the absolute unconditioned maximum, depends in any community upon two things, the way in which income and other relevant economic conditions are distributed among the population, and the way in which " handles " capable of having lump-sum taxation of the poll-tax type attached to them are distributed.

§ 2. In a community all of whose members were similar in family estate, income and all other relevant circumstances, a tax scheme which took equal sums of money from all of them by means of a uniform poll-tax would clearly attain to, and not merely approach, the absolute *optimum*. Even in a community where incomes and other relevant circumstances were not distributed evenly conditions are conceivable in which the *optimum* could be attained. For taxable handles might be distributed so as to fit exactly with the distributional facts. Thus, it might so happen that, for every man, the number of hairs on the head exactly corresponded to the levy in £'s which it was desirable, from the distributional point of view, to make upon him. On the assumption that no individual can voluntarily alter the number of his hairs and that the taxing authority possesses a practicable machine for hair-counting, a tax could be assessed on each man of a number of £'s equal to the number of his hairs. This tax would be perfect alike in announcement and in distributional aspects, and would yield its revenue with least sacrifice in the absolute sense. If acres of land were distributed in the way that we have imagined hairs to be, by assessing taxes upon them we should get the same result. In real communities, however, there are no handles distributed with this miraculous fore-thought for the tax-gatherer's convenience ; and it is not possible to raise revenue through any system of general rules in a manner conforming to the absolute *optimum*.

§ 3. It is necessary to distinguish between two types of tax, according as they are and are not innocent of injurious announcement effects when they are set out in the form of general rules. As will appear presently, taxes assessed on true rents, windfalls and monopoly revenue belong to the former type: death duties, income tax and taxes, whether specific or *ad valorem*, on particular commodities, to the latter. Taxes of the former type being ideal from the announcement point of view, the question how far resort should be had to them must be settled by balancing their advantages in this respect against any disadvantages they may have in worsening the distributional effects of the tax system as a whole — due account being taken of costs of administration and so on. Analytically the problem is a simple one, though, as will appear in later chapters, the practical working out of it presents considerable difficulty. Taxes of the latter type are, however, also certain to be needed. At first sight, indeed, it seems that here too we have merely to seek a straightforward compromise between distributional and announcement considerations. This way of looking at the matter is, however, unduly simple, and further analysis is required.

§ 4. The argument of Chapter V was concerned with the comparative announcement effects of various tax formulae, as addressed to a group of persons similar, not only in temperament, family estate and so on, but also in the amount of their incomes. It was shown that, when a given revenue is being raised by imposts assessed on income derived from work, proportionate taxes are less damaging than progressive taxes, and regressive taxes than proportionate taxes; the best tax being a poll-tax, which is the most regressive type of tax here admissible. If these propositions held good also of tax formulae as addressed to a group of persons with different incomes, the *prima facie* advantages of progressive taxes from a distributional point of view would have to be weighed against their disadvantages from an announcement point of view; and, so far as analysis goes, nothing further would need to be said. But the above propositions do not hold good in this wider sense. Thus consider two formulae designed to yield the same revenue addressed to a community whose members have unequal incomes. Let the formulae be $r = \psi_1(x)$ and $r = \psi_2(x)$, where r is the amount of revenue collected from each individual taxpayer in receipt of an income x. One of these formulae, say $r = \psi_1(x)$, is unambiguously more progressive than the other if, and only if, $\psi_1''(x) > \psi_2''(x)$ for all values of x that are represented by incomes actually extant in the community we are investigating. I postulate that neither formula imposes upon any person a rate of tax in excess of the rate which would extract from him the maximum possible revenue ; for to do this would be to defeat the purpose of the revenue officials. It then follows that, in order for the two formulae to yield equal revenues, the one which is less progressive must impose higher rates of tax than the other on small incomes. There will be a value of x, dependent on the amount of revenue required, the nature of the formulae, the way in which incomes are distributed and the attitude of the several taxpayers towards work and income, in respect of which $\psi_1'(x) = \psi_2'(x)$. For all values of x greater than this critical value — call it X — $\psi_1'(x)$ will be greater, and for all values less than this critical value, smaller than $\psi_2'(x)$. In these circumstances, it is not possible to prove in a general way that the aggregate announcement damage will be greater under the more than under the less progressive formula. Whereas in a community made up of people with equal incomes the demerits in respect of announcement effects of highly progressive income taxes stand out clearly, this is not so, or at all events is less markedly so, in a community the incomes of whose members differ widely.

§ 5. From the above analysis, imperfect as it is, a broad practical inference can, I think, legitimately be drawn. This is that, in constructing tax schemes of the second of the two types distinguished in § 3, we should not give predominant weight to announcement considerations. This conclusion is further strengthened when account is taken of what was said in § 9 of Chapter V. For there, it will be remembered, we found that, for all income groups, the great majority of people are likely to supply their work in a very inelastic manner, so that not much difference will be made to the amount of work performed by substituting one tax formula for another. No doubt an extreme formula, such as that illustrated at the end of § 6 of Chapter V, may properly be ruled out on announcement grounds ; but this type of formula, in view of its reactions on capital accumulation, is also objectionable from the distributional standpoint. Generally speaking, formulae which are *prima facie* good in respect of distribution ought not to be rejected merely because, from an announcement point of view, something less progressive would be better.

CHAPTER VII

THE STRUCTURE OF AN EQUAL-SACRIFICE INCOME TAX WHERE THERE ARE NO SAVINGS

§ 1. SOME popular writers assert that tax systems in general ought to be so arranged as to impose equal sacrifice upon all taxpayers. What has been said in the preceding chapters will have made it plain that there is no ground for this claim. Moreover, it is *a priori* highly improbable that least aggregate sacrifice would be brought about by *any* method of distributing sacrifice which was independent of the amount of revenue required. The more modest claim that the particular amount of revenue, which is being raised, say, in this country at the present time, would best be collected on an equal-sacrifice plan is not, of course, exposed to this logical objection. Any such plan implies, however, the imposition of *some* taxation even upon the very poorest persons, and this is *prima facie* incompatible with the principle of least sacrifice: and, even if this point be waived, there is still no positive ground for asserting that the principle of least sacrifice will be best promoted by a tax system conforming to the canon of equal sacrifice. Nevertheless, some enlightenment can be gained from an attempt to work out in the concrete the implications of a system of that kind.

§ 2. It is easy to see that the equal-sacrifice ideal cannot be attained by any system of commodity taxes with different rates on different commodities. For different people with equal incomes often have different tastes, and so are accustomed to spend their incomes in different ways. If expenditure on whisky is taxed at a high rate and expenditure on beer at a low rate, the man who spends £50 on whisky is penalised as against the man who spends £50 on beer. On these lines there was for many years an Irish grievance. It was given in evidence before the Royal Commission on the Financial Relations between Great Britain and Ireland of 1896 that: "Whilst the tax on spirits, the article more generally consumed in Ireland, is equal to from two-thirds to three-fourths of the price, the tax upon beer, which is the popular article of consumption in England, is only about one-sixth of the price ".[1] It may be added that, under non-uniform commodity taxes not only will different persons of equal incomes suffer different burdens at the same time, but the relation between their burdens will vary as their tastes change. Thus in his Budget speech of 1904 Mr. (later Sir Austen) Chamberlain observed that the substitution of expenditure on excursions for expenditure on drink was substantially modifying the distribution of tax burdens. There is also a more subtle point. Suppose that there are two persons of equal income and general economic status, that in the aggregate of their tastes they are similar, in the sense that they would get equal satisfactions from equal incomes if they were permitted to spend them as they chose, but that one likes and purchases commodity A and not commodity B, the other commodity B and not commodity A. Suppose, further, that taxes are imposed upon commodities A and B in such wise that both these persons pay the same amount of tax. It will not necessarily follow that they suffer equal real burdens. If the demand of one for his commodity is more elastic than the demand of the other for his, the former will suffer the larger hurt ; because, while they both pay the same sum of money to the Treasury, he loses more satisfaction than the other in respect of consumption which is prevented by the tax from coming into being and so contributes no revenue. In this chapter, therefore, I shall assume that all the revenue required is raised through an income tax : and I shall inquire what form of income tax would impose equal sacrifices upon all taxpayers.

§ 3. It will be well, as a prelude to this study, to refer briefly to some of the familiar difficulties which hamper attempts to define the concept income for the purpose of the tax-gatherer. What he desires — and should desire — to strike is real income, income, that is to say, conceived as a flow of so much goods and services. It is possible to conceive a state of affairs in which the tax-gatherer should make assessment upon this directly without any mediation. In actual life, however, apart from the services which an occupying owner derives from his house, it is generally held that only that part of real income which has a money counterpart can

[1] *Report*, p. 21.

be brought into account; to bring in other parts would involve such high administrative costs as not to be worth while. In general, therefore, the tax-gatherer has to content himself, for his object of assessment, with money income. In resorting to this makeshift he does not, of course, obtain quite the same result as he would have obtained if he had been in possession of a more efficient technique. He leaves outside his net, and so differentiates in favour of, certain forms of real income, not because he wishes to do so, but because he cannot help himself. Thus he neglects the benefit which the owner of a motor-car or yacht, when he uses it himself, obtains from it directly, only including what he obtains from it indirectly when he hires it out for money. He omits also certain parts of real income that some employees — *e.g.* a bank-manager with a rent-free house — receive in kind. Moreover, it is easy to imagine a type of society in which all the members should club together in a self-sufficing community, growing corn, baking bread, making clothes, digging out coal and building houses, and sharing the proceeds of their joint work among themselves without any money payment whatever being made. Conceivably, the whole nation might organise itself into an immense mutual association on this pattern, with the result that, though its real income remained as large as it is now, there would be no money income at all. If this happened, money income would no longer be even a plausible index of real income. In civilised communities as at present organised it so happens, however, that by far the greater part of real income is represented in money income,[1] so that

[1] In the co-operative societies of the United Kingdom it is sometimes suggested that a very large element of non-monetary income comes into being annually. This, however, does not seem to be so. On the side of labour, in the widest sense, there are paid managers, a paid staff and paid workpeople. There is also an unpaid committee, corresponding to the paid directorate of a joint-stock company. The work of this committee is the only item on the side of labour in which an income of real service is embodied without a money counterpart. Plainly it can only amount to a very trifling proportion of the whole. On the side of capital the contention that the co-operative form of business organisation enables a considerable amount of real income to be created which is not represented in money is more plausible. The service rendered by the share-capital of members has a fairly satisfactory money representative in the interest that is paid on it. But, so far as capital is obtained by contributions to reserve funds and by the retention on the part of the societies of moneys which are to become "divis" during the interval between the purchases by members of goods for cash and the dis-

the use of it in lieu of real income as the tax-gatherer's gauge involves only a small error.

§ 4. A second difficulty has to do with the relation between income and capital. The intention of an income tax on the English model, *i.e.* when savings are not exempted,[1] is to strike that part of the gross incomings of a year which is left over after provision has been made for maintaining capital equipment intact. Practically, however, it is not easy to draw a precise line in this matter. If a machine, which cost £100 at the beginning of the year, is worn-out during the year and a new similar machine can still be had for £100, in order to get the net income of the user of the machine we should clearly deduct £100 from his gross income. But, if during the year the price of this type of machine has risen or fallen, what exact allowance should be made? Again, when capital equipment suffers depreciation otherwise than through physical wear and tear, difficult questions arise. What allowance is to be made for the loss of value suffered by a physically perfect machine in consequence of somebody else having invented a better one; what allowance for the disappearance of the value of a mineshaft when the mine is worked out? Again, if a man buys a piece of property — a house or a necklace of pearls or the ordinary shares of some company — and the value of the property rises 50 per cent during the year, is this accretion of value to be counted as income or as

tribution of the " divis ", and so far as this capital is employed in the societies' own business, with the result of lowering prices or increasing the rate of " divi ", there is no taxable money representative of the real services that it renders. Thus we may imagine a society buying up a mill out of its accumulated reserves. If this mill had previously been earning £10,000 and were run now with exactly equal efficiency, no earnings of capital would appear as money profit, but the whole £10,000's worth of real income would remain, and would take the form either of lower prices or of larger dividends on purchases. But quantitatively this consideration is not important. Thus the reserve fund of the whole body of British Retail Co-operative Societies amounted in 1925 to a little over £6,000,000. If we take the average amount of " divis " to have been 17 millions a year, distributed quarterly, the average amount of capital held by the societies in respect of " divis " would have been $2\frac{1}{8}$ millions. If we reckon the real rate of return on the $8\frac{1}{8}$ millions capital composed of these two sums to be 10 per cent, we have some £812,000 a year of real income not represented in money income. This, belonging as it does to a body of nearly 5,000,000 persons, amounts to about 3s. 3d. per head per annum. On the (optimistic) assumption that co-operators on the average were liable to income tax at one-half the then standard rate, the aggregate revenue due on this £812,000 would have been £81,200.

[1] Cf. *post*, Chapter X.

an addition to capital? Is it to be treated in the same way when the appreciated property is held and when it is sold in the market and the profit realised in cash? Nobody would seriously propose to count it if it is not realised. But, if it is realised, it would seem that, with an income tax under which savings are not exempted, it should, for consistency, be counted. Administrative considerations, however, compel us to leave this type of profit out of account except when it is made by professional dealers.[1]

§ 5. A third difficulty concerns expenses. Plainly, what we wish to assess is not gross income, but net income, that is gross income minus whatever expenses are specially involved in the process of earning it — the purchase of tools or materials, travelling to and from work, and so on. In a sense, of course, a man's expenditure upon food and ordinary clothing constitutes a part of the expenses involved in earning income, for, if he did not eat and wear clothes, he certainly would not earn anything. But it is everywhere agreed that, for our present purpose, only expenditure which is incurred in immediate and special connection with the work or equipment from which income is derived should be reckoned as expenses. Even so, there will be some difficult points to settle; what part of the expenditure of the Head Master of a school in entertaining parents may properly be reckoned as expenses; what part of a doctor's bill for petrol for his car may be so reckoned; and so on. Though the principle in this matter is perfectly clear, the practical application of it is not free from doubt.[2]

§ 6. There remains a fourth and more serious difficulty. It was said in § 3 that what the tax-gatherer desires — or should desire — to strike is real income. But, while money raised in taxation from one set of people to be transferred to another (or the same) set in interest on war loan[3] or gratuitous pensions may be taken to represent real income *either* before it is transferred *or* after it is transferred, it cannot be so taken on both occasions; any more than the £200, which a father with a £1000 a year allows to his son, represents real income in both their hands. If national income

[1] Cf. *post*, Chapter XII, § 2.

[2] For a fuller discussion of the subject-matter of this chapter, cf. *The Economics of Welfare*, part i, chap. iii.

[3] Unless indeed we are prepared to regard not having been conquered in past wars as an *amenity* entering into current real income.

apart from transfers works out at £7000 million and transfers come to £500 million, the money income that represents real income is £7000 million, not £7500 million. Under the British Income Tax Law, however, the whole £7500 million is assessable to tax ; so that what is struck is not merely real income — social income as it is usually called — but this plus something else besides. To this extent the income of our Income Tax commissioners is a hybrid and illogical concept.[1] With this cautionary observation I leave the problem of definition.

§ 7. It is plain that no income tax could impose equal sacrifice upon all taxpayers if the amount of tax to be paid by each of them depended merely upon the size of his income without regard to other elements in his economic situation. For equality of sacrifice taxation must be adjusted, not merely to the various amounts of income received by persons whose incidental circumstances are similar, but also to the various incidental circumstances of persons in receipt of equal incomes. This is a well-worn topic, and I shall content myself with a very summary discussion of it.[2]

§ 8. Imagine three men, each with an income of £1000, but one a bachelor, another a married man without children whose wife has no income, and another a married man with two children whose wife and children have no income. It is evident that equal sacrifice will not be imposed if these three men are taxed to an equal extent. More generally, since equal incomes, each legally belonging to a single owner, often have to support different numbers of people, allowance must somehow be made for that fact in any income-tax scheme which aims at equal sacrifice. Ideally, of course, the scale of the allowance should be related to many other conditions besides the mere size of the family. " It is manifestly absurd to assume that a family with four daughters in high school or college can live as well on the same income as can a family with four children under 10 years of age." [3] Practically,

[1] The British income tax violates the condition of a true income tax in two further matters. First, terminable annuities are treated as taxable income without deduction being made of that part of them which constitutes repayment of capital. Secondly, that part of income which is saved through insurance premiums is — within certain limits — not treated as taxable income.

[2] Cf. my article on " The Report of the Royal Commission on the Income Tax " in *Essays in Applied Economics*.

[3] King, *Journal of Political Economy*, vol. xxix, p. 583.

however, this class of consideration cannot be taken into account. We must perforce content ourselves with a rough adjustment based on the number of dependants — what constitutes a dependant being defined by more or less arbitrary rules — that an income receiver has to support. This being granted, it becomes necessary to decide how large allowances should be made for differences in number of dependants, or, more loosely, in family estate. Plainly *some* allowance ought to be made at all levels of income, for at all levels a bachelor has more free money than a man with an equal income who has children to support. But, if the principle of equal sacrifice requires a man with a wife and three children to be taxed one *r*th part of what a bachelor is taxed at a given income level, it will require the family man to be taxed more than one *r*th part of what the bachelor is taxed at a higher income level. More generally, it will require the fraction which the family man's tax forms of the bachelor's tax to rise as the income level rises. Thus, if at the £500 level a man in family situation A should be made to pay 50 per cent of what one in family situation B pays, at the £50,000 level he should be made to pay much more than 50 per cent, and at the £500,000 level very nearly 100 per cent. Under the British system in 1927 allowances were so arranged that a married person with three children paid £36 less tax than a bachelor at all income levels from £800 onwards; in 1937–8 he paid £65 less and in 1941–2 £105 less for all levels from £500 upwards. Expressed in proportions, when incomes are wholly earned, the fraction of the bachelor's tax paid by the married man with three children at 1941–2 rate works out approximately as follows:

At £350 . . .	9 per cent
£500 . . .	33 ,,
£1,000 . . .	57 ,,
£1,500 . . .	70 ,,
£2,000 . . .	88 ,,
£20,000 . . .	99¼ ,,

We have no means except vague guess-work to determine whether this arrangement is in reasonable conformity with the principle of equal sacrifice. The Colwyn Committee reported: "Some of us think that, if regard is had solely to ability to pay, the amount of the family allowances ought to vary to some extent with the size of the taxpayer's income, instead of being absolutely fixed ".[1] This means that the percentages ought to be smaller than they are in the lower half of the preceding table.

§ 9. Alongside of differences in family situation should be set differences in respect of the possession of property that will yield income after the owner has ceased to work. From the present point of view it is immaterial whether the owner of such property is now deriving his income from it or from his own work. The essential fact is that in it provision is made for his children after his death, and that, therefore, he need not use so large a part of his present income to make such provision as he would feel called upon to do if he did not possess devisable property. Consequently, if two men have equal incomes but one has property and the other not, equal taxation will inflict a larger sacrifice upon the latter, and, in order to secure equal sacrifice, some allowance must be made in his favour. Since, however, the amount of income which a man feels under obligation to provide for his children is largely determined by the amount of his present income and the standard of life implied by that, a rich man with an exclusively earned income is certain to withdraw from current expenditure a much larger absolute sum than a poor man similarly situated would do. Hence, if the allowances are given by way of abatement from assessable income, it is certain that the amount of the allowances in this sense ought to be progressive. Under the British scale ruling at the date of the Colwyn Report (1926) each £ of earned income was counted as equivalent to $\frac{5}{6}$ths of a £ of investment income until a maximum allowance of £250 assessable income (not tax) was reached. For a bachelor the tax on wholly earned income worked out at the following percentages of that on wholly unearned income :

At £200 . . .	48 per cent
£400 . . .	65 ,,
£500 . . .	67 ,,
£800 . . .	75 ,,
£1,000 . . .	78 ,,
£2,000 . . .	86 ,,
£20,000 . . .	99·3 ,,

[1] *Report*, p. 345.

The Colwyn Committee expressed the view: "The earned income relief is in itself (*i.e.* when the Income Tax is viewed apart from the death duties) entirely inadequate to mark the difference in ability to pay between an income wholly earned and one consisting wholly of investments".[1] This means that, if there were no death duties, the percentages ought to have been much smaller than they were throughout the above table. In fact, of course, there are in England heavy progressive death duties, which, if reckoned as post-dated taxes on investment income, greatly augment the relative weight of tax upon investment income for other than poor persons. In 1937–8 the earned income allowance stood at $\frac{1}{5}$th and the maximum assessment allowance at £300. In 1941–2 figures were $\frac{1}{10}$th and £150.

§ 10. Assuming that appropriate adjustment can be and has been made for the foregoing differences in economic status, it has next to be observed that, if an equal sacrifice income tax is to be possible, certain conditions must be satisfied. The most important of these is that, apart from differences based on objective facts, which can be allowed for in the terms of our tax formula, different people with equal incomes must be so far similar that equal reductions in their incomes involve equal sacrifice. If this condition is not fulfilled, if, for example, one man in a given economic situation with a £1000 income is so constituted that to take any sum, say £100, away from him causes him more hurt than another man in a like economic situation with an equal income would suffer from a like bereavement, no income-tax formula is conceivable which will impose equal sacrifices upon these two men. This condition, therefore, unreal as it is, is a vital one. It implies, we may note, that the satisfaction which people in a given economic situation derive from income depends solely on the amount of that income, and is not affected at all by the amount (if any) or the nature of the work that they do to earn it. A second condition is that the amount of revenue required is such that it is possible to raise it without imposing upon any rich man a tax so heavy that the satisfaction taken away from him is greater than the total satisfaction which some poor man would be enjoying if he were subjected to no tax at all. This condition, while

[1] *Report*, p. 135.

not less necessary than the other, is less important, in the sense that it does not involve so wide a breach with reality.

§ 11. Before the argument can proceed, it is necessary further that we agree upon the way in which income that is not consumed, but is saved and invested, shall be regarded. In order that an equal-sacrifice formula may be *possible*, people in each separately definable category (*e.g.* bachelors) who have equal incomes must save equal amounts. This condition is implicit in the first condition laid down in the preceding section. It means that of any income x, belonging to persons in a given category, $f(x)$ is always saved and $\{x - f(x)\}$ always consumed. On this basis it is open to us to do either of two things. On the one hand, we can accept the fact that saved income does not yield any satisfaction to the saver in itself, but only in the fruits which are derived from it later on; and, therefore, that such part of taxation as is paid out of what would have been savings involves directly no sacrifice. On the other hand, we can adopt a convention under which each unit of saved income is conceived as yielding now "virtual satisfaction", derived from the actual satisfactions which are looked for from it in the future and measured by the saver's desire for it. That is to say, if I desire to save a hundredth £ as much as I desire to spend a fiftieth £ on clothes, I am, on this convention, said to obtain equal satisfactions from saving a hundredth £ and from spending a fiftieth £ in that manner. The former plan is, in some ways, nearer to reality than the latter, but to adopt it would complicate the argument without rendering it more illuminating. I shall, therefore, here adopt the latter plan. For the present I shall ignore the fact that a continuing — as distinguished from an isolated single-year — tax assessed upon income without remission either of savings or of income derived from savings involves an element of differentiation against the savings use. This matter is deferred to Chapter X.

§ 12. Though the ground is now fully prepared, it will be convenient to pause for a moment before attempting a constructive argument, in order to clear away a false opinion which appears to be somewhat widely entertained. This opinion is to the effect that, in all circumstances, in order to secure equal sacrifice, the tax formula must be, in some measure, *progressive*, in the sense that the rate of taxation per £ of income grows as incomes grow. This proposition is supposed to be logically deducible from the law of diminishing utility. That supposition is incorrect. All that the law of diminishing utility asserts is that the last £1 of a £1000 income carries less satisfaction than the last £1 of a £100 income does. From this datum it cannot be inferred that, in order to secure equal sacrifice — nor even, we may add, equal proportionate sacrifice [1] — taxation must be progressive. In order to prove that the principle of equal sacrifice necessarily involves progression we should need to know that the last £10 of a £1000 income carry less satisfaction than the last £1 of a £100 income; and this the law of diminishing utility does not assert.

§ 13. Remembering the condition set out in § 10, that all members of our tax group are similar, in the sense that the function connecting quantities of income and quantities of satisfaction is the same for all, let us write x for quantity of income, $F(x)$ for the quantity of satisfaction derived by any taxpayer from the use of a net income x, and $\psi(x)$ for the quantity of tax that is taken from a gross income x. Then, *provided that the amount of work done is not altered by the announcement effects of taxation*, it is easy to see that an equal-sacrifice income tax is constituted when ψ is such that, for all values of x, whatever the amount of the revenue required may be, $[F(x) - F\{x - \psi(x)\}] = k$ (k being a constant). The condition that the amount of work done shall not be altered by the announcement effects of taxation is that the satisfaction derived from increasing a gross income x by a small increment is not altered by the imposition of the tax. With the notation employed above this condition may be written

$$\frac{dF(x)}{dx} = \frac{dF\{x - \psi(x)\}}{dx}.$$

But the equation $[F(x) - F\{x - \psi(x)\}] = k$ implies that this condition is satisfied. In other words, it so happens that the tax formula, which would constitute an equal sacrifice income tax, provided that the amount of work that people do is not modified by the announcement effects of taxation, also ensures that the amount of work that they do shall in fact not be modified.

§ 14. To this conclusion an important objection may,

[1] Cf. Edgeworth, *Papers relating to Political Economy*, vol. ii, p. 240.

indeed, be made. Let the conditions be such that the scale given by the above tax formula assesses a £1000 income to £200 of tax and a £1001 income to £200 : 4s. Then, *ex hypothesi*, the work done to produce the 1001st £ yields to the taxpayer the same net satisfaction as it would do if there were no tax. But, it may be argued, though this is so, the taxpayer does not realise that it is so. All he realises is that, by working less and cutting down his gross income to £1000, he will save 4s. in taxation, and it is his opinion about the facts, and not the facts themselves, which governs his conduct. This objection, plausible as it is, has, however, an answer. Though the taxpayer may not realise the truth explicitly, he will realise it implicitly : for the fact that, if he refrains from securing the 1001st £ of gross income, his net income will be only £800 instead of £800 : 16s., will be just as patent to him as the fact that he will pay 4s. less to the Exchequer. Thus, let us start from a state of things in which the taxpayer is producing an income of £1001 and paying a tax of £200 : 4s. He reflects that, by cutting his income to £1000, he will get off 4s. of tax, and reflects about nothing else. Let us suppose that he does in fact, in consequence of this, cut his income to £1000. When he has got there, he finds that the utility of his last £ of income is more than it was before, because his income is smaller : while the disutility of the last unit of work is less than it was before, because he is doing less work. Therefore he will again increase the amount of his work, and, in the conditions here assumed, it will pay him to go on increasing it till his gross income again becomes £1001. Any departure, which, owing to a misconception of the facts, he may make from an income of £1001, will be corrected in this way.[1] What he thinks is happening may determine his first step,

[1] It is thus immaterial what technical form is given to the tax scale. A formula that announces a tax-rate of 5s. in the £ with abatement of £500 obviously raises the tax of a man, who increases his income from £1000 to £1001, from £125 to £125 : 5s. The same effect is produced by a formula which allows no abatement, but taxes £1000 at 2s. 6d. and £1001 at 2s. $6\frac{1}{40}$d. Under the former plan a man with a £1001 income may well think — mistakenly, of course — that by contracting his income he will escape more taxation than a similar man subject to the second plan would do, and, consequently, as a first step, may contract his income more. But, if he does this, the forces impelling him to take a second step in the reverse direction will be proportionately stronger; so that ultimately both men alike come to rest in the same position.

but what is really happening determines his final position. It is, therefore, true in the actual world, and not merely in a world of perfectly intelligent beings, that the tax formula $F(x) - F\{x - \psi(x)\} = k$ leaves the amount of work that people do unmodified, and so, subject to the conditions stated above, constitutes an equal-sacrifice income tax formula of general application. From that formula, when the function F and the constant k are given, the arithmetical value of $\psi(x)$ for every value of x can be determined. The list of these values is the tax scale, which, in the conditions given, will conform to the principle of equal sacrifice. It is evident that the magnitude of the constant k depends on the form of the function F, the aggregate amount of the community's income, its distribution among the taxpayers and the amount of revenue required. When, therefore, these things are known, the derivation of the required scale is a matter of mathematics.

§ 15. A study of the equation set out above shows that in one special case a very simple formula, and one, moreover, which is independent of the value of k, and so of the amount of revenue required, will provide an equal-sacrifice income tax. This special case is that in which $xF'(x)$ is constant for all values of x, in which, that is to say, the curve whose ordinates represent quantities of marginal satisfaction and its abscissae quantities of income is a rectangular hyperbola. From the equation $F(x) - F\{x - \psi(x)\} = k$ we derive

$$F'(x) - \{1 - \psi'(x)\}\frac{dF\{x - \psi(x)\}}{d\{x - \psi(x)\}} = 0.$$

Since $xF'(x)$ is constant for all values of x, this yields

$$\frac{1}{x} - \{1 - \psi'(x)\}\frac{1}{x - \psi(x)} = 0,$$

$$\therefore \quad \psi'(x) = \frac{\psi(x)}{x}.$$

Since everybody would agree that it is unreasonable to collect any tax from a nil income, we know that $\psi(0) = 0$. Hence the above equation is satisfied when $\psi'(x)$ is a constant; that is to say, when the rate of tax is the same for all values of x. In other words, in the special case in which the income-utility curve of the representative taxpayer — and in this matter, it will be remembered, we are assuming all taxpayers to be alike — is a rectangular hyperbola, a proportionate income tax will impose equal sacrifice upon all taxpayers.

§ 16. To this result it is easy to add another. If the income-utility curve is such that, for all values of x, $xF'(x)$ increases as x increases, that is to say, if the income-utility curve is flatter than a rectangular hyperbola, $\psi'(x)<\frac{\psi(x)}{x}$; and in the contrary case $\psi'(x)>\frac{\psi(x)}{x}$. To allow the former of these inequalities $\psi''(x)$ must be negative; to allow the latter positive. It follows that, if the income-utility curve is flatter than a rectangular hyperbola, we shall require, so as to impose equal sacrifices on all taxpayers, a tax formula whose rates are regressive: if the income-utility curve is steeper than a rectangular hyperbola, we shall require one whose rates are progressive. Should the income-utility curve be flatter than a rectangular hyperbola in some parts of its course and steeper in others, our formula will have to be regressive for some values of x and progressive for others. But complexities arise here into which it is not necessary to enter.

§ 17. In order to apply these results, we need, of course, to know whether, in the community we are considering, the income-utility curve of the representative taxpayer has the form of a rectangular hyperbola or a flatter form or a steeper form. When Sidgwick writes, "If equalisation of burdens were the sole consideration, the equity of a graduated rate of taxation, rapidly increasing as incomes rise, could hardly be gainsaid", he is implicitly asserting, "The proposition that the income-utility curve of the representative taxpayer is steeper throughout than a rectangular hyperbola can hardly be gainsaid". We desire to know whether this proposition is true, and, if not, what proposition should be substituted for it. To say that the income-utility curve is a rectangular hyperbola is to say, as is implied in the argument of § 15, that to subtract 10 per cent (or any other percentage) from a man's income always causes the same loss of satisfaction whatever the size of the income: that £10 off a £100 income means the same in terms of sacrifice as £100 off a £1000 income and £1000 off a £10,000 income.[1] Plainly it is impossible to decide whether

[1] That the above condition is in fact the condition of a rectangular hyperbola can be shown otherwise as follows. With our previous notation,

the income-utility curve of the members of our community (all of whom are assumed to be alike) is of this character or of some other defined character by any process of general reasoning. Nor is the Weber-Fechner law as to physical stimuli and the reactions found to be associated with them in physiological laboratories of direct relevance to our problem, though it affords a suggestive analogy. The only procedure available is to ask ourselves directly a series of questions in the form: Given that a £10 cut from £100 income involves so much sacrifice to the representative man, what size of cut from an £800, or a £1000, or a £10,000 income would involve about the same amount of sacrifice? The questions must be put carefully. We are concerned, not with a single-event tax, but with continuing tax systems. Therefore, when we speak of "cuts" from incomes of different sizes, we must not imagine the people affected to have developed their life and tastes to fit with the incomes named. That would run counter to our supposition that everybody is to be regarded as a representative man in respect of tastes. Tastes must be taken as given and alike for all. An accurate formulation of our questions, therefore, is: Given the difference in satisfactions yielded to a representative man by a £200 and a £190 income respectively, what is the income, the difference between which and £1000 income will represent that amount of satisfaction?; and so on for all other incomes. It is extraordinarily difficult to give, even within wide limits, any confident answer to this type of question. I feel fairly certain that the gap between £200 and £190 means more than the gap between £1000 and, say, £980. But does it mean more or less than the gap between £1000 and £970, or between £1000 and £940? I hesitate to say. Bernouilli's familiar hypothesis amounts, in effect, to the proposition that, in respect of incomes in excess of what is required to yield the necessaries of life, the income-utility curve of the representative man is a rectangular hyperbola. *Prima facie*, this seems not unplausible — much more plausible than Cramer's hypothesis, which Marshall mentions, that the

and it being taken for granted that the curve in debate slopes downwards towards the right, let h be any constant fraction. Then, in order that $\int_0^x F(x) - \int_0^{hx} F(hx)$ may be constant for all values of x, it is necessary that $xF(x) = hxF(hx)$; a condition which, in general, implies that $xF(x)$ is constant for all values of x.

satisfaction derived from income varies as the square root of its amount. But the plausibility is, I think, due to the fact that we have left out of account an important consideration. There is an ambiguity in the concept of an income-utility curve. This may refer either to an actual individual, whose consumable income is supposed to vary while the consumable incomes of the rest of the community are taken as fixed, or to a representative individual whose income, *along with the consumable incomes of all other similar individuals*, is supposed to vary. Income-utility functions conceived in these two ways are different from one another; for the reason that the satisfaction which a man derives from the possession of a given income depends, not only on the absolute amount of the income, but also on the relation subsisting between it and the incomes of other people. Obviously, since taxation is concerned with groups, and not with isolated individuals standing among untaxed neighbours, it is the second and not the first kind of income-utility curve that is of interest to us. For small and moderate incomes the difference between the two is probably slight. But for large incomes the proportion of the satisfaction-yield which is due to their *relative* magnitude is certainly high. While it would hurt a man in the £10,000 class a great deal if he had to make shift with £5000 while other people similarly situated were left with £10,000, the difference between the aggregate satisfaction enjoyed by the £10,000 class in a community where there were no taxes and in one where all members of this class were mulcted regularly in 50 per cent levies — on the assumption, of course, that other rival classes were subject to a like order of taxation — would, I submit, be extremely small.[1] So soon as this distinction between the two sorts of income-utility curve is grasped, we perceive that, for incomes above a moderate level, the relevant curve will be inclined much more steeply than *prima facie* impressions, derived from contemplation of the curve which is not relevant, at first blush suggested. It is *not* plausible to hold that cuts of £10,000 from incomes of £100,000, £1000 from incomes of £10,000, £100 from incomes of £1000, and £50 from incomes of £500 all imply about the same sacrifice. The first of these cuts, if imposed in a general form, would, apart from temporary dislocations, involve practi-

[1] Cf. *The Economics of Welfare*, 4th edition, p. 90.

cally no sacrifice, the second very little, the third a substantial amount, and the fourth a great deal. I suggest, therefore, that, in the passage cited on p. 89, Sidgwick's instinct was a true one. An equal sacrifice income tax would require large incomes to be taxed at *much* higher percentage rates than moderate incomes. Even if only a small revenue were required, not far from the whole excess amount by which large incomes exceed, say £5000, would need to be absorbed into the Treasury.

§ 18. Professor Irving Fisher has discovered and published a method by which it may prove feasible to deduce from statistics of prices and family budgets important information about the shape of income-utility curves.[1] To the best of my judgement this method is theoretically valid, but much laborious statistical work will need to be done before it can yield practical fruit. It is, none the less, interesting to learn from Professor Fisher that the results of a preliminary and partial application made by him to certain statistics of the United States Bureau of Labour " confirm the common idea that progressive rather than regressive taxation of incomes is justified ".[2]

§ 19. It remains to make one final observation. If we decide that the income-utility curve is a rectangular hyperbola, this carries with it the implication that, for equal sacrifice, proportionate taxes should be imposed whatever the amount of revenue required. Should we decide, however, that the income-utility curve is not a rectangular hyperbola, and that, therefore, something other than proportionate taxation is needed, the relation between the formulae appropriate to different quantities of revenue will not be thus simple. This point has some practical importance, because it is often tacitly assumed that, if a given tax scale is equitable in respect of one amount of revenue, a scale in which all the rates imposed are increased in an equal proportion must necessarily be equitable when 10 per cent or 50 per cent more revenue is needed. Pressed to the extreme, indeed, this thesis manifestly breaks down. For example, while a rate of 10s. 6d. in the £ for the highest incomes may well be equitable in relation

[1] Cf. *A Statistical Method for Measuring Marginal Utility and Testing the Justice of a Progressive Income Tax* (1927).

[2] *Loc. cit.* p. 193.

to certain budget needs, a rate of 21s. in the £ could not possibly be equitable in relation to a revenue double as large; for to reduce an income of £100,000 to zero is bound to inflict more sacrifice than results from reducing, say, a £10,000 income to some sum in excess of zero. The thesis is not, however, merely false in extreme cases: it is false in general. If the formula $R = \psi(x)$ furnishes an equal-sacrifice income tax in respect of a revenue R and the formula $mR = \phi(x)$ in respect of a revenue mR, $\phi(x) = m\psi(x)$ only in the case of proportionate taxes. In all other cases the equal-sacrifice formulae appropriate to revenues of different magnitudes will belong, not to the same, but to different families.

CHAPTER VIII

TAXES AND BOUNTIES TO CORRECT MALADJUSTMENTS

§ 1. In the course of the second Part of *The Economics of Welfare* I discussed at length a number of maladjustments in the allocation of resources between different employments, which tend to come about when private self-interest has free play. I was not concerned in that discussion, nor am I concerned now, with what are sometimes called " errors of distribution " in the aggregate income of the community as between rich people and poor people. The facts of distribution in this sense being taken — provisionally — as an unalterable *datum*, there still remain important maladjustments, which prevent resources from being allocated in the *optimum* manner. Of these maladjustments there are two principal causes. The first is that, in respect of certain goods and services, the return at the margin which resources devoted to making them yields to their makers is not equal to the full return which the community as a whole receives, but falls short of or exceeds that return. In other words, the value of the marginal private net product of resources so employed is greater or less than the value of the marginal social net product. The second cause is that in respect of certain goods and services, the ratio, so to speak, between people's desire and the satisfaction which results from the fulfilment of desire is greater, or less, than it is in respect of other goods and services. In view of the detailed discussion contained in *The Economics of Welfare* it will be sufficient here to illustrate these statements in a summary way.

§ 2. The value of the marginal social net product exceeds that of the marginal private net product when resources yield, besides the product or service which is sold and paid for, other products or services for which no payment can be collected. Thus, as Sidgwick observes, " it may easily happen that the benefits of a well-placed lighthouse must be largely enjoyed by ships on which no toll can be conveniently levied ".[1] Again, uncompensated services are rendered by investments

[1] *Principles of Political Economy*, p. 406.

made in establishing in cities private parks, which improve the air of neighbouring houses, and in planting, in dry districts, forests which improve the climatic conditions of the surrounding country. Such services are also rendered by investments on the part of factory owners in smoke-consuming devices; for these, besides economising fuel for their owners, also diminish the washing bills of people living near by. They are rendered, again, by resources devoted to developing industries of decreasing supply price, in which expansion of aggregate output makes possible the introduction of new external or (in single-firm industries) internal economics. *Per contra* the value of the marginal social net product falls short of the value of the marginal private net product when resources yield, besides the commodity which is sold and paid for, a dis-commodity for which those on whom it is inflicted are unable to exact compensation. Thus incidental uncharged disservices are rendered to third parties when the owner of a site in the residential quarter of a city builds a factory there and so destroys a great part of the amenities of neighbouring sites; or when he invests resources in erecting in a crowded centre buildings which, by contracting the air space and the playing room of the neighbourhood, injure the health and efficiency of the families living there. In like manner uncharged disservices are rendered by resources devoted to developing industries of increasing supply price from the standpoint of the community, if there are any such, *i.e.* industries in respect of which an increase in output involves an increase in the supply price to the community.[1] It would be easy to multiply examples of these two sorts of divergence between the values at the margin of private and of social net products. The existence of these divergences is bound to lead to maladjustments. It is, of course, possible to conceive a state of affairs in which the value of the marginal private net product of the resources employed differs from the value of the marginal social net product, whether by defect or by excess, to exactly the same extent in all occupations. In this case there would be no maladjustments. But the case is

[1] As is pointed out in *The Economics of Welfare*, industries of increasing supply price, in which higher prices are associated with larger outputs merely because the use of land has to be paid for at a higher rate, do not fall into this class. Cf. *loc. cit.* part ii, chap. xi, § 5.

fanciful and unreal. In fact it is certain that there will be maladjustments, investments being stopped off too soon in some occupations and carried too far in others.

§ 3. The line of analysis sketched out in the preceding section is relevant to the choice made between competing methods of obtaining commodities which it is physically possible to obtain either by home manufacture or by importation. Apart from temporary borrowings and so on, when an article is imported from abroad, it is, in effect, obtained by the manufacture and export in exchange for it of something else. The play of self-interest, in the absence of fiscal intervention, determines how much of any commodity, which is physically capable of being made at home, shall be secured by the direct process of manufacturing it here and how much by the indirect process of manufacturing its purchase price in exports. In certain circumstances the balance which is thus set up will not be the best possible. Suppose, for example, that this country is exceptionally well qualified to make some commodity which it is now importing, so that, if the early difficulties could be got over, home manufacture would ultimately involve less real cost than importation. The distant and diffused gain from investments directed to building up the industry which makes the commodity in question may well fail to enter at full value into the profit envisaged by potential investors; with the result that too little of the commodity is obtained by home manufacture and too much by sending exports to purchase it. This type of maladjustment, which will be considered more at length in a later chapter,[1] is on the same footing as the maladjustments discussed in the preceding section.

§ 4. Of abnormal relations between desire and the satisfaction obtained from the fulfilment of desire there is one, and, I think, only one, example of large practical importance. This has to do with people's attitude towards the future. Broadly speaking, everybody prefers present pleasures or satisfactions of given magnitude to future pleasures or satisfactions of equal magnitude, even when the latter are perfectly certain to occur. But this preference for present pleasures does not — the idea is self-contradictory — imply that a present pleasure of given magnitude is any *greater* than a

[1] Cf. *post*, Chap. XXIII, § 4.

future pleasure of the same magnitude. It implies only that our telescopic faculty is defective, and that we, therefore, see future pleasures, as it were, on a diminished scale. That this is the right explanation is proved by the fact that exactly the same diminution is experienced when, apart from our tendency to forget ungratifying incidents, we contemplate the past. Hence, the existence of preference for present over equally certain future pleasures does not imply that any economic dissatisfaction would be suffered if future pleasures were substituted at full value for present ones. The non-satisfaction this year of a man's preference to consume this year rather than next year is balanced by the satisfaction of his preference next year to consume next year rather than to have consumed this year. Hence there is nothing to put against the fact that, if we set out a series of exactly equal satisfactions — *satisfactions*, not objects that yield satisfactions — all of them absolutely certain to occur over a series of years beginning now, the desires which a man will entertain for these several satisfactions will not be equal, but will be represented by a scale of magnitudes continually diminishing as the years to which the satisfactions are allocated become more remote. This reveals a far-reaching economic disharmony. For it implies that people distribute their resources between the present, the near future and the remote future on the basis of a wholly irrational preference. When they have a choice between two satisfactions, they will not necessarily choose the larger of the two, but will often devote themselves to producing or obtaining a smaller one now in preference to a much larger one some years hence. The inevitable result is that efforts directed towards the remote future are starved relatively to those directed to the near future, while these in turn are starved relatively to efforts directed towards the present. Suppose, for example, that a person's telescopic faculty is such that he discounts future satisfactions, which are perfectly certain to occur, at the rate of 5 per cent per annum. Then, instead of being ready to work for next year, or a year ten years hence, so long as a given increment of effort will yield as much satisfaction as an equal increment devoted to work for the present, he will only work for next year so long as the yield of an increment of effort employed for that year is 1·05 times, and for a year ten years hence so long as it is $(1 \cdot 05)^{10}$ times, the yield of an increment employed for the present.

§ 5. Nor is this all. Since human life is limited, such fruits of work or saving as accrue after a considerable interval are not enjoyed by the person to whose efforts they are due. This means that the satisfaction with which his desire is connected is not his own satisfaction, but the satisfaction of somebody else, possibly an immediate successor whose interest he regards as nearly equivalent to his own, possibly somebody quite remote in blood or in time, about whom he scarcely cares at all. It follows that, even though our desires for equal satisfactions *of our own* occurring at different times were equal, our desire for future satisfactions would often be less intense than for present satisfactions, because it is very likely that the future satisfactions will not be our own. This discrepancy will be more important the more distant is the time at which the source of future satisfaction is likely to come into being; for every addition to the interval increases the chance of death, not merely to oneself, but also to children and near relatives and friends in whom one's interest is likely to be most keen. No doubt, this obstacle to investment for distant returns is partly overcome by stock-exchange devices. If £100 invested now is expected to reappear after 50 years expanded at, say, 5 per cent compound interest, the man who originally provides the £100 may be able, after a year, to sell his title in the eventual fruit for £105; the man who buys from him may be able similarly to get his capital of £105 back with 5 per cent interest after one year; and so on. In these circumstances the fact that any one man would require a higher rate of interest per annum to induce him to lock up £100 for 50 years than he would to induce him to lock up the same sum for one year makes no difference. But, of course, in actual fact this device is of very narrow application. As regards investments, such as planting a forest or undertaking drainage development on one's own estate, which can only be accomplished privately, it is not applicable at all; and, even where investment is undertaken by a company, investors cannot seriously expect to find a smooth and continuous market for non-dividend paying securities. Thus the free play of self-interest will cause resources to be turned more than they ought to be — maximum aggregate satisfaction being taken as our goal — to the use of immediate consumption, and less than they ought to be to the use of distant consumption, the proportion directed to the service of some (unknown) intermediate future being presumably about right.[1]

§ 6. When maladjustments have come about or are threatening to come about from either of the two causes which I have been describing, it is always possible, on the assumption that no administrative costs are involved, to correct them by imposing appropriate rates of tax on resources employed in uses that tend to be pushed too far and employing the proceeds to provide bounties, at appropriate rates, on uses of the opposite class.[2] There will necessarily exist a certain determinate scheme of taxes and bounties, which, in given conditions, distributional considerations being ignored, would lead to the *optimum* result. There will also be a range of schemes, which, while falling short of the *optimum*, would, nevertheless, increase aggregate satisfaction above the level attainable under the free play of self-interest. Of course, in real life considerable administrative costs would be incurred

[1] In an important article in the *Economic Journal* for December 1928, Frank Ramsey showed how to determine, on certain hypotheses, how much of their incomes people of different incomes would need to save in order to maximise satisfaction. This is a step beyond the results reached in the text, but is not, of course, inconsistent with them.

[2] It will be noticed that these results, so far as they refer to industries of increasing and decreasing supply price, though similar to those reached by Marshall in the *Principles of Economics*, book v, chap. xii, are not identical with them. Marshall shows that sometimes, though not always, the payment of a bounty on the production of a commodity obeying the law of decreasing supply price will add to consumer's surplus (measured in money) more than the money cost of the bounty, and suggests that there is a *prima facie* case for a bounty only when this condition is satisfied. My thesis is that there is a *prima facie* case for a bounty *in all cases* where the payment of it adds to consumer's surplus (as measured in money) more than the addition made to aggregate real costs of production (as measured in money); and that, where conditions of decreasing supply price (from the standpoint of the community) prevail, there must *always* — under conditions of simple competition — be some rate of bounty that will accomplish this. The amount of money actually disbursed by the State in paying the bounty, being in large part a transfer and not a using-up of resources, is not, as such, a factor in the problem. Marshall's test and mine give the same results — abstraction made of my distinction between decreasing supply price from the standpoint of the community and from the standpoint of the industry — in the special case of a commodity for which the demand curve, in the relevant part of its length, has the form of a rectangular hyperbola: for in this case the sum disbursed in bounty payments is equal to the addition made to aggregate real costs (as measured in money).

in operating schemes of this kind. These might prove so large as to outweigh the benefit even of the *optimum* scheme, and, *a fortiori*, of the others. Again, it must be clearly understood that, unless the rates of taxes and bounties imposed fall within certain determined limits, more harm than good will be done even though there are no administrative costs. Yet again, since different commodities are purchased in different proportions by rich and poor persons, no tax-bounty scheme could be worked in practice without modifying distribution. These considerations would need to be taken into account before a final judgement could be passed upon any scheme.

CHAPTER IX

DIFFERENTIATION IN TAXATION BETWEEN DIFFERENT SORTS OF EXPENDITURE

§ 1. THE relation between the present chapter and the preceding one must be made clear. In the preceding one we were concerned with the correction of maladjustments in the allocation of resources between different uses, and it was shown that these maladjustments could, in theory, be corrected by the collection of appropriately chosen taxes from some uses and the employment of the proceeds in bounties on other uses. *In the present chapter we assume that either no corrections are required, or, alternatively, that whatever corrections are required have been made.* We thus postulate that a certain revenue, over and above whatever it may have been necessary to collect and expend in the tax-bounty system, is required; and we ask whether and in what conditions it is better to raise this revenue by means of a uniform tax on all uses of income or by means of taxes which differentiate between various uses; differentiate, it will be understood, in addition to and independently of any differentiation that may have been involved in the aforesaid tax-bounty system. In conducting this inquiry, I shall speak, for simplicity, as though all incomes were earned. Apart from savings, to be considered separately in the next chapter, a general expenditure tax and an income tax are obviously equivalent to one another. Our task is to compare, from the standpoint of least aggregate sacrifice, a uniform tax scheme with differentiating tax schemes. This involves a threefold inquiry. We have to examine the rival schemes in respect of (1) their announcement aspects, (2) their distributional aspects, and (3) technique and costs of administration. I shall take these three topics in order. Throughout I shall assume that competitive, as distinguished from monopolistic, conditions prevail.

I

Announcement Aspects

§ 2. Under this head our first need is to state with precision the problem to which a solution is being sought. It is very natural to put the issue to ourselves in the form : " Given that 200 millions of revenue are required, is it better to collect them by means of a general income tax or by means of taxes assessed at different rates upon different sorts of expenditure ? " Ninety-nine persons out of a hundred would take this to be a definite and completely unambiguous question. But in fact it is not so. To obviate irrelevant complications let us imagine a community all of whose members are exactly alike and have equal incomes. Even so, as was shown in Chapter V, there are likely to be a large number of formulae, with income as the object of assessment, by means of which 200 millions may be raised, these formulae differing in respect of the amount of sacrifice which they impose. An exactly analogous statement holds good of a tax yielding 200 millions that is confined to particular sorts of expenditure. Hence it is impossible to make any *general* comparison between the effects of raising 200 millions by a tax differentiating between various uses of income and those of raising the same sum by a non-differential tax on all uses of income. For, while some differential schemes would involve less aggregate sacrifice than some non-differential schemes, other differential schemes would involve more aggregate sacrifice than some non-differential schemes. The result of the comparison would, in short, depend on the choice made of schemes to be compared.

§ 3. We have, therefore, to decide upon this choice. It is clear that the rival levies, one assessed on the whole of a man's income, the other assessed, at least as regards some portion of it, on the part of his income spent in a particular way, must be represented by defined formulae. This is necessary in order to give our question *any* meaning. In order to give it an *interesting* meaning, it seems at first blush that the formulae should be identical save only in respect of the object of assessment embodied in them. It is, however, impossible to raise the same revenue by imposing a given formula on the whole of a man's income and by imposing it on a part of his income. Hence the formulae to be compared must necessarily be different. Though different, however, in order that the comparison may be interesting, they must be members of the same family. Thus, if x be the aggregate of income and y the part of it that is expended in a particular way, say, on beer, and if $R = \psi(x)$ be the tax formula in the first case, the tax formula in the second case should be $R = m\psi(x) + n\psi(y)$, it being understood that R has the same value in both formulae. Our problem then becomes: Given that a revenue R can be raised either by a tax assessed in the form $R = \psi(x)$ or in the form $R = m\psi(x) + n\psi(y)$, on which plan will the aggregate sacrifice imposed on the taxpayers be smaller? The simplest special case of this general problem is presented when $\psi(x)$ has the value kx, k being a constant. That is to say, it is premised that, whatever taxes are imposed, whether on income as a whole or on certain particular ways of spending it, shall be simple proportionate taxes.[1] I shall confine my detailed analysis to this simple case. There is some presumption that the broad results attained hold good as a general rule, though not universally, for more complex cases also.

§ 4. Given that adjustment has been made so as to eliminate all divergences at the margin between private net product and social net product (together with the second set of different but analogous divergences considered in Chapter VIII), then, *so long as no revenue has to be raised*, any further fiscal interference with "natural" arrangements — distributional factors are, of course, here excluded — is bound to be harmful. For the satisfaction obtained from the marginal unit of work devoted to any one use is equal to that obtained from the marginal unit devoted to any other, and each of these satisfactions again is equal to the dissatisfaction involved in the marginal unit of work performed in each and every use; which, distribution apart, is obviously the *optimum* possible situation. There is a temptation to step from this thesis to the further thesis that, given equality between private and social net products at the margin, together with the other condition referred to above, fiscal differentiation must still be

[1] The complications arising out of the fact noted in Chapter V, § 10, that *progressive* income taxes differentiate between safe and risky uses of productive resources need not, therefore, be brought into account here.

injurious and wasteful even though revenue has to be raised. We have proved that any differentiation (over and above that provided for in Chapter VIII) is harmful when operated alone: we infer that it must also be harmful when superimposed upon the collection of a given revenue by non-differential taxes. This inference suggests itself almost immediately to the mind; for, if a differential arrangement is bad, how should the fact that a revenue is needed do away with its badness? A proof that differentiation is bad, so to speak, in itself is thus made to serve for a proof that differentiation among taxes required to raise a revenue is bad. With great deference I venture to suggest that even Marshall fell into this trap. For in chapter xi of *Money, Credit and Commerce*, which is concerned to show that protective import duties are evil because they are differential, the argument and the illustration used in support of it relate to conditions in which differentiation is being practised but no revenue is being raised.[1] Where a Marshall is caught the trap must be subtle indeed!

§ 5. One further preliminary remark is required. A careless reader might imagine that our problem could be solved by some simple development of Marshall's proposition that, distributional considerations being ignored, a given revenue can be raised with less sacrifice by a tax imposed on a commodity for which the demand is inelastic than by one imposed on a commodity (produced under similar conditions of supply) for which the demand is elastic: and of the analogous proposition that, given similarity between the conditions of demand for two commodities, a given revenue can be raised with less sacrifice by a tax on the one of relatively inelastic supply than by a tax on the one of relatively elastic supply.[2] To prove, however, that it is better to tax commodity A exclusively than commodity B exclusively throws no light on the question whether it is better to tax A exclusively or to obtain the same revenue by taxing A and B at equal (*ad valorem*) rates. Still less does it help us to decide what, if any, degree of differentiation between the rates on A and B will minimise aggregate sacrifice. Our problem is, in short,

[1] *Loc. cit.* p. 211.

[2] These propositions hold good whether we measure sacrifice by loss of consumers' surplus or by loss of consumers' *plus* producers' surplus as depicted in the familiar geometrical constructions.

an entirely different one from Marshall's, and cannot be successfully attacked by his methods.

§ 6. Let us begin with the consideration of two highly simplified special cases. Thus, suppose that there are only two uses, one, A, of elastic, and the other, B, of inelastic demand, and that supply is conducted under conditions of constant return in both. If the demand in B is *absolutely* inelastic, the same amount of commodity will be produced and the same amount of work done there, whether a given revenue R is collected by a uniform rate of tax on both A and B or by a higher rate of tax concentrated upon B alone. Under the former system, however, people will be prevented by the threat of the tax from performing as much work in A as, in the circumstances, if left alone, they would wish to perform. Under the latter system they are not prevented from doing this. Hence the latter system involves the smaller sacrifice. By analogous reasoning it can be shown that, when one source of production yields an absolutely inelastic supply, so that, whatever tax system prevails, only an infinitesimal amount of work will be withdrawn from it (because any finite withdrawal causes the marginal physical productivity of work there to rise infinitely), a given revenue can be raised with less sacrifice by concentrating taxation upon this use than by imposing uniform rates of tax on all uses. From these cases of absolutely inelastic demand and absolutely inelastic supply it is easy to pass to cases of highly inelastic demand and highly inelastic supply: and the mind is prepared for the suggestion that the best way of raising a given revenue, when the supply of work is *not* rigidly fixed, is by a system of taxes, under which the rates become progressively higher as we pass from uses of very elastic demand or supply to uses where demand or supply are progressively less elastic. In order, however, to obtain definite results a more powerful engine of analysis is needed.

§ 7. Frank Ramsey examined the problem by mathematical methods and obtained a very interesting solution. He means by " a given revenue " for the purposes of his problem a given *money* revenue, and he postulates that money income is so adjusted as to make its marginal utility, which, since distributional considerations are here ignored, is taken to be the same for everybody, constant. With this very important proviso we start, as hitherto, from a state of things in which either there is no divergence at the margin between social and private net products, or whatever divergence there may have been is already corrected by appropriate adjustments. This, it will be observed, for practical purposes implies that there are no monopolies. Ramsey assumes further that the money collected by the government in revenue is either re-transferred to holders of war loan and then allocated among different purchases in the same proportions in which its original owners would have allocated it had it remained in their possession, or, alternatively, that the government, in spending it on its own needs (and so using up resources), allocates it in these proportions. Then, provided that all the functions involved are quadratic — this implies that such independent demand and supply curves as exist are straight lines — it can be proved, differences in the marginal utility of money to different people being, of course, ignored, that the *optimum* system of proportionate taxes yielding a given revenue is one that will *cut down the production of all commodities and services in equal proportions*. This is true, not merely of independent commodities, but also of commodities of complementary or rival demand or of complementary or rival supply. Thus, whether we are dealing with independent commodities, such as iron and beer, or with jointly supplied commodities, such as beef and hides, or with jointly demanded commodities, such as tea and sugar, or with wheat grown in Kent as against wheat grown in Norfolk, or with steel made by one process as against steel made by another process, we ought always so to arrange our taxes as to preserve the proportions in which these diverse things are severally produced.

§ 8. This result is subject to the assumption about the method of spending money collected in revenue that is set out above. If this money is not allocated among different purchases in the same way in which it would have been allocated had it been left to " fructify in the pockets of the people ", the demand schedules for the several commodities will be shifted. *These* shiftings will involve shiftings in the proportions in which the several commodities are produced of a sort which are not anti-social and ought, therefore, to be allowed to occur. Since their scope will depend on the manner in which the money raised is spent, Ramsey's result would need to be modified, should they be admitted, in different ways according to their detailed nature. It is important to add, however, as Ramsey's mathematics imply,[1] though he does not explicitly say so, that, if and in so far as the State spends its revenue on commodities of a kind not purchased by the public (and, of course, not themselves subject to tax), *e.g.* battleships, the rule that the taxes imposed should be such as to reduce all sorts of production subject to tax in equal proportions holds good in exactly the same way as it would do if the State spent its revenue on different commodities in the same proportion as the public.

§ 9. What then, in the conditions supposed, is the system of taxation that will reduce the production of all taxed goods in equal proportions? Obviously when several commodities have interdependent demands and supplies, the answer in respect of any given revenue will vary according to the nature of the interdependence. In certain circumstances some commodities may need to be subjected to a negative tax, *i.e.* a bounty. For example, a reduction in the supply of sugar consequent upon taxation might so affect the demand for very sour types of damsons that without a bounty on these it would be impossible to prevent their production falling off in a larger proportion than the production of sugar.[2] For such cases any formula for relating together the appropriate rates of tax would need to embody elements describing the detailed character of the interdependencies of demand and supply actually existing.

§ 10. On the assumption — a highly unrealistic one, no doubt — that the demand and supply schedules are all completely independent, a very simple formula, built upon the elasticities of these independent demand and supply schedules in respect of the quantities that would be produced and sold in the absence of any taxation (beyond the taxes considered in the last chapter), can be found. Writing η (defined as negative) for the elasticity of demand in respect of pre-tax output, e_r for the corresponding elasticity of supply[3] of the

[1] Cf. *Economic Journal*, March 1927, p. 60.

[2] Cf. *ibid.*, p. 54.

[3] I have substituted this notation, to which I am accustomed, for that employed by Ramsey. It should be observed that whereas he, following Marshall, defines elasticity of demand as (small) *proportionate increase* of quantity divided by (small) associated proportionate *decrease* in price, so

rth of commodity and t_r for the *ad valorem* rate of tax on it, it can be proved that, in the conditions supposed, production will be cut down in the same proportion for all commodities purchased by the public when the rates of tax are such that $\dfrac{t_r}{\dfrac{1}{e_r}-\dfrac{1}{\eta_r}}$ has the same value for all values of r. That is to say, the rate of tax on any commodity must be larger, the less elastic in respect of pre-tax output is the demand for it, and the less elastic, if positive, or more elastic, if negative, is the supply of it. If the elasticities of all the supplies are infinite, *i.e.* if all commodities are produced in conditions of constant return, the rates of tax on them must be inversely proportionate to their elasticities of demand. If there is any commodity for which either the demand or the supply is absolutely inelastic, the formula implies that the rate of tax imposed on every other commodity must be nil, *i.e.* that the whole of the revenue wanted must be raised on that commodity. In spite of the fact that e_r for some values of r may be negative (*i.e.* conform to increasing returns), the formula cannot warrant any bounties, other than those described in the last chapter, because it is a condition of stable equilibrium that, when e_r is negative, $\left\{\dfrac{1}{e_r}-\dfrac{1}{\eta_r}\right\}$ must be positive.[1]

§ 11. On the assumption that the several commodities have independent demands but are complete substitutes on the side of supply, *e.g.* if they are all produced at constant returns by one kind of labour only or by packets of constant com-

that it is in general positive, I define elasticity as (small) proportionate increase of quantity divided by (small) associated proportionate *increase* in price, so that my elasticity is in general negative. Thus in place of his ρ I have to write, not η, but $-\eta$. Strictly this should entail that, when he writes "the more elastic is the demand" I should write "the more elastic (numerically) is the demand"; but I shall not trouble to do this except where there is real scope for misunderstanding. Ramsey and I both define elasticity of supply as (small) proportionate increase of quantity divided by small proportionate *increase* in price. Since e may be either positive or negative, we have both, therefore, strictly to say "the larger (numerically) is the elasticity of supply if positive or the smaller if negative", or alternatively "the less sharply supply obeys the law of decreasing or the more sharply it obeys the law of increasing returns".

[1] Cf. Ramsey *loc. cit.* For this value to be negative implies that the demand curve lies below the supply curve to the left of their point of intersection, in which case the equilibrium is unstable.

position made up of several kinds, and if we write ϵ for the elasticity of supply of things in general, Ramsey shows that, to secure an equal contraction of all sorts of output, $\frac{t_r}{\frac{1}{\epsilon}-\frac{1}{\eta_r}}$, and so $\frac{\epsilon\eta_r t_r}{\eta_r-\epsilon}$ must have the same value for all values of r. This implies that, for any given positive value of ϵ, the rate of tax must be heavier on any commodity the less elastic is its demand ; and that, given the elasticities of demand, the rates of tax must approach one another as the elasticity of supply, if positive, becomes smaller. In the limit, when $\epsilon=0$, *i.e.* when the supply of things in general, and so, in our case, of labour, is absolutely inelastic, the rates of tax must be equal on all commodities.[1]

§ 12. The above analysis, as stated in § 7, depends on the proviso that the functions involved are quadratic, *i.e.* in the case of commodities with independent demand and supply schedules, that the demand and supply curves are straight lines. If this proviso is satisfied, the conclusions set out above are valid for revenues and tax rates no matter how large. If it is not satisfied, the range is narrower, the conclusions only being demonstrable strictly for infinitesimal, approximately for small taxes. How large the taxes may be while yet qualifying as "small" for this purpose depends on the closeness with which the relevant functions approach to being quadratic — with independent commodities on how closely the curvatures of the demand and supply curves approach to zero.[2]

[1] In this special case it is evident that, if all the revenue raised is spent by the State on various commodities in the same proportions in which private persons spend, the proportionate cut in the output of these commodities, which as we have seen must be equal for all, is nil. If the State spends a part or all of its revenue on things not purchased by private persons, the proportionate cut in the output of things so purchased is, of course, not nil. It is larger the larger the proportion of its revenue that the State does not retransfer but spends on commodities special to itself. This part of its revenue is not equal to, but, in general, may be expected to be much less than its non-transfer expenditure as defined previously ; for that is sure to contain items of the kind that private persons also purchase. We need not here trouble ourselves with complications due to such facts as that resources used by the State to provide, *e.g.*, free education are also partly a substitute for resources which private persons would have to devote to securing education if the State did not provide it (cf. *ante*, pp. 20-1).

[2] Cf. Ramsey, *loc. cit.* p. 60.

§ 13. There remains a more difficult matter. The whole of this argument, as was stated above, proceeds on the assumption that money income is so adjusted as to make its marginal utility (to the representative man) constant irrespective of variations in production. The proof of the proposition that, in order to minimise the sacrifice entailed in raising a given money revenue, the taxes imposed must be such as to reduce all sorts of output in equal proportions is built up on that basis. For that proof depends on equal quantities of money offered or asked for representing throughout all parts of the argument equal quantities of satisfaction. The above assumption is also required — though this is less fundamental — to warrant us in regarding any pair of commodities as having absolutely independent demand or supply schedules ; for, if it is not made, we must anticipate — apart from freak cases — that an alteration in the purchase or production of one commodity will affect the marginal utility of money and, through that, the supply and demand schedules of all other commodities, even though their marginal utility and marginal disutility schedules are absolutely independent. Thus, for example, if money income is fixed, the demand schedules for productive resources in various uses must necessarily be so adjusted that the elasticity of the demand for them in all uses together is equal to -1, even though the elasticity of the marginal desire for (*i.e.* the marginal utility of) them in all uses has a value quite different from that.

§ 14. Now, in discussing the effect of taxes imposed on single (small) commodities, Marshall regularly assumes, for demanders, that the marginal utility of money stands constant automatically without any need for deliberate adjustment. He recognises, indeed, that this might not always be so for suppliers. Thus a rise in the price offered for the services of coal miners might so far lower the marginal utility of money to them that they would supply less service at the higher than at the lower price. So far, however, as demanders are concerned, he relies on the common-sense consideration that, since the proportion of their income that people spend on any single ordinary commodity is very small — this does not, of course, apply to such a thing as the hiring of house room — a prospective change, even of several hundred per cent in expenditure on it, would only entail a minute proportionate change in the income left over for spending on other things, and could not, therefore, affect the utility of the marginal £ in an appreciable degree. When however, we are considering, not a tax on one commodity, but a whole system of taxes, this way of approach is obviously not appropriate. For the expenditure on all the commodities subjected to taxation may well constitute a substantial proportion of aggregate expenditure. What then is to be said about this matter ?

§ 15. Let us suppose first that all the revenue collected by the State is retransferred to the taxpayers in the manner described in § 7, *e.g.* as interest on war loan. The announcement effect of any system of proportionate taxes is probably, as Ramsey implies, to cut down the aggregate output of real income to some extent; which entails that the marginal utility of real income is somewhat increased. In order then that the marginal utility of money income may be held constant, money income must stand in such a relation to real income that the price per unit of real income is expanded in direct proportion to the expansion in the marginal utility of real income. Thus write I for money income, A for real income and $f(A)$ for the marginal utility of A units of real income. We require that $\frac{Af(A)}{I}$ shall be constant. If the curve representing the marginal utilities yielded by successive quantities of real income is a rectangular hyperbola, this condition will obviously be satisfied provided that money income I is kept constant. If, as we have seen reason to believe,[1] the marginal utility curve in respect of real income is steeper than a rectangular hyperbola, so that $A.f(A)$ increases as A decreases, in order to satisfy the required condition money income must be increased along with the imposition of the tax system.

§ 16. Let us suppose next that part of the revenue collected by the State is not retransferred to the taxpayers, but is expended on public objects such as battleships. Then obviously the real income left available to private persons is smaller and, therefore, its marginal utility larger than in the preceding case. If the marginal utility curve in respect of real income is a rectangular hyperbola, in order that the marginal utility of money income may be the same as it was

[1] Cf. *ante*, Part II, Chap. VII, § 17.

in the absence of taxation, money income must, as in the previous case, be kept constant; and, if the curve is steeper than a rectangular hyperbola, it must be increased. But, with the curve steeper in a given degree than a rectangular hyperbola, it must be increased *more* in this case than in the other, because the marginal utility of real income multiplied by its amount will be increased more.

§ 17. In view of the multiform nature of output there are in real life elements of ambiguity which this summary account has slurred over. Still, for a rough approximation what has been said may serve. Whether in given circumstances the marginal utility of money income in the face of tax changes will hold constant automatically or would need to be kept constant by deliberate adjustment can, of course, only be decided when the nature of the monetary and banking system in use is known. With a system of the kind that I have called elsewhere[1] "normal" we might expect a contraction in real income, since it would entail diminished savings and, therefore, a fall in the rate of interest, to be accompanied by an automatic contraction in money income. Hence, if our curve is steeper than a rectangular hyperbola, in order that the marginal utility of money may be unaffected by the imposition of a general tax system, deliberate adjustment of money income in an upward direction, *e.g.* through manipulation of the bank rate, will be needed.

§ 18. The results reached by Ramsey throw an interesting light on the question whether, as a means of raising revenue — apart from the considerations brought under review in Chapter VIII — advantage is likely to be found in taxing the imports of any commodity at a higher rate than the competing home products. For the purposes of this section the possibility of obtaining a contribution from foreigners in general, as distinguished from the particular foreign producers of the taxed commodity, which will be examined in Chapter XXII, is ignored. Since only a small part of our exports exchange against any particular foreign import, we may reasonably regard the production of our exports, from the point of view of this problem, as conforming approximately to conditions of constant return. Then the real supply schedule of the import, to be set against that of the competing

[1] Cf. my *Employment and Equilibrium*, p. 60.

home product, is approximately regulated by its supply schedule in terms of money in our market. The question whether a higher rate of tax should be imposed on the imported product than on the home product turns, therefore, on the question whether the imported supply in this sense or the home-made supply is the less elastic. In certain cases there can be no doubt that the imported supply will be the less elastic. When there is a surplus in some foreign country of a commodity for which England is the only available large market, it will pay the foreign manufacturer to accept what price he can get, and the amount he offers will scarcely be altered by (moderate) variations in the price obtainable. Special duties upon imports of this character, if they could be worked in practice, would, therefore, from a purely national point of view, be an excellent means of raising revenue. The case of ordinary foreign goods imported in ordinary circumstances is, however, different. Here the presumption is that the domestic supply is the less elastic of the two. For, presuming, as, in the absence of special knowledge, is reasonable, that the elasticity of *production* is the same at home and abroad, the elasticity of the home supply will be equal to, but that of the foreign supply to our market will be greater than this. The reason is that a given rise of price in England will increase the *proportion* of the foreign production that comes to us as well as the aggregate amount of that production.[1] It follows that, in the absence of special knowledge, there is a presumption — of course when we have special knowledge the presumption may be overthrown — in favour of taxing imports at a *lower* rate than competing home products. There is certainly no presumption in favour of the opposite and more popular form of differentiation. This result is subject to the condition that no significant contribution to our revenue can be obtained from foreigners in general ; a proviso the validity of which will, as was said above, be considered in Chapter XXII.

[1] Let A be the foreign production and D the foreign consumption. Let e be the elasticity of production, both in England and abroad, and η the elasticity of the foreign demand. Then, for a one per cent rise of price in the English market the foreign import rises from $(A+D)$ by $\{eA-\eta D\}$ times one per cent. Therefore the elasticity of the foreign supply to our market is equal to $\frac{eA-\eta D}{A+D}$. Since η is negative, this is $>e$.

II

Distributional Aspects

§ 19. In comparing differential and non-differential tax systems from the standpoint of distribution we have to consider two things: the treatment of people of equal incomes and dissimilar economic situations; and that of people of unequal incomes and similar situations. Since our objective is least aggregate sacrifice, it is clear that members of the first group should be taxed equally, subject to allowances for the differences in their economic situations; and that members of the second group should be taxed in such a way that people pay progressively heavier *rates* of taxation the larger their incomes are. We have to inquire how far these *desiderata* point towards differentiation between various commodities and uses.

§ 20. As between people of equal incomes but unlike economic situations, it is possible to accomplish *certain* desirable adjustments by a particular kind of differentiation; namely, by superimposing on a general income tax certain special taxes upon luxury expenditure. Thus, of two men with equal incomes, one may have heavy obligations of a kind which it is not possible to schedule for allowance under income tax: for example, an obligation to support financially a sick friend not related to him. The man free from this obligation may be expected to spend a much larger proportion of his income on personal luxuries; and a heavy tax specialised upon luxuries may thus serve to bring into account the difference between his true "taxable capacity" and that of the other man. This is not, however, a very important matter.[1]

§ 21. As between people of unequal incomes it is, no doubt, theoretically conceivable that a progressive scale of taxation should be constructed on the basis of a number of commodity taxes with rates steepening as we pass from commodities mainly purchased by the poor to those mainly purchased by the rich. As will be shown more in detail in the next chapter,

[1] When no other provision is made to eliminate the differentiation against savings, which, as will appear in the next chapter, is involved in an ordinary income tax, special imposts upon luxuries may also be advocated as a partial set-off to this.

the practical difficulties in the way of this arrangement are, however, insuperable ; and, even if this were not so, it would need no argument to prove that whatever scale of graduation we decide upon can be established far more exactly, as well as far more easily, by the imposition of a general income tax than by any combination of various commodity taxes.

§ 22. In sum, then, it appears that distributional considerations are, in the main, opposed to differentiation between tax rates on different sorts of expenditure, but that there is a case for superimposing some special duties on luxury consumption upon a general income tax. It need hardly be pointed out that the detailed arrangements which this kind of differentiation would involve are entirely different from those suggested by announcement considerations.

III

Technique and Costs of Collection

§ 23. For practical purposes a non-differential tax system means an income tax or a general expenditure tax ; because, to collect commodity taxes [1] at a uniform, or, indeed, at any rate upon all goods and services is not administratively feasible. Whenever, therefore, considerations of technique exclude an income tax, the system adopted must be a differential one. In certain conditions an income tax cannot be made to work except at inordinate cost ; in a highly scattered community of farmers, for example, with bad means of communication and a weak central government. Where this is so, technical considerations may compel us to rely on a limited number of import duties collected — if our community is an island — by officials stationed at the ports. Again, it is possible to imagine conditions in which direct taxes are so unpopular and administrative machinery so inefficient that an income tax would be rendered unworkable by evasion. In England, of course, at

[1] It is usual to speak of taxes of this kind as *indirect* taxes, on the ground that they are supposed to be paid ultimately by people other than those from whom they are collected. To make a definition depend on questions about incidence that may be disputed is, however, very inconvenient. Moreover, if it be assumed, for example, that duties on imports are paid by the consumer, these duties are only indirect provided that they are levied when the goods affected are in the hands of dealers. To collect them from consumers would turn them into direct taxes.

the present day, there is no question of anything of this kind. What measure of evasion is in fact practised is a matter of controversy. But over a wide range the device of taxation at source stops it altogether ; while over other parts of the field the administrative machinery wielded by the Treasury is admittedly well equipped. For this country, therefore, so far at least as what are known as the income tax paying classes are concerned, considerations of technique and cost of collection give no ground for preferring commodity taxes, which, as we have seen, entail differentiation, to a general income tax.

§ 24. Until recently the issue was more doubtful as regards that large part of the community which is made up of manual wage-earners. Before the 1914–18 war it was regarded as axiomatic that the difficulty and cost of collecting income tax from these persons would be so great that whatever levy it is decided to make from them *must* be made through commodity taxes. Before the Royal Commission on the Income Tax, 1919, however, evidence was adduced which showed that, by the device of quarterly (since 1925 half-yearly) assessments on wages, income tax was being collected at a very reasonable cost from a large body of weekly wage-earners. Though, therefore, there were still difficulties and inconveniences to be overcome,[1] it could not any longer be held that the income tax method of levy is out of the question for small incomes. During Hitler's war this method has been carried much further, and, by arrangements which provide for the tax to be collected at the time when incomes are earned, instead of later on when they may have dwindled or ceased, the most serious objections to it have been removed. To grant this, however, is not to deny that technical and administrative considerations still tend towards commodity — and so differential — taxes as a means of collecting revenue from *very* poor persons ; if, indeed, it is desired to tax these persons at all. The sort of differentiation required would, of course, be quite different both from that suggested by announcement considerations and from that suggested by distributional considerations.

[1] Cf. Stamp, *Current Problems in Finance and Government*, p. 223.

IV

§ 25. From each of the three points of view distinguished in § 1 we have thus found that a case can be made out for some measure of differentiation as against a tax system which, after the manner of income tax, draws no distinction between the various ways in which income is expended. The kinds of differentiation which the three points of view suggest are, however, different from, and incompatible with, one another. They are also — all of them — different from, and incompatible with, the main body of differential taxes that are likely to find advocates among practical politicians dependent upon votes and subject to the pressure of powerful interests.

CHAPTER X

INCOME TAX AND SAVINGS

§ 1. Up to this point I have deliberately slurred over the difference between a general income tax and a general expenditure tax; tacitly assuming that a general income tax does not differentiate between different uses of income. This assumption is not, however, correct, and the time has come to go into the matter more fully. There are two main uses, each, of course, containing numerous subdivisions, into which income can be turned; saving—so defined that in the aggregate it is equivalent to investment—and expenditure upon consumption. The latter use is ordinarily spoken of as "spending" in contradistinction from saving, and, though the term is unfortunate, since, of course, net saving is itself a form of spending, namely, spending upon the purchase of machines and other new capital objects, it may, with this explanation, be allowed to stand. A general income tax, as understood in England, can be shown to differentiate against the investment, *i.e.* the savings, use of income, and so to differentiate in favour of its rival.

§ 2. The proof of this proposition is as follows. A general income tax, since it hits equally income that is saved and income that is spent, appears at first sight to be neutral between these two things. This appearance is, however, illusory. If we had in mind a tax to be imposed for one year only, or for a short period only, at a given rate, it would, indeed, be correct. But, in relation to a system of taxation that is expected to continue indefinitely with constant rates, an expenditure tax is neutral as between saving and spending, and not differential in favour of spending. For resources that are saved are taxed indirectly, through their subsequent yield, to the same extent as resources that are consumed at once. An income tax, on the other hand, differentiates against saving, by striking savings both when they are made and also when they yield their fruits. Thus a general permanent income tax at the rate of x per cent strikes the part of income that is spent at this rate. But, if £100 of income is put away for saving, this tax removes £x at the moment and, thereafter, removes also some parts of the fruits yielded by it.[1] How large this secondary taxation will be depends on the subsequent conduct of the saver; *i.e.* on whether he withdraws his savings with a view to spending them soon or late or never; and also, *if* he withdraws them, on the current rate of interest. If the saver's investment is a permanent one, so that the principal is never withdrawn, the secondary taxation amounts every year to $\frac{x}{100}$ths of the fruit of the £$(100-x)$ that are actually turned into the investment. The primary and secondary taxation together are thus equivalent to a tax now of x *plus* the present value of a perpetual annuity of $\frac{x}{100}(100-x)i$, where i is the rate of interest at which the investment is made; *i.e.*, in all, to $\left\{x+\frac{x}{100}(100-x)\right\}$, that is, to $x\left\{2-\frac{x}{100}\right\}$. Thus the effective rate on saved income is practically double the rate on spent income when the tax is small, and substantially more than equal to, though less than double, that rate when it is large. For example, a general rate of 10s. in the £ implies a tax, not of 10s., but of 15s. in the £ on saved income. If the principal is presently withdrawn for spending, the primary and secondary taxation together work out as equivalent to a single tax now smaller than the above.[2] The general formula, with withdrawal of principal after n years and rate of interest i per cent, is $x+\frac{x}{100}(100-x)\left\{1-\left(\frac{100}{(100+i)}\right)^n\right\}$. For a withdrawal after ten years at a 5 per cent rate of interest, this works out at rather more than $1\frac{1}{3}x$ when x is small.

[1] Cannan objected to this way of stating the matter on the ground that "we save and spend out of what the government leaves us after we have paid over our income tax" (*Economic Journal*, 1921, p. 213), so that to speak of £100 as being put away for saving and, thereafter, as being taxed is illegitimate. If, however, we put the issue in Cannan's way, the result is still the same. For then the saved part of income (income being interpreted as what is left over after taxation) is taxed on its fruits and the spent part is not taxed at all.

[2] The contention that, since, if the principal is presently withdrawn for spending and taxed then, the situation will be the same as if it were taxed now, is, of course, a gross fallacy.

§ 3. The edge of this analysis is, indeed, found, when looked at closely, to be less sharp than it seems to be. For, first, it has been tacitly assumed that investment always yields future fruits subject to taxation, while expenditure upon consumption does not. This is incorrect. On the one hand, some saving yields nothing at all. On the other hand, some expenditure, *e.g.* upon food, clothing and house-room, builds up the efficiency of human instruments, just as investment in the ordinary sense builds up the efficiency of mechanical ones, and, therefore, like it, leads to the production of future income. Secondly, it has been tacitly assumed that the rate of tax on the fruit of savings will be equal to the rate on savings as made. This is not always so. If, as in England, unearned, or investment, income is taxed at a higher rate than earned income, the fruit of savings made from earned income will be taxed at a higher rate than the original savings, so that such part of earned income as is saved is really exposed to severer adverse differentiation than the formula given above indicates. But, *per contra* — and this is practically more important — where, as in England, there is steep graduation against large incomes, income which is saved by a rich man and left to a relatively poor man, on whose income the income tax (including sur-tax) rate is lower, is not differentiated against so heavily as the formula indicates. Though, however, these considerations leave our results less clear-cut than might be wished, the broad conclusion that a general income tax on the British plan differentiates, in some measure, against income that is saved remains unshaken.

§ 4. In considering in this place whether or not this differentiation against saving is in conformity with the principle of least sacrifice, we are met with the awkwardness that taxes assessed on the savings of individuals may to some extent hit "hoarding" as distinguished from investment. For the fact that, on our definition, savings and investment in the aggregate must be equal — for the reason that hoarding by one man destroys an equivalent amount of income, and so of saving, by other men — does not preclude there being individual hoarders. I shall, however, ignore this complication. On this understanding three principal sorts of consideration are relevant.

First we have to inquire whether, in the absence of any

taxation on income, income is likely to be shared between consumption and investment (*i.e.* savings) in such a way that, distributional considerations being ignored, the marginal contributions to satisfaction will be equal in both uses, and, therefore, aggregate satisfaction a maximum ; or, more practically, to which of the two uses too much income would be devoted. The fact that the ownership of capital, to which investment leads, yields an amenity in the form of prestige, security against misfortune and so on over and above its annual contribution of money income, is not relevant here, since this amenity value is presumably taken into account by potential savers. But the argument of Chapter VIII, §§ 4-5, shows clearly that the general tendency to discount the future against the present together with the limitations of human life tend to reduce investment below what, in the interests of least aggregate sacrifice, it ought to be. This points to the propriety of differentiating in favour of savings, *e.g.* through a tax on consumption to be used as a bounty on savings, even though no net revenue were to be raised ; and so, by implication, to this kind of differentiation when revenue *is* being raised.

Secondly, Ramsey's important article on the Mathematical Theory of Saving,[1] in which he shows that the rate of investment required to promote maximum satisfaction is much larger than is actually found in practice, or, indeed, would ordinarily be thought suitable, gives strong support to the view that, from the announcement standpoint, investment ought at least to be exempted from taxation.

Thirdly, as regards distribution, it may be argued that saved income ought to be struck more lightly than other income, because, as between savers and non-savers or less-savers among people of equal incomes, the savers probably have greater needs — the greater needs being the cause of their extra saving. This argument, of course, loses its force if the fact that some persons (*e.g.* the recipients of earned incomes) have greater needs than other persons (*e.g.* the recipients of investment incomes), the amount of whose incomes is no greater, is allowed for in other ways. *Prima facie*, however, differentiation in favour of saved income has the advantage that it takes account of the extra sums which particular propertyless men actually do withdraw from consumption to

[1] *Economic Journal*, 1928, p. 548.

provide against the future, not of estimates and guesses as to what normal propertyless men might be expected to withdraw; though it must be admitted that to treat with special favour only those savings of propertyless men which are made on account of their greater needs is not feasible. On the other hand, as between persons of unequal incomes, since there is reason to believe that rich people save more, not merely absolutely but proportionately also, than poor people,[1] to exempt savings from income tax and to do nothing else would involve the distributional evil of giving a substantial bounty to the rich. This objection might be met at least in part if remissions of taxation on saved income were coupled with a steepening of the upper part of the general graduation scale.

When all these various considerations are taken into account there would, I think, be general agreement that, whether or not it may be proper to differentiate in favour of the savings use, there is certainly no case for differentiating against it. As a means to least aggregate sacrifice, a tax under which consumption and saving are placed on an equal footing is superior from this standpoint to one under which, as with a general income tax, an extra and special impost is laid on savings.

§ 5. *Prima facie*, by substituting for a general income tax a general expenditure tax — assessed on expenditure for consumption — yielding the same revenue, we should get rid of all anti-saving differentiation and secure a completely neutral system. But this is not really so. The fact that saved income yields an amenity return, as described in § 4, as well as an interest return, and that an expenditure tax would only hit the interest return, entails that such a tax differentiates *in favour* of saved income. I should not, however, expect it in a general way to do this to an extent beyond what, from the announcement point of view, the principle of least sacrifice requires; certainly not to an extent less conformable to that principle than a general income tax yielding equal revenue. Nor is the distributional damage that results from omitting to hit the amenity returns from saved income likely to be very serious. A general expenditure tax, therefore, is *prima facie* preferable to a general income tax. What is there to say about it from the standpoint of practical administration?

[1] Cf. *ante*, Part II, Chapter IV, § 7.

§ 6. If all saved income were saved *permanently*, the principal never being withdrawn for expenditure, a general expenditure tax on consumption would be the same thing as a general income tax from which savings were exempted. This kind of tax would, like a general income tax, be compatible alike with graduation and with family allowances. Moreover it would be possible, if it were so desired, to make a rough adjustment for the fact that some expenditures upon consumption are, in effect, investments yielding income in the future [1] and, therefore, liable under an ordinary income tax to a double impost. Thus charges incurred for children's education might be exempted *eo nomine.*[2] In spite, however, of these possibilities the idea of constituting a general expenditure tax by means of a general income tax from which savings are exempted is exposed to a very powerful objection. Income that is saved need not be saved permanently. In so far as what has been saved is subsequently withdrawn for spending, when, not counting as income, it would not be taxed, there would be an element of differentiation *in favour* of saving,[3] an element which, if the withdrawal took place soon after the saving had been made, would be very large. Moreover, and this is the decisive point, under an income tax from which savings were exempted dishonest citizens might make a practice of saving in one year, thus escaping taxation, and secretly selling out and spending their savings in the next year. The skill of revenue officials in this country has succeeded in mastering many forms of dishonesty, but the opinion is widely held among experienced administrators that this form would prove too much for them ; that so wide a door for evasion would be opened as seriously to impair the efficiency of the income tax as an engine of revenue.

§ 7. If on this ground it is decided that an income tax with exemption of savings is impracticable, so that the hope of establishing a general expenditure tax directly through

[1] Cf. *ante*, p. 120.

[2] It would be clearly impracticable to treat in this way expenditure upon other " necessaries for efficiency ". The compromise device of exempting, not actual expenditure upon these things, but fixed sums estimated to cover them, would not eliminate adverse differentiation.

[3] Cf. Benham, " Notes on the Pure Theory of Public Finance ", *Economica*, November 1934, p. 442, where an error in what was said in early editions of this book is corrected.

that device must be abandoned, we have to consider the feasibility of establishing one directly. Unfortunately, even apart from the fact that some commodities have a double use and may on one occasion serve as consumable and on another as capital goods, there are insuperable difficulties in the way of this arrangement.

A general 5 or 10 or 20 per cent tax on consumable *imports* is, indeed, feasible. But a tax on all consumable commodities and services — for services, of course, would also have to be included — produced at home for home consumption could hardly be worked successfully. For things normally bought in shops substantial purchase taxes were, indeed, imposed with success during the special emergency of the war. But in times of peace such taxes would almost certainly be very unpopular, while the administrative task of preventing evasion would be difficult and costly. To collect purchase taxes otherwise than through shopkeepers is even less feasible. It would be necessary to set up a system of production in bond for all consumable articles made at home! Thus, even if it were a proportionate tax on expenditure of which we were in search, it would be very difficult in practice to attain it by way of commodity taxes.

The construction of a *progressive* expenditure tax would present other and more formidable difficulties; for it would be necessary to impose upon each commodity, not a single rate, but a number of different rates adjusted to the incomes of the various purchasers. Such an arrangement would be absolutely unworkable. The utmost we could hope for would be to secure a rough progression by taxing articles mainly consumed by the rich at higher rates than those mainly consumed by poorer persons. There are, however, serious obstacles in the way even of this. A large part of the income of the rich is spent, not on commodities, but on services, *e.g.* foreign travel, of a sort that it is very difficult to hit by taxes. Moreover, the expenditure of the rich is scattered among a large number of different things, no great amount being directed to any one of them. To tax things of this sort involves very high administrative costs. Experience shows that "the lucrative revenue-yielders are the staples consumed in great amounts, and consumed chiefly by the masses".[1] It is idle,

[1] Taussig, *Principles of Economics*, vol. ii, p. 558.

therefore, to look in practice for a system of commodity taxes that shall be better than proportionate. Nor is this all. Should we be forced for administrative reasons to confine ourselves to "lucrative" revenue-raisers, a system made up of commodity taxes is likely to prove actually regressive. If food articles of large consumption are included, this is almost certain to happen. "The man who possesses an income of £1000 a year does not, as a rule, drink ten times as much whisky, tea or beer, or smoke ten times as much tobacco, as the man who possesses an income of £100 a year."[1] Again, if raw materials, a technically fairly easy thing to tax, are assessed in preference to more complex finished goods, there will be regression, because equal quantities of raw material are worked up (with more labour) into finer articles bought by the rich and into the coarser articles bought by the poor. When this happens a raw material tax carries off a less proportion of rich men's than of poor men's expenditure. The same thing is true for the same reason of taxes on machinery. The danger of regression, to which these considerations point, is actually realised in that part of the British revenue system which consists in taxes on commodities. Thus for 1937–8 Messrs. Shirras and Rostas offer the following estimates[2] of the percentage burden on fully earned incomes, for a married couple with two dependent children, due to commodity taxes (*i.e.* indirect taxes exclusive of Social Insurance contributions), on the assumption that "moderate" amounts of alcohol and tobacco are consumed, and, for incomes of £500 and over, a moderate amount of private motoring:

Income, £	% Burden	Income, £	% Burden
100	14·4	1,000	9·0
150	14·1	2,000	7·1
200	13·5	2,500	6·2
250	12·5	5,000	4·2
300	11·9	10,000	2·8
350	11·3	20,000	2·0
500	12·8	50,000	1·1

[1] Sir D. Barbour in the *Report of the Royal Commission on the Financial Relations between Great Britain and Ireland,* 1896, p. 122.

[2] *British Taxation,* pp. 52-3.

Obviously all calculations of this sort rest on a precarious basis, depending, as they must, on particular assumptions about incidence and about the comparative consumption of the several taxed articles by representative members of different income classes. But there is no reason to doubt that the general drift is correct. The tendency of commodity taxes towards regression would not, indeed, be important in a community all of whose members were about equally wealthy. Thus, " it should not be forgotten that the Russian population has been to a large degree reduced to a common level, so that indirect taxation does not bear that anti-democratic character which it does in capitalistic countries where sharp inequalities in property exist ".[1] In such a country as England, however, they are exceedingly important.

Yet again, systems of commodity taxes cannot be adjusted to differences in the family estate of different people. Indeed, it may easily happen that commodity taxes, on the things on which it is easy to impose them, will not only fail to make allowance in favour of large families, but will actually take more from a man with a large family than from one with a small family ; because the former is obliged to buy a larger amount of ordinary articles of food and clothing. It is sufficient for our purpose, however, that the positive allowances for differences in family estate which fairness requires cannot be made under a system of commodity taxes.

The considerations set out in the preceding paragraphs taken in combination make it plain that our promised way of escape is in fact a blind alley. If the differentiation against savings present in the British income cannot be eliminated by direct exemptions, there is no hope of eliminating it by the manipulation of commodity taxes.

[1] G. Sokolnikoff, *Manchester Guardian Supplement*, July 6, 1922, p. 225.

CHAPTER XI

DIFFERENTIATION BETWEEN SOURCES OF INCOME

§ 1. INCOME may be distinguished into parts, not only according to the uses to which it is put, but also according to the sources from which it is derived. In the present chapter it is the latter distinction which interests us. For this country Dr. Bowley has estimated that the proportionate share of income derived from property, as against work, was round about $37\frac{1}{2}$ per cent in 1880 and also in 1913; and, further, "that there was no important change in the proportion of earned to total income between 1880 and 1913 or between 1911, 1913 and 1924";[1] while the proportionate share derived from *manual* labour from 1880 to 1935 lay between 40 and 43 per cent.[2] Within each of the two main groups, work and property, there are, of course, innumerable subdivisions embracing incomes from different parts of each.

§ 2. Since the incomes received from particular sorts of work and of property are derived from the sale of the commodities or services which they produce, it is clear that differentiation between various parts of work income and various parts of property income comes to much the same thing as differentiation between income spent on various sorts of products. The general analysis of Chapter IX is, therefore, applicable.

§ 3. The only important instance of differentiation in accordance with source *within* either of the two main groups of income (work income and property income) to be found in this country is afforded by the assessment to local rates of income derived, not from property in general, but from property in land and houses. The adverse differentiation against this particular kind of property income is the result of complex historical causes, which cannot be examined here, but in which considerations of administrative convenience probably played the chief part. Nobody would seriously maintain that this differentiation, which must militate seriously against investment in houses and agricultural improve-

[1] *Wages and Income since 1860*, pp. 96-7. [2] *Ibid.* p. xvi.

ments, is defensible either from an announcement or from a distributional point of view. It has, indeed, for many years been common ground that the system on which local rates are assessed in this country is thoroughly unsatisfactory.

§ 4. It is not, however, within the scope of this volume to attack that difficult problem. I leave, therefore, differentiation *within* the main groups, work income and property income, and proceed to ask whether the principle of least sacrifice requires that there should be differentiation *between* these groups, *i.e.* whether work income as a whole and property income as a whole should be put upon the same or upon disparate footings as objects of tax assessment. I shall study this question first from the point of view of announcement and then from that of distribution. I assume, of course, that the same given amount of revenue is to be raised in any event.

§ 5. With tax formulae of the type $t = \frac{k}{x}$, that is to say with lump-sum taxes, it is obviously immaterial, on the announcement side, to what object of assessment the formula is nominally directed. If £1000 is to be taken from a man in any event, it makes no difference whether we assess it on work income or on property income or on both. Exactly the same consequences will follow. But with tax formulae in which a man is told that, if his holding of the assessed object increases, the aggregate amount of the levy made upon him will increase in *any* degree, the choice of the object to be assessed is not, in general, immaterial. In practice it is certain that taxes assessed upon any division of income will be at least as progressive in respect of aggregate levy as a proportionate tax, and it is likely that they will be more progressive than this. I shall, for simplicity, conduct my analysis on the assumption that we have to do only with proportionate taxes. With tax formulae of a more complicated nature the argument would be more difficult, but the broad results would, I think, be the same.

§ 6. If property income were rigidly fixed, in such wise that no threats to it through taxation could cause its amount to be altered, the announcement of a tax assessable upon it, at no matter what rate, would have exactly the same effect as the announcement of a poll-tax. On the other hand, the announcement of any tax — other than a poll-tax — assessable upon income from work must lessen everybody's expectation of monetary return from work, and, therefore, must cause a smaller addition to be made to work, if not a contraction to be made in it, than is desirable from the standpoint of least aggregate sacrifice. It follows that, so far as announcement effects are concerned, if property income were rigidly fixed, the principle of least sacrifice would require the revenue to be raised by taxes assessed wholly upon it, and not at all — poll-taxes being ruled out — upon income derived from work.

§ 7. In real life, of course, property income is not rigidly fixed in the sense of the preceding section. On the contrary, if property owners fail to make good the wear and tear which their equipment normally suffers, property income will decline, whereas if they make new investments, it will presently increase. In these circumstances the issue is considerably more complicated. Let us start from a position in which a uniform rate of tax is imposed on all income from whatever source it is derived, this uniform rate being ten per cent and the resultant revenue being R. It is required to determine the effects of various departures from that arrangement. Let us consider first the complete exemption of investment income, coupled with whatever consequential increases in the rates imposed upon earned income are required to keep the revenue yield up to R.

§ 8. A proposal to exempt investment income from taxation seems at first sight too paradoxical to be worth considering. A little reflection shows, however, that there is a real purpose behind it. It was argued in the last chapter that the British income tax suffers from a serious defect, in that it differentiates against savings ; but our discussion there revealed no means of removing that defect. It is easy to see that the exemption of investment income from taxation would provide a remedy ; for the differentiation against savings can be removed equally well by exempting saved income when it yields its fruits as by exempting it when it itself comes into being. Unless, therefore, it can be shown that this advantage would be outweighed by counterbalancing disadvantages, it will follow that, *on the announcement side*, the exemption of investment income is in line with the principle of least aggregate sacrifice. Are there then counterbalancing disadvantages

— distributional considerations are not yet to be brought into account — sufficient to refute this conclusion? If the amount of annual savings were normally equal to the amount of investment income, remission of taxes on investment income would reduce the revenue by approximately the same amount as remission of taxes on saved income. Therefore the remainder of income would have to bear the same addition of taxation. With the remission made off investment income, this remainder would consist in the whole volume of earned income: with the remission made off savings it would consist partly of earned and partly of investment income. In either event the rate of tax on the remainder, and so the rate of tax on earned income, would have to be raised to about the same extent. Hence, on the announcement side, the adverse reactions set up by the exemption of investment income would be no worse than those set up by the exemption of saved income. Since, then, we know that, from the announcement side, the exemption of saved income would on balance conform to the principle of least sacrifice, it follows that, failing that exemption, the exemption of income derived from investment income would also on balance conform to that principle. This conclusion, however, only holds good on condition that annual savings are normally equal in amount to investment income. In a community where annual savings are substantially smaller than investment income it does not hold good. For there the exemption of investment income would involve a much larger reduction of revenue and, therefore, if that is to be prevented, a much larger increase in the rate of taxation upon earned income than the exemption of savings would do. Thus, suppose that a third of a community's income comes from property, while one-fifteenth of its income is saved — roughly the situation in England in 1938. Then the remission of a 15 per cent tax on saved income would necessitate the rate of tax on other income being raised by about 1 per cent: but the remission of a 15 per cent tax on investment income would necessitate the rate on other income being raised by nearly 7½ per cent. Obviously there is much less chance of a net benefit resulting in the latter case than in the former. Obviously again in the latter case this chance will become progressively smaller the larger is the amount of property income relatively to the normal amount of annual savings.

This fact creates a strong presumption, from the announcement point of view, against the remission of taxes upon investment income.

§ 9. From the distributional point of view the presumption is, of course, of overwhelming force. For, whereas to remit taxation upon saved income would, as has been shown, confer a considerable bounty upon the rich, to remit it upon investment income would confer an enormous bounty. Statistical calculations in this country are made difficult by the fact that business incomes under schedule D are counted as wholly earned, no reckoning being made of the part of them that is due to invested capital. As stated, however, at the beginning of this chapter, Dr. Bowley has estimated that for three widely separated years income from property (including, of course, property held abroad) amounted, for the United Kingdom, to 37½ per cent. Out of the 37½ per cent of property income he reckoned that only about one-fortieth part was accruing in 1913 to persons with incomes below £160, among whom at that time nearly the whole of the wage-earning class would be comprised. Practically all of it went to persons assessed to income tax, *i.e.* to some 1,100,000 [1] persons, constituting, with their families, about one-ninth of the whole population. There are no statistics to show the way in which property income was distributed within the class of persons assessed to income tax. But the predominant part of it almost certainly went to people with more than £700 a year, the total number of whom in 1910 amounted to only a little over 200,000. Further light is thrown on this matter by Daniel's and Campion's study of *The Distribution of the National Capital*. On the basis of death duty assessments they find that, in the period 1924–30, for England and Wales, 1 per cent of the persons aged over twenty-five owned 60 per cent of the total capital and 5 per cent owned 8 per cent of it.[2] Further, nearly half of the total capital owned by males over twenty-five belonged to men with more than £25,000 each, not far short of two-thirds to men with over £10,000 each, and nearly 72 per cent to men with over £5000 each; while among women over twenty-five, whose ownership of capital was naturally on the lower scale, 28 per cent belonged

[1] *The Change in the Distribution of the National Income*, p. 22.

[2] *Loc. cit.* p. 53.

to those with more than £25,000 each, 44 per cent to those with more than £10,000 each, and 56 per cent to those with more than £5000 each.[1] It is thus evident that property income must be concentrated enormously more closely than work income. It must, therefore, be in great part directly responsible for the extreme concentration of income in general. It has a further indirect responsibility in this sense, because the possession of property income permits of training that is likely to augment its owners' earned income also. In these circumstances to exempt property income from income tax is a plan that nobody would seriously contemplate.

§ 10. When to the foregoing distributional argument are added the considerations set out in § 8, it becomes plain, not merely that the exemption of investment income from taxation would be highly objectionable, but that there is a strong *prima facie* case for taxing it at a higher rate than earned income. At first sight it seems that, if, in the interests of distribution, we decide to do this, we must necessarily intensify the differentiation which even a flat-rate general income tax would impose against savings. It is possible, however, to devise, at least in theory, a compromise plan, by which, in some measure, the best of both worlds would be attained. In order to eliminate differentiation against saving it is not necessary to exempt any investment income as it stands at present. It is sufficient to announce that incomes derived in the future *from investments to be made from now onwards* shall be exempt. This arrangement would not require us to give up the present tax on income derived from existing property, and so would not force us to raise the general rate of income tax to any great extent. On the contrary, for some time forward, *i.e.* until the annual income resulting from investments made subsequent to the date of change rose above annual savings, the general rate of income tax would not have to be raised so far as would be necessary were saved income exempted. In real life, it must be conceded, nobody would believe that a pledge to exempt for ever the fruits of investment made after a given date would be kept. Therefore, the only practical form of this plan is a limited form, in which the pledge is to exempt the fruits of saving for a defined term of years after they are made. Marshall, on these lines, sug-

[1] *The Distribution of the National Capital*, p. 56.

gested that improvements should not be assessed to local rates till after the lapse of twenty years, in order that the making of improvements may not be discouraged. This idea can be generalised and fashioned into a proposal that property and the income from property shall remain free from taxation till twenty years after the property has been created. This means that the fruits of saving are exempt for twenty years. The plan is actuarially equivalent (interest being reckoned at 5 per cent) to cutting the rate of tax on saved income by something more than one-half. It would eliminate a large part of the differentiation against saving without necessarily *ever* causing the general rate of income tax to rise as high as it would do under a simple exemption of savings. *Prima facie* there is much to be said for it.

§ 11. Here again, however, as with the devices discussed in the preceding chapter, the issue cannot be decided by analysis alone without reference to administrative technique. To an outsider it would seem that, when a business man builds a new factory or when a company starts operations with a definite amount of subscribed capital, the income yielded by these investments could, without great difficulty, be ear-marked as " free of tax " for a defined period of years. But much new saving is devoted from time to time to enlarging and developing concerns which already exist. If the fruits of saving were to be exempted for any period, it would, therefore, be necessary, in respect of every concern, to analyse its total income every year and to assign an appropriate part to the new capital that was invested at each separate date. This could only be done in practice by highly arbitrary rule-of-thumb methods. Even so, elaborate machinery would probably be needed to safeguard the revenue against fraud. But these are matters for technical experts. No final judgement can be passed upon the merits of the policy here sketched out except in collaboration with them.

CHAPTER XII

TAXES ASSESSED ON INVESTMENT INCOME *VERSUS* TAXES ASSESSED ON PROPERTY

§ 1. SINCE property yields income and has a value determined by the amount of the income which it is expected to yield, there is plainly no far-reaching difference between assessing annual taxes at a given rate on investment income and assessing them at a rate — when interest rules at 5 per cent — one-twentieth part as high upon the capital value of property. Broadly, the two methods come to the same thing both from the point of view of announcement and from that of distribution. There are, however, certain secondary differences, some of which, on the practical side, have considerable importance. In the brief paragraphs that follow these will be summarily set out.

§ 2. First, a tax assessed on property will bring under review certain elements, so to speak, of psychic income, which are not reckoned with in an ordinary tax on investment income because they are neither represented in money nor can easily be given a money value by tax commissioners. Thus, such anomalies of the British income tax as taxing the annual value of a yacht or motor-car when it is let out to somebody else, but not when it is used by its owner, are eliminated. Again, there are certain elements, which do have a money representative, but are not of a kind which ordinary income taxes include. The chief of these are profits resulting from appreciations in the capital value of property; *e.g.* a house, a pearl necklace, or the shares of a joint-stock company.[1] The British practice is that profits of this sort are never counted for income-tax purposes unless they are "realised" by sale of the property. If they are realised, they are, in general, counted when to seek them is a part of the normal business of their recipients, but not otherwise. Thus, a stockbroker's profit from the purchase and sale of shares of changing value is counted as income, but any profit that a philosopher might make from this form of activity would not be counted. The

[1] Cf. *ante*, Part II, Chap. VII, § 4.

Royal Commission on the Income Tax recommended a change in this respect. They inclined to make the issue depend on the intention of the income-receiver. "Any profit made on a transaction in which the subject matter was acquired with a view to profit-making should be brought within the scope of income tax, and should not be treated as an accretion of capital simply because the transaction lies outside the range of the taxpayer's ordinary business."[1] Clearly there are great practical difficulties here. These could be avoided, and, moreover, casual profits not realised through sales would also be brought into account, if property instead of income were made the object of assessment.

§ 3. Secondly, however, there is a very important respect in which property is an inferior object of assessment to its rival. If every piece of property yielded an equal flow of income every year, there would be no difference at all between a 10 per cent tax on the income derived from it and (with interest at 5 per cent) a $\frac{1}{2}$ per cent tax on the property itself. But in actual life some pieces of property do not yield a continuous equal flow of income. Thus, consider two men of equal wealth, one of whom buys with £10,000 a property reckoned to yield a permanent income of £500 a year, and the other buys for the same sum a property of equal present value reckoned to yield a series of oscillating incomes, in the aggregate of equivalent present value, but individually different in different years. Under a property tax the two men will pay equal sums to the Treasury every year; under an income tax the man with variable income will pay more when his income is large and less when it is small. Obviously, the second plan is the more convenient and the less irritating. But there is also a second and subtler difference. Suppose that one of the two £10,000 properties yields, not merely an oscillating income, but an income which begins at a low figure and is destined, and known to be destined, to grow progressively larger; that, for example, there is to be no income at all for ten years and, thereafter, a perpetual income of large amount. A property tax in this case is not merely inconvenient, in that it forces a man to make payments (possibly by borrowing) before he has any income to pay with. It is also guilty of an inequity, for, since the two series

[1] *Report*, p. 20.

of incomes have, *ex hypothesi*, the same present value, they ought to be subject to taxes of the same present value. But, whereas a permanent 10 per cent income tax on the first series beginning now will have the same present value now as a permanent 10 per cent income tax on the second series, a permanent $\frac{1}{2}$ per cent property tax beginning now on the property yielding the second series will have a substantially larger present value than a permanent $\frac{1}{2}$ per cent property tax beginning now on the property yielding the first series. What happens in effect is that the incomes which are to begin ten years hence are, under property taxes, assessed both when they arrive and also in anticipation of their arrival. There is here, clearly, a distributional evil.

§ 4. Finally, there remain certain considerations of administrative convenience. Against assessment on income it may be argued that, when a business man derives an income from a business which he manages himself, there are difficulties in disentangling the part of his income which is due to his investment from the part that is earnings of his work. These difficulties are so serious that in the United Kingdom it has been found necessary, as was observed in the preceding chapter, to circumvent them by treating incomes of this class as wholly earned, in spite of the fact that this procedure is not only logically indefensible but also confers a differential favour on one form of industrial organisation, *i.e.* the private business, as against the chief rival form, *i.e.* the joint-stock company. With taxes assessed on property this differentiation would not occur. The administrative puzzle which leads to it would not, however, be solved ; for, presuming that there is also in existence a tax on earned income, the earned part of a business man's income would still need to be disentangled from the unearned, or investment, part. This class of consideration, therefore, does little to help the advocates of property taxes. On the other side there are three important considerations. First, it is much less easy to make arrangements for tax graduation if there is an income tax on earned income coupled with a property tax than if the whole of everybody's income is brought under review — whether the rates on earned income and investment income are the same or different — in some form of general income tax. Secondly, whereas a tax on investment income can, by the device of taxation at source, be levied easily, cheaply and without any opening for evasion, there is no way in which that device could be applied to a property tax. Thirdly, and this is a point of great practical importance, whereas, when general rules of definition have been laid down, investment income is a thing the size of which can be determined by counting, property is a thing the size of which must be established by some process of valuation. For many sorts of property, speculative stock-exchange securities, for example, values undergo large and frequent changes, to keep track of which for taxation purposes would constitute a serious administrative problem. For other sorts, private businesses, lands, and so on, special appraisers would have to be employed, not merely at long intervals, as has to be done now for death duties, but at very short intervals. Hence, we should be compelled either to make shift with very unsatisfactory valuations or to undertake enormous trouble and expense in perfecting them. These administrative considerations are, I think, decisive in favour of the income tax as against the property tax method of assessment.

CHAPTER XIII

DEATH DUTIES AND TAXES ON INVESTMENT INCOME

§ 1. In turning to the subject of death duties we may conveniently begin by clearing out of the way a time-worn controversy of an ethical nature. It used to be, and is still sometimes, urged that, though ordinary taxation is an unobjectionable and, indeed, an essential function of the State, taxes on the scale and in the nature of present-day death duties violate fundamental natural rights, and are thus ethically wrong. After what was said in Part I, Chapter II, on "The Principles of Compensation" I need not delay over this matter. The point of view I have been describing was refuted once for all by Sir William Harcourt in the following passage from his Budget speech in 1894: "Upon the devolution of property of all descriptions the State takes its share first — before any of the successors in title are benefited. The reason on which this is founded is plain. The title of the State to a share in the accumulated property of the deceased is an anterior title to that of the interest to be taken by those who are to share it. The State has the first title upon the estate, and those who take afterwards have a subsequent and subordinate title. Nature gives man no power over his earthly goods beyond the term of his life. What power he possesses to prolong his will after his death — the right of a dead hand to dispose of property — is a pure creation of the law, and the State has the right to prescribe the conditions and the limitations under which that power shall be exercised."[1] Nothing further needs to be said.

§ 2. The characteristics peculiar to death duties are easily set out. From our point of view these duties are occasional property taxes, thus standing in contrast with annual property taxes. Instead of collecting a relatively small sum from each property every year, they collect a large sum from each property at intervals averaging about thirty years and associated with the death of the proprietor. This is the essential point. The fact that some owners of property, universities

[1] Quoted in Soward and Willard, *The Taxation of Capital*, p. 59.

and other like corporations, do not die and, therefore, would pay under property tax but not under death duties, is a minor matter and need not be considered here. In the preceding chapter it was shown that annual property taxes do not differ fundamentally from taxes on unearned, or investment, incomes. Since these latter taxes are a well-established fiscal instrument, it will be convenient to use them, rather than annual property taxes, as a standard of comparison for our present study. It is evident that, in the matter of distribution, death duties and taxes on investment income can be so contrived as to have closely similar results. Attention may, therefore, be confined to what I have called " announcement aspects ". Thus, we have to contrast, without reference to distribution, death duties designed to yield a given revenue with taxes on investment income designed to yield an equal revenue, these latter taxes being confined to incomes derived from pieces of capital on which death duties are paid. In other words, we have to contrast them with taxes on investment income at rates for each several taxpayer equivalent to the rates required to yield full insurance against death duties. It being assumed, of course, that the revenue collected is employed in the same way whichever method of raising it is adopted, the comparative effects on aggregate sacrifice of adopting one or other of the two sorts of tax will then depend upon the comparative effects which they respectively produce upon work and saving. In view of the analysis carried through in Chapter V, § 9, we may fairly presume that the effects upon work will not be significantly different. If saving is affected to about the same extent, heirs, as a body, will start equally well-off on either plan, and so will have no inducement to work with different amounts of energy ; and, even though savings are affected substantially more under one plan than under the other, the aggregate difference made to the amount of energy heirs display is unlikely to be other than small. Hence, attention may be concentrated on the comparative effects which the two plans may be expected to produce upon the volume of savings.

§ 3. Popular opinion makes short work of this problem. According to it, while all other taxes are paid, at least in part, out of economies in consumption, death duties, being taxes on capital, are necessarily paid wholly " out of capital ".

This is a gross confusion. Some of those who fall under the spell of it recognise, indeed, that what the government receives is not actual capital, but resources against which the taxed persons sell actual capital, and which, but for this transaction, would themselves have become new capital. But the assertion that taxes on capital are necessarily paid out of resources which would have become capital is no less false than the assertion that they are necessarily paid out of actual capital. It springs from a failure to distinguish between *object of assessment* and *source of tax payment*. The object of assessment is the channel through which the source of tax payment is reached; it is not identical with it. For commodity taxes everybody recognises this. Nobody maintains that a tax assessed on beer is necessarily paid out of beer, or even out of resources which would otherwise have become beer. The position is essentially the same with income and capital. Merely to know that a tax is assessed upon one or other of these objects tells us nothing as to how far it is paid out of resources which would have been used as income, *i.e.* chiefly for consumption, or out of resources which would have been wholly turned into new capital, *i.e.* saved. Our problem cannot be solved by means of this popular short-cut.

§ 4. As a first approach towards it it is convenient to concentrate attention upon the peculiar time-incidence of death duties, without regard for anything else. To that end let us imagine a community consisting of a number of family groups of similar wealth and income, and let us set over against one another two systems of lump-sum taxes, under one of which £100 is taken from each family group every year, while under the other £3000 is taken from each on the occasion of the death of the head of the family, which is assumed to occur, on the average, once in thirty years. On the above assumption it is evident that the two tax-systems will yield equal annual revenues to the government. We have to inquire in what, if any, respects, their effects upon the volume of savings are different.

It is easy to see that, when a tax levy is small in amount relatively to a man's annual income, a considerable part of the funds for it may easily be provided by economies in consumption. When, however, the tax levy is large — under death duties it is often equivalent to several years' income —

this is impossible. A large part of the funds required *must* be provided by a sale of capital, which means, as we have seen, out of resources which would normally have become new capital. With levies made at the moment of death the case is still stronger. Since heirs as a rule look to what actually comes to them and are little interested in what would have come to them on the hypothesis that there had been no death duties, they are very unlikely to meet any part of a death-duty levy by cutting down their consumption. Even small levies made at that moment would, therefore, be paid to practically their full amount out of capital in the sense described above. *A fortiori* this will be true of large levies. Practically, we may conclude that the whole of death-duty levies will in fact be so paid ; in other words, that, so far as the present argument goes, they will deplete the volume of savings by their full amount.

If we had to do with imposts required only in a single isolated year, the above result might stand without qualification. In fact, however, we are concerned with regular annually recurring imposts ; and, consequently, there is another side to the picture. For, whereas in any year only about one-thirtieth of the sum-total of estates become subject to tax, the fact that death duties (here conceived, it will be remembered, as simple lump-sum taxes) exist, and that all privately owned estates will eventually fall under them, reacts, or may react, upon the conduct of the owners of the other estates. The total effect of death duties upon savings is not, therefore, determined by the fact that the actual payment of death duties is made at the expense of what would have been savings. To obtain a true comparison between large lump-sum taxes levied at death and small lump-sum taxes designed to yield the same revenue and levied annually a more difficult inquiry is needed.

§ 5. The issue is perfectly precise : will the representative man over the whole period of his life restrict his consumption as much when he knows that £3000 will be taken from his estate at death as he would do if he knew that £100 would be taken from it in every year of his life ? In other words, will a group of thirty men, one of whom is to be taxed £3000 now, a second £3000 next year, a third £3000 a year later, the impact of the tax in each case to coincide with death, contract their consumption as much as they would have done were all of them to be taxed £100 every year? To resolve this issue let us begin by supposing that all the men concerned are completely indifferent to personal death, and are just as much interested in their heirs as in themselves. On this assumption, if everyone were perfectly rational, it would seem that the two systems ought to affect the aggregate volume of savings to an exactly equal extent. In fact, however, people are not perfectly rational. They are apt to procrastinate; to turn their eyes away from events that lie in the future, particularly if the date of these events is unknown. For these reasons they are not likely to economise so largely to meet occasional large lump-sum payments as they would do in order to meet equivalent smaller annual payments. The circumstance that the vast majority of persons are not indifferent to personal death and are not just as much interested in their heirs as in themselves obviously reinforces this conclusion, the more so if the large lump-sum imposts are to be levied at the moment of death. Nor can the conclusion be rebutted by reference to the conduct of heirs. For, under the death-duty plan, since the former owners have economised less than they would have done under annual taxation, the heirs inherit less and so have smaller investment incomes. This may perhaps cause them to work somewhat harder — though, as urged above, this effect will be slight — but it cannot, in any ordinary circumstances, cause them to save more. I conclude, therefore, that, as between lump-sum taxes assessed on the occasion of death and equivalent lump-sum taxes assessed annually, the former are practically certain to prove more injurious to saving than the latter.

§ 6. If the relation between large occasional lump-sum taxes and death duties were precisely the same as that between small annual lump-sum taxes and taxes on investment income, it would follow that death duties are more injurious to saving than taxes on investment income of like distributional character. In fact, however, I shall submit that the two relations are not the same, and that the excess damage, as against lump-sum levies, is certain to be substantially smaller under death duties than under the rival form of tax. The grounds of this conclusion have now to be set out in detail.

§ 7. The desire to build up capital possessions is not a

simple thing. It is made up of various elements blended in various ways among different men. One element is the desire to be able to exercise the constructive force, which a strong man may find in himself, in conjunction with a large-scale undertaking: another is the desire for that power in society or, perhaps, in politics which great wealth confers: another is the desire for fame or notoriety: another the desire for a large income accruing without effort in later life: another the desire for posthumous glory in dying very rich: another mere inertia — inability to spend in consumption the whole of a large income. All these motives are concerned only with the lifetime of the man who contemplates saving under the stress of them: the fact that after his death his fortune does not also die is, so far as they are concerned, an irrelevant accident. Alongside of them there is the desire to hand on accumulated capital to his children after the accumulator's death. This desire is most urgent when a family of young children is being supported by a father out of a considerable earned income backed by little property; for the father knows that, if he dies, his children will be very badly off, so that each extra £ of property accumulated for them will have a high marginal utility. In such a case even a man who cared little for his children's *satisfaction* as compared with his own, might, nevertheless, be ready to give up many £'s from his own consumption in order to provide even one £ for them. But the desire may also be strong where considerable heritable funds already exist, since these may have to be divided among a number of children, and, even if this is not so, the father may have ambitions to found a wealthy family. When, however, a man stands possessed of an estate which is already *very* large, he can hardly desire to increase it still further for the sake of his children, and he may even reflect that too large an inheritance is likely to prove injurious to them. On the other hand, a man who is, and expects to remain, childless may still desire, though perhaps not very keenly, to have property at his death to leave to relatives, friends, or public objects in which he is interested.

§ 8. Death duties and taxes upon investment income alike are exactly equivalent to their lump-sum counterparts in the amount of money that they take from those who have to pay them. Consequently, the effects of both are the same as those of their respective lump-sum counterparts so far as reactions through the marginal utility of income in fact or in prospect are concerned; they differ from these only because the tax formulae employed involve a differential element. Since both death duties and taxes on investment income have this characteristic, the one striking accumulated savings directly, the other the fruit of these savings, it appears *prima facie* that their effects will differ from those of their respective lump-sum counterparts in equal measure. The analysis of motives that was set out in the preceding section shows, however, that this is not so. In so far as a man's motives for saving are confined to happenings during his lifetime and at the moment of his death, a death-duty levy will affect his conduct in exactly the same way as an equivalent lump-sum levy: he will save to exactly the same extent as he would have done under that type of levy. As regards the whole of this important class of motives he is not discouraged in any degree. A tax on investment income, however, strikes, not only at this class of motives, but also at the other class. Consequently, such a tax must always check saving more than an equivalent lump-sum tax. Hence, we may lay it down that the excess damage to saving done by death duties, as compared with their lump-sum counterpart, is smaller than the excess damage done by taxes on investment income, as compared with their lump-sum counterpart. This is true even when the death duties are imposed on estates passing to the children of the decedents. The relative advantage is obviously still greater when they are imposed on estates left to remoter relatives or to friends.

§ 9. It thus appears that, in attempting to compare the effects on saving of death duties and of taxes on investment income, designed to yield equal revenues and alike in respect of distribution, we are confronted with conflicting considerations. The lump-sum counterpart of death duties is more injurious to saving than the lump-sum counterpart of taxes on investment income; but, on the other hand, death duties are not so much worse than their lump-sum counterpart as taxes on investment income are than theirs. There are no means by which these two factors can be measured. We may, if we will, guess on which side the balance of advantage lies; but we cannot know. All that can be said with confidence is that neither of the two rival means of raising revenue is likely to be *much* superior to the other. It will not make *much* difference either to saving or to anything else whether the one or the other is chosen.

§ 10. It remains to call attention to one further point. From the concluding sentences of § 8 it is easy to see that death duties specialised upon bequests other than in the direct line, after the manner of the British legacy and succession duties,[1] are, in respect of a given levy distributed in a given way, less injurious to saving than general death duties. An extension of this line of thought leads naturally to Rignano's proposal that a man's savings, when left by him in the first instance, should pay one rate of duty, and that, when left a second time by his legatee to the legatees' heirs, they should pay a higher rate of duty. The theoretical basis of the proposal is the presumption that most men will care very little about the fortunes of the heirs of their heirs, and that, therefore, other things being equal, death duties at the second remove, so to speak, would enjoy the same kind of advantage as duties on bequests out of the direct line. This is, I think, certainly true ; and it follows from it that, provided the practical difficulties could be overcome, the compound type of death duty contemplated by Rignano, or some variation of it, would enable a given revenue to be raised with somewhat less damage to saving than is possible under death duties of the ordinary type. There is, of course, no reason why the Rignano plan should not be superimposed upon arrangements providing for progression in tax rates as the size of estates increases and for differentiation between the rates charged on legacies to the testator's children and on legacies to other people.

§ 11. The practical difficulties in the way of this plan are, however, very serious. The first heir might be tempted to squander his legacy or to dispose of it by gifts *inter vivos* to

[1] These duties which are, of course, of small importance compared with the main death duty, estates duty, are assessed upon the amount received by beneficiaries without reference to the aggregate size of the estate passing at death. They are at the rate of 1 per cent when the beneficiary is the husband, wife, or lineal issue or descendant of the author of the benefaction, subject to certain exceptions ; 5 per cent when the beneficiary is a brother or sister or a descendant of a brother or sister ; 10 per cent in all other cases. (Cf. *Report of the Committee on Taxation and the National Debt*, p. 195.)

such effect that, when he died, his inherited property and his earned property together would be insufficient to pay the tax due on his inherited property. Moreover, it would be very difficult to allow properly for changes in the value of the inherited property when that property and property newly created by the first heirs were mixed together. If no allowance were made, and the inherited property had fallen in value, owing either to a general cause such as a rise in the rate of interest, or to a cause special to the property itself, a portion of the first inheritor's savings sufficient to make good the depreciation in the value of his inherited property would find itself, contrary to Rignano's intention, treated at his death on the same footing as that property. These difficulties might, indeed, be met by a rule requiring all legacies to be "settled", in such wise that the heirs could neither spend the principal nor, except under close restrictions, shift it from one form of investment to another. Rules of this kind would, however, obstruct the free movement of capital in ways that might prove injurious to enterprise. Attention may, therefore, be directed to an ingenious alternative plan that was suggested some years ago, apparently independently, by Mr. Hugh Dalton and Mr. H. D. (now Sir Hubert) Henderson. This plan proposes that, when an estate passes at death, there should be levied on it one death duty of the ordinary sort and also a second death duty in respect of its next descent. Against this second death duty, however, the State would pay to the first heir during his lifetime an annual sum representing interest upon it, so that he would not suffer and, until he in turn died, the State would not gain. At his death the State would stop paying interest, and so would hold the principal of this second death duty free, so to speak, of mortgage. This plan would dispense with the need for compulsory settlements. Sir Hubert Henderson suggested that the rate charged in respect of the second death duty should depend, not on the aggregate amount of the fortune left, as the rate of the primary death duty would do, but, as against each separate legatee, on the amount of the fortune accruing to him. This, however, is not essential to his plan.[1]

[1] Cf. Henderson, *Inheritance and Inequality*, pp. 17-26.

CHAPTER XIV

TAXES ON THE PUBLIC VALUE OF LAND

§ 1. It has become apparent in the course of our study that, when a tax is assessed on anybody by reference to the value of some object in his possession of such a sort that that value cannot be altered by any action on his part, the tax, in its announcement aspect, works like a poll-tax and is, in that aspect, an ideal tax from the standpoint of least aggregate sacrifice. In order that it may possess this quality it is not necessary that the object of assessment should be inalienable by the present owner. He may be free to sell it — of course at a price diminished by the discounted value of the tax — and the tax will remain, in its announcement aspect, wholly innocuous. The essential point is that the object of assessment is such that its value, and, therefore, the amount of the impost to be collected, cannot be altered by anything that the owner, whoever he may be, decides to do.

§ 2. Now, if we select any piece of durable property, determine its value in 1936, and decree that henceforward its owner shall pay a tax based on that value, we have an object of assessment of the type contemplated above. There is, however, a certain appearance of absurdity in basing taxes on historical values of this kind. It is easy to imagine how anomalous taxes so based would seem when they had continued for 100 years. In practice, if any value is to be taken as an object of assessment for taxation, it must be current, or, at all events, very recent value. The values of all ordinary sorts of property are, however, liable to be altered by work or investment on the part of the owners or occupiers. Taxes assessed upon them will, therefore, vary in amount according to what these persons do, and, therefore, will react upon their conduct. Thus these taxes do not conform to the poll-tax type. There is, however, one current value, taxes upon which do so conform. This is what is called in Australia the " unimproved value " of land.

§ 3. In Great Britain up to the present time, apart from the small " undeveloped land " duty of the 1909 Budget, no resort has been had to this taxable object. In New Zealand and the Australian colonies, however, it has for many years played an important part both in local and in national finance. In South Australia a special national tax on unimproved land values was first imposed in 1884. One halfpenny in the £ was levied on all unimproved (capital) values ; an extra halfpenny on unimproved values exceeding £5000 ; and an absentee tax, amounting to 20 per cent, on absentee owners.[1] In New South Wales : "The land tax of the State is levied on unimproved value at the rate of 1d. in the £. A sum of £240 is allowed by way of exemption, and, when the unimproved value is in excess of that sum, a reduction equal to the exemption is made ; but, when several blocks of land within the State are held by a person or company, only one amount of £240 may be deducted from the aggregate unimproved value. In cases where land is mortgaged the mortgagor is permitted to deduct from the tax payable a sum equal to the income tax paid by the mortgagee on the interest derived from the mortgage on the whole property including improvements."[2] In 1910 the Commonwealth of Australia introduced a central tax on unimproved land of the same general character as the State taxes, with a graduated scale rising from $\frac{1}{30000}$ of a penny on the first £ of taxable balance to 6d. on each £ in excess of £75,000. The rates were raised substantially during the first world war, subsequently reduced, and in 1940–41 raised again to approximately the 1914–17 level.[3] In New Zealand : "In 1891 the Property Tax Act then in force was repealed and replaced by the Land and Income Assessment Act, under which a land tax was imposed on land and mortgages of land, and an income tax on all income other than income derived from land and mortgages of land. Improvements on land were exempted up to £3000. In 1893 an amending Act was passed by which all improvements on land were entirely exempted, and in 1896 an Act was passed by which the principle of taxation on the 'unimproved value' was extended to local rating, by enabling local authorities to adopt the system on a poll of the ratepayers being taken and a majority voting in favour of its adoption."[4] The amount of

[1] [Cd. 3191], p. 20.
[2] [Cd. 3191], p. 21.
[3] *22nd Report of the Commissioner of Taxation Commonwealth of Australia*, 1940, p. 7.
[4] [Cd. 3191], p. 24.

the national tax in this colony was ordinarily one penny in the £ on unimproved (capital) value. "Land in possession of natives is treated specially, and, out of consideration for small peasant farmers, plots worth less than £500 are exempted and plots worth less than £1500 are allowed an abatement. In addition to the ordinary land tax, the same Act imposed a graduated State tax on large estates, commencing at one-sixteenth of a penny in the £ on land of an unimproved value of £5000, and rising to threepence in the £ on land of an unimproved value of £210,000 or more." [1] The arrangements existing in 1940 are summarised in the New Zealand official Year Book for that year as follows. "Land tax is assessed on the unimproved value of land after deductions provided for by Statute have been made by way of special exemptions. An owner of land the unimproved value of which does not exceed £1500 is allowed an exemption of £500; . . . [and with larger values an exemption gradually diminishing, so that no exemption is allowed when £2500 is reached. . . .] When the unimproved value, on which land tax is payable, does not exceed £500, the present rate of land tax is 1d. in the £. The rate is increased by $\frac{1}{8000}$ of a penny for every £ in excess of £5000, with, however, a maximum of 6d. in the £." [2]

§ 4. In all these arrangements the essential matter is the distinction between improved and unimproved value. Some light on the precise way in which this distinction is drawn may be gathered from a very interesting explanatory memorandum furnished by the Valuer-General of New Zealand, Mr. G. F. C. Campbell, in the Report [Cd. 3191], from which extracts have been quoted above. Mr. Campbell cites the definition clauses of the Government Valuation of Land Act, 1896, and adds certain comments of his own. The principal points to be noted are the following:

First: "The increased value attaching to any piece of land due to the successful working of other lands in the district or to progressive works effected by the State, the general prosperity of the country, high markets for produce, etc., form a portion of the unimproved value under the New Zealand law. Any increased value, however, which is represented by the improvements effected by the individual pos-

[1] Chorlton, *The Rating of Land Values*, p. 160.
[2] *Loc. cit.* p. 587.

sessor, either past or present, does not form part of the unimproved value."[1]

Secondly: "Improvements can only be valued *to the extent to which they increase the selling value of the land.* This fact should not be forgotten; the valuer must, therefore, value an improvement at the proportionate sum which it represents in the selling value of the whole property. We sometimes find a large house built on a small area of farming land. The ordinary farmer who would purchase such a property would not be likely to pay for the house anything approaching its cost — he would only pay the price of a house which suits the requirements of the farm. The selling value of the house must, therefore, be put at what the ordinary purchaser would be likely to give for it, or, in other words, at the sum by which it increases the selling value of the property. Sometimes an owner will expend his capital and labour injudiciously, and the result will prove detrimental to the land instead of being an improvement. Some lands hold grass better without first being ploughed than they do after the plough. The effect of ploughing in such cases would not be to improve the selling value. Some improvements, such as ornamental shrubbery, orchards, lawns, vineries, etc., rarely increase the selling value to the full extent of their cost, and should, therefore, be valued accordingly. . . . No work can be considered an improvement if the benefit is exhausted at the time of valuation. . . . The amount at which improvements are to be valued is defined by the Act as the sum by which they increase the selling value of the land, *provided that the value must not exceed the cost,* although it may be below the cost if their condition warrants it. The cost of an improvement is not necessarily its selling value, as its suitability and condition must be taken into consideration."[2]

Thirdly: "It is the actual improvement which is valued, not the effect of that improvement. For instance, suppose that the expenditure of a small sum in cutting an outlet for water has converted a swamp into first-class agricultural land. The fact that the swamp was capable of easy drainage would enhance its unimproved value, and the cost only of cutting the drain would be valued as the improvement."[3]

[1] [Cd. 3191], p. 37.
[2] *Ibid.* pp. 39-40.
[3] *Ibid.* pp. 40-41.

Lastly: An improvement, to be classed as such, must be made by the owner. Suppose that there are two pieces of land adjacent to one another, and that the cutting of a drain or the erection of a fence upon one of them would enhance the total value of both. If the two pieces are owned by the same person, their unimproved value, both before and after the drain is cut, would appear to be equal to their total value *minus* the cost of cutting the drain. If, however, they are in different hands, the unimproved value of the piece on which the improvement is not required is enhanced so soon as the improvement on the other piece is carried out. The same point arises in connection with collective improvements. Thus Mr. Campbell observes: "It has been argued that public works done by small communities, and for which those communities agree to rate themselves, shall be valued as an improvement" for the purpose of the national land tax.[1] The New Zealand Act, however, does not accept the view.[2]

§ 5. The general nature of the distinction between improved and unimproved value has long been familiar to economists. It corresponds to the Ricardian distinction between true economic rent and profits from capital invested in land. Unimproved value is the capitalised value of the true rent, and improvement value that of profits. A terminology for some purposes more convenient was suggested many years ago by Marshall. True rent is that part of the annual value of land which arises from its position, its extension, its yearly income of sunlight and heat and rain and air. "The (annual) value of the land", he wrote, "is sometimes called its 'inherent value'; but much of that value is the result of the action of men, though not of its individual holders; and, therefore, it is perhaps more correct to call this part of the annual value of land its 'public value', while that part of its value which can be traced to work and outlay by its individual holder may be called its 'private value'."[3] Public value capitalised corresponds to the unimproved (capital) value, and private value capitalised to the improvement (capital) value of the Australasian laws.

[1] [Cd. 3191], p. 40.

[2] For an account of some of the difficulties of valuation, cf. Scheftel, *The Taxation of Land Value*, pp. 69 *et sqq*.

[3] *Memorandum on Imperial and Local Taxes* [Cd. 9528], p. 115.

§ 6. Having thus found in the unimproved or public value of land a taxable object, which, from the standpoint of "announcement", conforms perfectly to the principle of least aggregate sacrifice, we have now to inquire how far it conforms to that principle in its distributional aspects. In attacking this problem, we have to apply the general method of Chapter IX, §§ 19-22, to the facts of this particular case. In this country, among people at any given income level, the proportions in which their incomes are drawn from the public value of land vary enormously. One rich man's income is made up almost entirely of rents, another's contains scarcely any rents. Hence, as between persons of equal incomes, this type of tax will act very unequally, and, so far, will be distributionally bad. On the other hand, the ownership of rents is in this country concentrated in a high degree upon rich people. Hence, as between people of different incomes, this type of tax is distributionally good.

§ 7. There is, however, a *special* consideration which commends this type of tax up to a point from the distributional angle. It is, in a measure, preventive of distributional evils, which government expenditure of taxation otherwise tends to bring about. Thus Marshall wrote: "There may be great difficulty in allocating the betterment due to any particular improvement. But, as it is, the expenditure of such private societies as the Metropolitan Public Gardens Association, and much of the rates raised on building values for public improvements, is really a free gift of wealth to owners who are already fortunate." [1] It is true, no doubt, that those who have purchased urban land recently may have partially discounted this betterment in their purchase price; but they are not likely to have discounted it entirely; while those owners who are not recent purchasers will not have discounted it at all. Consequently, it is to be expected that the special burden which new taxes upon site-values would impose upon site-owners — at all events in urban districts — would be partially offset by a special increment in no way due to their own effort and expenditure.

§ 8. In view of the excellence of a tax on the public value of land from the standpoint of announcement we should plainly need proof that, taken all in all, it was abnormally

[1] *Memorandum on Imperial and Local Taxes* [Cd. 9528], p. 125.

bad distributionally before being justified in rejecting its claims to a place in the tax system. If it were proposed to put a very high rate of duty upon the annual — still more upon the capitalised — public value of land, owners of valuable sites would, indeed, have ground for complaint that *gross* discrimination was being practised as between them and other equally wealthy persons. Even with a fairly low rate of tax the discrimination may be considerably more important than it is at all likely to be in the case of, say, a tea tax ; because some persons draw a proportion of their income from true rents larger than the proportion of their income that any persons spend on tea. Moreover, taxes on true rents, if imposed with an expectation of continuance, are apt to become amortised : that is to say, the present owners of land, should they wish to sell their property, are forced to accept a purchase price reduced by the discounted value of the future annual imposts. When this happens they are hit, *pro tanto*, with greater severity. This is a sound reason against imposing very high rates of tax on true rents.[1] It is of little weight, however, against low or moderate rates ; for, after all, *every* single tax taken by itself is bound to be in *some* degree unfair between individuals. On the whole, therefore, I conclude that, in any tax system which relies on a number of different imposts, there is a strong case for including among the rest a moderate tax assessed at a moderate percentage upon the (annual) public value of land.

[1] If a tax of this sort is in existence and has been in existence long enough for a large proportion of the affected property to have changed hands by sale or inheritance, these same considerations constitute a strong argument against remitting it ; for, just as the imposition of the tax mulcted one arbitrarily selected set of men who are to receive no compensation, so the removal of it gives a present to another arbitrarily selected set who have suffered no previous hurt. It is with this consideration in mind that Marshall writes : " Any relief as regards old rates should, therefore, apply only to new buildings and other fresh investments of capital " (Marshall, *Memorandum on Imperial and Local Taxes* [Cd. 9528], p. 121).

CHAPTER XV

TAXES ON MONOPOLY REVENUE

§ 1. It is a commonplace of economic text-books that, when a monopolist is making full use of his monopolistic power over prices, a tax assessed upon monopoly revenue will not affect in any way his or anybody else's conduct. Hence, this kind of tax, like a tax on the public value of land, is, in its announcement aspect, ideal. Again, then, we turn at once to distributional aspects. As with taxes on the public value of land, so also with these taxes, people who happen to possess shares in monopolistic concerns are treated unequally as against people with like incomes whose investments are in other things. Nor can this inequality be excused by the argument that shareholders in monopolistic concerns are making an income " unduly " large relative to their investment: for most shareholders will have bought their shares in the market at prices in which the high returns, if there are such, due to monopolistic exactions are already discounted. To set against this distributional evil, as between people of similar economic situations, there is the fact that many of the persons interested in monopolistic concerns are wealthy, so that, as between people of dissimilar economic situations, monopoly revenue taxes are, *pro tanto*, distributionally good. Perhaps, too, it may be claimed for such taxes that, in some measure, they discourage people from attempting to form monopolies with a view to exercising monopolistic power over prices.

§ 2. If, then, the State takes no direct steps to prevent the mulcting of the public by the exercise of monopolistic power, there is a good *prima facie* case for the imposition of, at all events, moderate taxes upon monopoly revenue, *i.e.* that part of a monopolist's income which results from the exercise of monopolistic power in forcing selling price above supply price.

§ 3. The exercise of monopolistic power is, however, in general, highly anti-social, since it involves deliberately restricting the output of the monopolised good below the most advantageous output. Though, in respect of the output which is actually produced, the loss which the public suffers through high prices is offset by an equivalent gain to the monopolist, in respect of the output which high prices prevent from coming into existence there is a loss of consumer's surplus unbalanced by any gain. Hence it will, in general, be more in the interest of the community as a whole for the State to prevent the exercise of monopolistic power than to permit it and to tax the proceeds. Even if the tax were approximately a 100 per cent tax this would be so. In that case the monopolist would secure nothing out of his exactions, the whole of what he had tried to gain going to the State. But the tax would be equivalent to a tax assessed on the commodity at the rate calculated to yield maximum possible revenue : and it is easy to see that a tax on any assessable object at so high a rate as this tends to inflict an abnormal amount of sacrifice on the community relatively to the revenue which it yields. For the State to allow monopolists to mulct the public and then to force them to disgorge to it a part, or even the whole, of their spoils is, therefore, only defensible where the better policy of preventing an anti-social exercise of monopolistic power is not politically practicable.

CHAPTER XVI

TAXES ON WINDFALLS

§ 1. By windfalls I mean accretions to the real value of people's property that are not foreseen by them and are not in any degree due to efforts made, intelligence exercised, risks borne, or capital invested by them. In the present chapter I propose to consider taxes assessed upon these objects. It is apparent immediately that in their announcement aspect such taxes conform to the ideal, for they take the same given amount of money from the taxpayer without reference to his conduct in any respect. What is to be said of them in their distributional aspect?

§ 2. It is possible to imagine a community in which, by a miraculous dispensation of Providence, windfalls are so distributed that large ones always go to poor people, moderate ones to men of middle incomes, and none at all to rich people. In actual life there is no reason to suppose that anything of this sort happens. On the contrary, if any general presumption can be made, it is that rich people are more likely to enjoy windfalls than anybody else, because most windfalls consist in unlooked-for changes in the value of some piece of material property, and pieces of material property are, in the main, owned by rich men. We have, therefore, no ground for supposing that windfalls as a whole are good for distribution or that taxes upon them would be distributionally bad. Something might be said, if it were administratively practicable, for exempting from taxation any windfalls (of moderate amount) that fall to poor people: but, apart from this, in so far as true windfalls can in practice be isolated, the general considerations set out in this volume point towards heavy taxation — perhaps 100 per cent taxation — of all of them. The principle of this matter is thus clear, and discussion may be confined to particular applications.

§ 3. It is necessary to distinguish first between what may be called integral windfalls and partial windfalls. By an integral windfall is meant an accretion, in the nature of a windfall, to the aggregate value of a person's property reckoned relatively to the whole period of his life ; by a partial windfall an accretion of this nature occurring at some definite moment to some definite part of a person's property. The distributional soundness of a tax upon integral windfalls has already been recognised. But with partial windfalls the issue is less clear. For a windfall increment to one part of a man's property in one year may be offset by a windfall decrement to another part of it in another year. If there were a presumption that an observed windfall increment would in fact be balanced by a windfall decrement that is not observed, distributional considerations would point against the taxation of partial windfalls. Integral windfalls would be proper objects of taxation, but partial windfalls would not. Since in practice it is quite impossible to ascertain by direct inquiry whether or not an integral windfall has occurred — for this would imply knowledge of the future as well as of the past — or, if it has, how large it has been, this conclusion would, in effect, rule all windfall taxation out of court. There is not, however, in fact, any presumption of the kind contemplated. When a partial windfall increment is observed, it *may*, of course, be cancelled by a partial windfall decrement to the same property ; but there is no presumption that it will be. Consequently, in the absence of definite knowledge that it is in fact so cancelled, we need not hesitate to tax it. Those windfalls that are observed are not rendered improper objects for taxation by the fact that windfall decrements and other windfall increments occur, which cannot in practice be brought into account.

§ 4. The exceptional circumstances of the two German wars brought into being a new and very important class of windfall, in the abnormal profits made by certain businesses as a direct consequence of them. The values of certain sorts of goods and services were enormously enhanced, with the result that those persons who had a store of these things or the means of making them quickly — shipowners, iron and steel makers, munition makers, farmers and many others — were in a position, except in so far as the government interfered by fixing maximum prices for the commodities in which they were interested, to reap undreamt-of fortunes. In these fortunes there was a large element of windfall. In order to isolate that element it was necessary to determine what the normal profit of the business was, to add on to that an allowance for extra profit due to new capital investments and additional work, and to take account of the fact that machinery set up and adaptations made specially for war purposes would be of little use, and might even be in the way, after the war was over. The estimate of normal profit ought strictly to have taken account, not merely of what the profits in the years immediately preceding the war actually were, but also of the prospects that then existed of their increasing. It ought further to have taken account both of the high level of general prices prevailing during the war, in consequence of which a given money profit represented a much smaller real profit than before, and also of the probability that prices would be high for some time after the war, in consequence of which larger reserves should properly be held against depreciation. The English excess profits duty, as operated in both wars, aimed, in a general way, at isolating the windfall element in war profits on these lines and at taxing this element at as high a rate as possible ; that rate being limited only by the prospect that, since it is not possible completely to isolate the windfall element, a tax above, say, 80 per cent would encourage laxity and wasteful administration and discourage enterprise in a dangerous degree.[1] The 100 per cent rate imposed in May 1940 had a political rather than economic justification. Its economic disadvantages were, however, mitigated by various adjustments and allowances.[2]

§ 5. Windfall taxation, as an instrument for raising revenue in normal conditions, was practically unknown until the present century. Some years, however, before the 1914–18 war, several attempts were made on the continent of Europe to tax windfalls of a particular kind, namely, those in respect

[1] The original American excess profits duty was based on the absolute rate of profit, not on the excess above the profits obtained before the war. It was, therefore, much less nearly a true tax on windfalls than the English tax. It was, moreover, open to the serious objection that it penalised inventions, the skilful seizing of opportunities and good management. " Something can be said for a graduated tax on income ; something can even be said for a graduated tax on capital ; but it is difficult to say anything in defence of a tax which is graduated on the varying percentages which income bears to capital. To penalise enterprise and ingenuity in a way that is not accomplished by a tax on either capital or income — that is the unique distinction of the law " (Seligman, " The War Revenue Act ", *Political Science Quarterly*, March 1918, p. 29).

[2] For a thorough discussion of E.P.T. cf. Hicks, *The Taxation of War Wealth*, Parts ii-iv.

of the public value of land, by means of increment duties. In Frankfort-on-Main, "if, since the previous change of ownership less than twenty years have elapsed, and if there has been an increase in value amounting to at least 15 per cent of the previous purchase price, after allowance has been made for expenditure on improvements, loss of interest and costs of transfer, increment duty is levied on the following scale: 2 per cent on the increase in value for increases between 15 and 20 per cent, 3 per cent for increases between 20 and 25 per cent, and so on, 1 per cent being added to the rate of duty for every 5 per cent increase of value, up to a maximum rate of 25 per cent".[1] In Cologne the general arrangements were similar. The scale of duty started at 10 per cent for increases of value of more than 10 and less than 20 per cent, and the rate increased by 1 per cent for every additional 10 per cent in the increase of value, up to the same maximum rate of 25 per cent. This scale was charged in its entirety when not more than five years had elapsed since the previous change of ownership, two-thirds of the scale when not more than ten years had elapsed, and one-third in respect of any period exceeding ten years.[2] In 1911 the Conservative party in the Reichstag carried a proposal for the introduction of kindred arrangements into the Imperial fiscal system, but "by the amendment of the law in 1913, the revenue accruing from the Wertzuwachssteuer was relegated entirely to the States and local authorities".[3] In the United Kingdom a cruder form of duty upon increments of land value was imposed by the Budget of 1909. It might be thought at first sight that these duties satisfy the conditions required of windfall taxes, and that nothing more complicated is necessary. This, however, is not really so; and it is desirable to show why it is not so. We shall thus be able to bring into clear light the practical difficulties by which any attempt to devise effective windfall taxes is confronted.

§ 6. To begin with, there are two classes of increment which are apparent and not real. One of these arises in this way. If the general level of prices during one decade is 50 per cent higher than in the previous decade, then the money value of unimproved land may increase 50 per cent and yet

[1] Cf. [Cd. 4750], p. 21. [2] *Ibid.* p. 18.

[3] Scheftel, *The Taxation of Land Value*, p. 145, footnote.

not experience any real increment. The income that the owner derives from it, or the capital sum that he would obtain by selling it, though 50 per cent larger than before in terms of money, is exactly the same as before in terms of the things which this money enables him to buy. This sort of difficulty does not exist as against *ad valorem* taxes, but it must exist wherever the taxed object is the difference between the money value which a particular thing has at different points of time. The only way to avoid it is to revise the valuation assigned to the basis period in the light of the new level of general prices which exists in the period when the amount of increment liable to duty has to be determined. This revision would be a difficult task. The method of performing it that naturally suggests itself is to multiply the original site value by the ratio which an ordinary index number of general prices in the assessment year bears to the corresponding index number in the original valuation year. This method, however, would not be satisfactory, because the capital value of an instrument of production does not vary in correspondence with the income derived from it in a single year, but depends upon the expectation of income for a number of years. Nevertheless, by a reasonable, and not a mechanical, application of index numbers, it would seem that a competent authority could eliminate from the field of taxation the main part of the merely apparent increments of this class that come into being. By a similar process, though here much popular prejudice would have to be overcome, a competent authority might be able, in times of depressed prices, to bring into the field of taxation real increments of value which appeared as decrements. When currency values are changing with the violence experienced in Germany, Austria and Russia in the years immediately following the 1914–18 war, the whole basis of this sort of taxation is destroyed. For its practical application reasonably stable currency values are essential.

§ 7. The other class of apparent increment arises when the general rate of money interest on long-period investments falls. This kind of change means that an investment yielding exactly the same annual return must rise in capital value. Such a rise is of no advantage to the owner of the investment — unless, indeed, he wishes to turn the proceeds into consumable income — because, even if he sells it, he will not be able to invest the proceeds in anything that will yield, on equal security, a higher annual return than he was obtaining before. Here, again, adjustment would be difficult. But, if account were taken of the place occupied by the year of the original valuation and the year of assessment in their respective credit cycles, it would seem that a competent authority could so qualify the original valuation that the increments assessed to taxation should not include this class of apparent increment.

§ 8. Our task, however, is not completed when apparent increments have been eliminated. For even real increments, when they are anticipated and discounted, are not windfalls. The point may be put in this way. The capital value of a site is the present worth of the annual income which it is expected to yield. Increments in capital value must, therefore, arise regularly as the date at which an increase in annual value will begin draws nearer. For simplicity of illustration, let us imagine an estate, which is not expected to yield any income at all for the next twenty years, but is, thereafter, expected to yield an income (apart altogether from expenditure on the land) of £500 a year. This example is typical of the condition of much land in the neighbourhood of towns, which is expected at a future date to become valuable for building purposes. Interest being reckoned at 5 per cent, a simple calculation shows that the capital site value of our imaginary estate will progress approximately as follows :

Value in	1940 . . .	£3,800
,,	1945 . . .	4,800
,,	1950 . . .	6,100
,,	1955 . . .	7,800
,,	1960 . . .	10,000

The increment of value over the fifteen years following 1940 is thus £4000, and a duty of 20 per cent on this increment, payable in 1955, is £800. A further simple calculation shows that, with interest at 5 per cent, £800 in 1955 is equivalent to a little less than £400 in 1940. This means that, if an owner wished to sell the estate we have been considering in 1940, the existence of a 20 per cent increment duty payable in 1955 would cause him to get some £3400 for it instead of £3800. The tax, in short, would be a direct impost on the present owner, and not in any sense a windfall tax.

§ 9. In practice, of course, many actual increments of value are partly windfalls and partly increments of this kind. When the element of appearance in actual increments has been removed, it is possible to distinguish the windfall element in the real increment in the following manner: If a piece of land in 1940 has a total value $(x+y)$, made up of a value x due to its present (agricultural or other) use, and a value y due to expectations of building rents after 1960, there should, interest being reckoned at 5 per cent, be a non-windfall increment in the value of the land by the year 1955 equal to about 108 per cent of y. In order, therefore, that increment tax may be confined to windfalls, it ought only to be levied on the excess of the then value of the land over its present value now *plus* 108 per cent of that portion of its present value which is due to its prospects as building land. For periods of greater or less length than fifteen years similar calculations could, of course, easily be worked out. The root idea of this plan was embodied both in the increment duties established at Frankfort and Cologne and also in the German Imperial increment tax. The fourth section of the Frankfort bye-law, for example, provided that, "in the case of unbuilt-on land which the vendor does not himself use for purposes of agriculture or industry", before the increment which has accrued at any time is calculated, there shall be added to the original basis valuation interest at the rate of 4 per cent.[1] Compound interest was, however — it would seem incorrectly — not allowed.

§ 10. Yet one more point remains. In some circumstances an increment, which is not definitely expected, nevertheless enters, in some measure, into present value, and is, therefore, not true windfall. I may, for instance, have a piece of land which is expected to yield for a long while £500 a year, but in regard to which it is recognised vaguely that either a rise or a fall may take place. This land — with interest at 5 per cent — will have a capital value of £10,000, and it, therefore, seems at first sight that the possibility of its rising in value is not being discounted. In reality, however, this possibility does enter into present value, acting there as a counterweight to the possibility of a fall. The measure of influence which this possibility, reckoned over the ensuing fifteen years, exercises

[1] Cf. [Cd. 4750], p. 21.

upon present value is given by the sum for which the right to all increment *of this class* — I am not, of course, now referring to the *anticipated* increment already discussed — accruing during the said fifteen years could be sold. It is fairly certain that the sum obtainable would, in general, be a very small fraction of the capital value of the land. Consequently, these increments are *predominantly*, though not entirely, windfalls ; and the passing of a law now for their taxation if and when they accrue would not strike present owners to any substantial extent. In order, however, to reduce the risk of this to a minimum, it might be well to provide for the exemption from duty of increments amounting to less than 10 per cent. This provision, combined with that suggested in the preceding section, would exempt from increment duty all increments arising in a fifteen-year period amounting to less than 10 per cent of the value x, plus, say, 120 per cent of the value y.

§ 11. The various safeguards, which this discussion shows to be required in an increment tax that is to strike windfall increments only, are probably too complicated for practical politics. The cause, however, is not yet lost. For it is still possible, at the expense, indeed, of letting some real windfalls go free, to avoid any serious risk of taxing increments that are not windfalls by the simple device of exempting all increments other than those which are very large. In normal circumstances, apart from war and its aftermath, we may reasonably expect that no enormous variations in general prices or in the general rate of interest will occur in the course of fifteen years. If, therefore, we decree that increment duty shall only be levied on land which in fifteen years has trebled in value, or, if our period be of some other length, has improved in a proportionate degree, it is very unlikely that anything other than true windfall increments will be enmeshed by our scheme. Nearly the whole amount by which, at the end of fifteen years, the unimproved value of any man's holding of land — it seems necessary to take the total holding as our unit — exceeds treble its original unimproved value might safely be taken by the State. If the unimproved values of land are periodically estimated for some other purpose, with a view, for example, to a direct tax on the body of these values, it should not prove a very difficult or expensive matter to collect a tax of this kind also. But the various complications, to which attention has been called, make it plain that such a tax is never likely to yield a large revenue from windfalls that accrue in landed property. The task of constructing a tax to catch analogous windfalls in other kinds of property, with the single exception of treasure trove, is so difficult that no attempt has yet been made to cope with it.[1]

[1] There is no resemblance between the arrangements discussed above and the German "property increment" tax introduced in 1913, which hit increments of property, *whether inherited or saved*, while exempting the general corpus of possessed property. (Cf Cohn, *Economic Journal*, 1913, pp. 543 *et sqq.*)

CHAPTER XVII

INTERNATIONAL REACTIONS OF DOMESTIC TAXES

§ 1. Up to this point I have taken no account of international relations, but have argued as though we had to do with a single isolated and self-contained community. When this assumption is removed, several new and large problems arise. The first of these concerns modifications in the effects of taxes, as considered in the preceding chapters, that may result from there being an outside area to which these taxes do not apply. For, when such an area exists, it may be feasible for a man subjected to taxation in the taxed area to make use of the untaxed area in such a way as to reduce the fiscal burden imposed upon him. *Prima facie* two sorts of reaction are liable to be set up. First, capital, which would otherwise have been invested in the territory of the taxing authority, may be driven abroad. Secondly, persons, who would otherwise have worked and lived within that territory, may be driven abroad. Plainly, in so far as either of these things happens, the revenue yielded by taxes is made smaller than it would otherwise have been, and also, the sum of net (post-tax) income having been diminished, economic welfare in the community is likewise diminished. More generally, the process of raising a given revenue inflicts further damage in excess of that considered hitherto. New and so far unexamined dangers are threatened. It is clearly important to gauge, so far as we can, the scope and range of these in the particular case of our own country.

§ 2. Much stress is laid in popular discussion upon the risk that high British taxation, particularly high income tax, may " drive capital abroad ". Clearly, a resident abroad can avoid British income tax on the proceeds of investments here by not making investments here; and, therefore, in the absence of international agreements to obviate double taxation, high British taxation on investment income must, *pro tanto*, impede the influx of foreign capital. Since, however, this country is, on the whole, not a capital-importing country, but a capital-exporting country, this fact is of small practical importance. The reaction that matters is not the reaction on foreign-owned, but on British-owned, capital. Here popular fears in great part arise out of a mistaken belief that a British citizen can escape British income tax on his investment income by merely investing abroad instead of at home. This is not so. A person technically resident in England is liable to British income tax in respect of the whole of his income, wherever it arises ; even, under the Act of 1914, of that part of his foreign income which is not brought home but is re-invested abroad. The result is that, if, while continuing to reside in England, he makes investments abroad, he will not only not escape British income tax, but will find himself subject both to that income tax and also to the income tax, if any, of the country in which he makes his investment. Under a later Act income derived by British residents from investments in the British Dominions is subjected to British income tax at only half the current rate ; the purpose being to mitigate the discouraging effect of double taxation upon inter-Imperial investment. But even here there is no question of a British resident being allowed, while continuing a British resident, to reduce the aggregate amount of his tax burden by making investments outside the country. No doubt, a man who wishes to break the law and avoid taxation by perjury may be able to do this more easily when his income originates outside than when it originates inside the national borders. Apart from fraud, however, a British citizen can gain nothing by investing abroad rather than at home, so long as he himself remains a resident here. High taxation has no tendency to drive British capital abroad *otherwise than in company with its owners*.

§ 3. The position is substantially the same as regards driving British work, mental or manual, abroad. A person who is resident in England — in the sense that he lives in England for not less than six months of the year, or maintains a house in England — is liable to British income tax on the proceeds of his work, wherever this is performed. Hence, if he wishes to avoid the tax, he must not merely transfer his work but also abandon British residence. Hence, for capital and work alike, the crucial question is whether and how far high taxation here is likely to induce people to abandon British residence.

§ 4. There is a strong surface tension holding people to their native land, which it needs a strong force to overcome. For poor persons taxation is, in general, a small item in their total economic situation and is not likely to play any significant part in determining their action in this matter. For rich persons, on the other hand, for whom taxation *may* loom large, the advantages to be obtained from a big income consist, in considerable measure, of social amenities which would be sacrificed if British residence were abandoned. Moreover, in the present state of the world, such persons will not easily find countries, suitable to their way of life, residence in which will not also render them subject to large taxation ; so that what they gain by leaving England they will, in large part, lose again by entering their new home. On the whole, therefore, we may conclude that, in the present state of the world, no very serious reactions in driving either British capital or British work abroad need be looked for as a result of our high taxation.

CHAPTER XVIII

TAXING THE FOREIGNER BY PERSONAL TAXES

§ 1. The next problem to which the separation of the world into different national groups gives rise is concerned with action by the government of one group designed to exact a contribution to its revenue from the subjects of other governments. Exactions of this sort are *prima facie* practicable either through the machinery of personal taxes, through lump-sum levies on governments in the form of reparations or through import or export duties. What has to be said under the last two heads is reserved for the chapters that follow. In the present chapter I shall briefly consider contributions secured through personal taxes.

§ 2. At the outset we encounter a difficulty of definition: what precisely constitutes a "national group"? For the present purpose it cannot be defined simply as all persons owing political allegiance to one sovereign; for, apart from the fact that in certain rare circumstances the same man may be claimed as a national by more than one government, it is plain that a British subject, for example, living permanently in Rumania and deriving all his income from there belongs, for economic purposes, to the Rumanian and not to the British group. Reflection along these lines suggests that a national group is best defined as all persons resident in the territory covered by its government. This, however, is only a first step; for, since people often move about from place to place, residence is an ambiguous term. Mr. Smith has one house in England, another in Germany, spends one month each year in each of them and, during the other ten months, is annually occupied in travelling round the world: where does Mr. Smith reside? Knots of this kind cannot be unravelled: they must be cut by adopting some more or less arbitrary convention. Since, however, the vast majority of persons live habitually in the same country with only occasional visits abroad, the precise significance given to the term residence — for individuals [1] — is not, for our purpose, im-

[1] For a discussion of the complicated problems connected with the residence of companies, cf. *Royal Commission on the Income Tax, Report*, section 14.

portant. People who habitually reside outside this country are non-residents, and non-residents are, for that purpose, foreigners.

§ 3. It is in the power of a government to collect revenue by personal taxes from persons not subject to it, if these persons either come themselves within its territory during any part of the year or draw from its territory any part of their income. Thus, personal taxes may be laid on tourists and on foreigners who come into a country temporarily to earn income therein — musicians and actors, for example — ; and the proceeds of investments made by foreigners may be taxed before they are remitted abroad. The amount of revenue which a government can hope to secure from foreigners by these means is, of course, limited. If the rates of tax are raised beyond a certain point, foreigners will be so far discouraged from visiting the country and making new investments in it that less may well be obtained than would have been obtained from lower rates. Still, the government of a country in which foreigners have in the past made and now hold large investments has the power, if it chooses to exercise it, to exact large sums from them in respect of their existing holdings ; and, by providing that holdings now in the hands of foreigners shall continue to be taxed even if they are transferred to nationals, it can prevent them from escaping the burden by selling their property. In actual practice most governments tax both income accruing to their residents wherever it originates and also income originating in their territory and accruing to foreigners : and they behave in an analogous manner in respect of property passing at death. Thus they often contrive to make a substantial levy upon foreigners.

§ 4. Now it is plainly no net advantage to the inhabitants of State A to collect £50 million towards its revenue from the inhabitants of States B, C, and D, if at the same time the inhabitants of those States collect £50 million towards their revenue from the inhabitants of A. What is won with one hand is lost with the other ; and the " representative State " would be equally well-off if all States confined their levies to residents within themselves. Nor is this all. When A taxes B's residents in respect of income arising, or property situated, in A, these persons must, unless B refrains from taxing them, be subject, in respect of the income or property, to "double taxation". This means that a resident in one country, who contemplates rendering service or making investments in another, is prevented from doing so unless the profits to be won are, not merely higher than those obtainable at home, but higher in a sufficient degree to compensate for the double taxation. A barrier is thus set up against the free movement of work and capital between countries. In so far as aggregate government expenses are really higher in respect of a man who resides in one country and earns or invests in another than in respect of one all of whose activities are confined to the same country, such a barrier corresponds to a true cost, and is *prima facie* desirable from the standpoint of world welfare. But any excess of aggregate government expense that may result from the splitting of residence and work or property is likely to be very small as compared with the additional taxation currently imposed on people who achieve this splitting. The barriers which are in fact set up by double taxation are, therefore, *not* desirable from the standpoint of world welfare, but are, on the contrary, calculated to reduce aggregate productivity and aggregate well-being. Hence, if all States were in an equally strong position for levying taxes on foreigners, it would be to the advantage of them all, both collectively and individually, to enter into an agreement not to make these levies. Since in real life some States are in a stronger position for mulcting foreigners than others, a mutual self-denying ordinance, though still in the interest of all States collectively, would not be in the interest of all of them individually, unless some arrangement were made to compensate those to whom the agreement would be detrimental at the cost of those to whom it would bring exceptional advantages. To find a practicable solution for problems of this class is the proper work of international diplomacy. The subject was studied by experts under the auspices of the League of Nations and a plan was devised.[1]

§ 5. Until comparatively recently "origin" was predominantly regarded as the primary title to taxation, so that, if, in order to obviate a double charge, either the right to tax residents in respect of income arising abroad or the right to

[1] Cf. League of Nations *Report on Double Taxation*, by Professors Bruins, Einaudi, Seligman and Sir Josiah Stamp, 1923.

tax foreigners in respect of income originating in the taxing country had to be surrendered, there would have been a wide consensus in favour of the former policy. Later studies, however, have reversed this view. Stress is laid on the fact that countries, whose citizens or governments wish to borrow money from foreigners, have the chief interest in removing the barrier of double taxation: and it has been observed that Great Britain, France and Brazil, during the course of the 1914–18 war, all raised loans in foreign countries, interest on which was guaranteed free of tax, thus giving up, in respect of that interest, the right to tax income originating inside themselves. The League of Nations experts recommended that, as between countries neither of which is predominantly debtor or creditor to the other, each should agree to exempt from taxation income originating in itself but accruing to citizens of the other, and to tax only income accruing to its own residents, no matter where that income has its origin. As between one country which is predominantly a debtor and another which is predominantly a creditor this arrangement would not, however, work out equally. The debtor country would be required to surrender much more revenue than the creditor country; for there would be much more income originating in its borders and accruing elsewhere. The League of Nations experts, therefore, suggested that in these cases conventions should, as before, be made for the mutual exemption of income passing out to non-residents, but that, in order to prevent this bargain from affecting the contracting States unequally, appropriate compensation should be paid to the governments of those which would lose by it by the governments of those which would gain.

§ 6. The purpose of this plan was simply to remove the anti-social barrier set up by double taxation, while leaving unmodified the relation between the levies made by government A on the nationals of B, and by government B on the nationals of A. Persons interested in political ethics will, however, wish to delve deeper than this. In so far as a government only subjects foreigners, in respect of income originating in its territory or of property situated there, to rates of taxation equal to those imposed on its own nationals, it may seem at first sight that the charges made can be justified as payments for, corresponding to costs of, services rendered. Reflection, however, shows that this plea is unsound. For an Englishman resident in England and drawing a £1000 income from England is protected by the British Government in respect of his person as well as of his property; whereas a non-resident foreigner drawing a £1000 income from England is protected in respect of his property only, and ought, therefore, on this line of argument, to pay less.[1] *A fortiori* discriminating taxes against foreign visitors and investors could not be thus justified. Hence we may conclude in a general way that, if a government taxes foreigners through non-discriminating income tax and death duties, still more if it taxes them through levies that discriminate against them, it makes, as regards some part of these levies, a simple predatory exaction from them. Now, it is commonly believed that the vegetable, and, within limits, the animal kingdom, are, so to speak, kingdoms for man; so that it is proper to treat them merely as means, and not at all as ends in themselves. To some ardent nationalists foreigners are in a very similar position; their interests as such demand no consideration from us; so far as they can be exploited without risk of danger to ourselves, they ought to be exploited. To a person holding that view our problem presents no difficulty. But persons who are educated do not hold that view. To them it seems plain that one government is not entitled to make a predatory exaction on the citizens of another country, any more than one individual is entitled to take money from another individual, unless some good reason can be given for doing this. There is only one sort of good reason available. If a foreign government can be shown to be collecting a contribution to its revenue from members of our community of, say, £10 million more than is "justified" by any services which it renders to them, this gives warrant for our government, if it can, collecting a like unearned £10 million from the subjects of that foreign government. No doubt, it will rarely be practicable to give an equivalent relief out of this money to those particular members of our community whom the foreign government has mulcted, and, therefore, the case for this retorted taxation is

[1] To retort that the resident pays for the protection of his person through commodity taxes, which the non-resident escapes, is obviously inadequate in the case of rich men; and this, from the present point of view, is the only important case.

weaker than it might have been. Nevertheless, there is a case; for it is not unreasonable to regard the British community *vis-à-vis*, say, Frenchmen, as, in a sense, a unitary body, and to seek to offset by levies on Frenchmen any levies that the French government may make upon it. Apart from this kind of compensatory retaliation, attempts to mulct the foreigner are not ethically defensible.

CHAPTER XIX

REPARATION LEVIES AND THE RATIO OF INTERCHANGE OR TERMS OF TRADE

§ 1. In this chapter I propose to investigate, not the whole effect of reparation levies on foreigners, but only their effect on the ratio of interchange between the reparations-receiving country's and the reparations-paying country's goods, usually called the terms of trade between them. We suppose the reparations levies to consist of *annual* payments of constant amount and also that wage rates and everything else have been adjusted to the fact of reparations in both reparations-paying and reparations-receiving countries, so that there is no reparations-induced unemployment in either of them. We disregard any complications which may arise through reparations being paid to one country alone among several others, and contemplate a reparations-paying country confronting a unified rest of the world.

§ 2. For this study, as also for the parallel study of general taxes on imports or exports, to be undertaken in the next chapter, we need to think away the complicating fact that international trade comprises many different kinds of articles. This is in line with traditional practice. Thus Mill, in his analysis of foreign trade, started from the simplifying hypothesis that all England's exports may be represented by so many yards of cloth and all her imports by so many yards of linen. Marshall proceeded along the same lines, writing, in the first exposition of this theory, as follows : " It is assumed that the pure theory of domestic values has provided the means of measuring the value in England of all the various wares exported by England in terms of any one of them. Suppose cloth of a definite quality to be one of them ; then the value in England of all the wares which England exports may be expressed as that of a certain number of yards of cloth. So the value in Germany [representing the rest of the world] of all the wares which Germany exports may be expressed as that of, say, a certain number of yards of linen." [1] In his final statement

[1] *The Pure Theory of Foreign Trade* [privately printed], p. 1.

he modifies these assumptions somewhat, writing: "Mill took a yard of cloth as representative of the products of one country and a yard of linen as representative of the products of the other. But it seems better to suppose either country to make up her exports into representative 'bales', that is, bales each of which represents uniform aggregate investments of her labour (of various qualities) and of her capital."[1] It is important to realise that this second assumption, though Marshall's phraseology does not reveal the fact, differs from the first in a fundamental manner. When several commodities enter into international trade, the first assumption necessarily conflicts with the facts unless conditions of constant return prevail everywhere; for any modification of international trade conditions, such as will result from the imposition of reparation levies or of general import or export duties, is bound to alter the relative values of the different commodities produced inside each country. The second assumption escapes this logical difficulty, but only at the expense of allowing a thing called a bale to have different real contents before and after taxation. If, however, constant returns prevail everywhere, both assumptions fit the facts and become equivalent to one another. An English yard of cloth is the same as an English bale, each being the fruit of a unit of English labour — I use labour as a short term to cover a composite "dose" of labour, capital and land — in all conditions: and a foreign yard oı cloth is the same as a foreign bale, each being the fruit of a unit of foreign labour in all conditions.

§ 3. In studying the effects, whether of reparations or of general uniform taxes on foreign trade, along these lines, we assume that approximately the same amount of productive effort is forthcoming everywhere as would be forthcoming in the absence of these things. This dispenses us from having to bring into account complications associated with diminishing or increasing returns, which, in the treatment of import or export taxes on particular commodities, necessarily play an important part. The assumption is not always in exact accordance with the facts. Heavy reparation levies, for example, might compel a country subjected to them to increase the length of its average working day. In my judgement, however, the assumption is legitimate, in the sense that it is, in general,

[1] *Money, Credit and Commerce*, p. 157.

near enough to the truth for results based upon it to be substantially correct. I shall employ Mill's cloth-linen terminology throughout.

§ 4. Reparation levies might be assessed in terms either of goods produced by the reparations-paying or of goods produced by the reparations-receiving country. If we suppose either country's general price level to be held approximately constant, to assess them in terms of goods produced by it is equivalent to assessing them in terms of its money. It is important to distinguish between the two sorts of assessment. For with assessment in terms of the reparations-paying country's goods or money the only limit to the scale of theoretically possible levy — what is practically possible is, of course, substantially less — is given by the margin between the country's productive power and its "necessary" consumption. But, with assessment in terms of the reparations-receiving country's goods or money, the scale of levy cannot be larger than the quantity of that country's goods or money that the reparations-paying country is able to buy from it with exports of its own goods; and if at a certain scale of levy the reparations-receiving country's demand for the other country's goods has an elasticity less than unity, it will be impossible for anything beyond that scale to be attained. The harder the reparations-paying country tries to meet its obligations by sending out its own goods, the less reparation goods or money it will succeed in acquiring.

§ 5. Provided, however, that the scale of the reparation levy is such that it is possible for the reparations-paying country to meet it, it is immaterial whether it is assessed in the form of R units of the reparations-receiving country's goods or money or of that number of units, say K, of the reparation-payer's goods or money which, in the circumstances, are required to purchase those R units. It is, therefore, immaterial which of the two types of assessment we suppose to be adopted. In what follows I shall work with the former of them. For this choice there is sufficient reason in the fact that the reparation levies imposed upon Germany after the 1914–18 war were intended to be assessed in that way. The likelihood of the value of gold, in which they were expressed, varying in value relatively to the reparations-receiving country's goods, was not taken into account by the politicians until the Dawes Report was published. Thus I shall regard the reparation receivers as producers of cloth and the reparation payers as producers of linen, and I shall take the annual reparation levy to consist in R units of cloth — an amount which is assumed to fall within the limits of what is feasible.

§ 6. If apart from the reparation levy the reparations-paying country had no foreign dealings, the reparations-receiving country would obtain annually for nothing the amount of linen needed to purchase there the R units of cloth that had to be handed over to its government; and nothing else would happen. But, if, apart from reparations, some linen was being traded privately against cloth, the imposition of a reparation levy would, in general, cause the quantity of linen imports on private account and the rates of interchange between linen and cloth, that is to say the terms of trade, to be different from what they were before. I propose in this chapter to examine the way in which the imposition of an annual reparation levy affects this ratio of interchange.

§ 7. It is important to be clear what this phrase is here used to mean. It means the quantity of cloth — produce of the reparation receivers — which purchases a unit of linen — produce of the reparation payers — *in the market.* This, if there are no reparations, is equal to the total quantity of cloth exported by the reparations-receiving country, say X, divided by the total quantity of linen imported by it, say Y. But, when there are reparations, and in consequence X is changed to $(X+\Delta X)$ and Y to $(Y+\Delta Y)$, it is not equal to $\frac{X+\Delta X}{Y+\Delta Y}$. It is equal to the total quantity of cloth exported by the reparations-receiving country *plus* the quantity bought with the reparations-paying country's exports, in discharge of reparations, divided by the reparations-paying country's exports of linen: namely, $\frac{X+\Delta X+R}{Y+\Delta Y}$.[1] What is the relation between $\frac{X+\Delta X+R}{Y+\Delta Y}$ and $\frac{X}{Y}$; more specifically, in what circumstances is

[1] Had we been reckoning reparations as K units of linen (not R units of cloth) the ratio of interchange would in like manner have had to be written $\frac{X+\Delta X}{Y+\Delta Y-K}$.

the former of these quantities larger and in what smaller than the latter ?

§ 8. I postulate that productive technique, tastes and so on are the same both at home and abroad after the reparation arrangement has been entered into as they were before. Further, abstraction is made of differences in taste and situation among individual Americans — for simplicity of language I use America and Germany throughout to signify the rest of the world and the reparations-paying country respectively — and among individual Germans, so that each of the two countries is depicted as consisting exclusively of representative citizens, all of them exactly alike and behaving in the same way. Finally, I assume that for each representative American the utility that he derives from a given quantity of American goods is independent of the quantity of German goods that he has, and *vice versa* ; and similarly for each representative German. These highly abstract assumptions, together with the assumption of constant returns and the cloth-linen simplification already referred to, obviate many complications. They do not, however, prevent the analysis that follows from being broadly applicable to real conditions, *provided we suppose the reparation tribute to have been established long enough to allow the industrial structures of the reparations-paying and the reparations-receiving countries to have become adjusted to it.*

§ 9. If there were the same number of Americans as of Germans, a representative American would deal in the same fraction of his country's imports and exports as a representative German would do. But, since the numbers are not the same, this is not so. If x measures total American exports and y total German exports, we must write for the representative American's exports and imports nx and ny, and for the representative German's mx and my.

Write then in respect of the pre-reparation period —

$\phi(nY)$ for the marginal utility to the representative American of (nY) German goods (linen) ;

$f(nX)$ for the marginal disutility to him of surrendering (nX) American goods (cloth) ;

$F(mX)$ for the marginal utility to the representative German of (mX) American goods (cloth) ;

$\psi(m\mathrm{Y})$ for the marginal disutility to him of surrendering (mY) German goods (linen).

"Marginal utility of" in the above expressions has the same meaning as "marginal desire for"; and "marginal disutility of surrendering" as "marginal aversion from surrendering". We know that the ratio of interchange between American and German goods is $\frac{\mathrm{X}}{\mathrm{Y}}$. We also know that in equilibrium the ratio of interchange between any two exchanged goods must be equal, for each exchanger, to the inverse ratio of their respective marginal utilities: and we can construct equations of the type employed by Jevons in the fourth chapter of his *Theory of Political Economy*. Thus

$$\frac{\phi(n\mathrm{Y})}{f(n\mathrm{X})}=\frac{\mathrm{X}}{\mathrm{Y}}=\frac{\psi(m\mathrm{Y})}{\mathrm{F}(m\mathrm{X})}. \quad \text{(I)}$$

By precisely analogous reasoning in respect of the post-reparation period we have

$$\frac{\phi\{n(\mathrm{Y}+\Delta\mathrm{Y})\}}{f\{n(\mathrm{X}+\Delta\mathrm{X})\}}=\frac{\mathrm{X}+\Delta\mathrm{X}+\mathrm{R}}{\mathrm{Y}+\Delta\mathrm{Y}}=\frac{\psi\{m(\mathrm{Y}+\Delta\mathrm{Y})\}}{\mathrm{F}\{m(\mathrm{X}+\Delta\mathrm{X})\}}. \quad \text{(II)}$$

In order that the new ratio of interchange may be equal to the old, it is, therefore, necessary that

$$\frac{\phi(n\mathrm{Y})}{f(n\mathrm{X})}=\frac{\psi(m\mathrm{Y})}{\mathrm{F}(m\mathrm{X})}=\frac{\phi\{n(\mathrm{Y}+\Delta\mathrm{Y})\}}{f\{n(\mathrm{X}+\Delta\mathrm{X})\}}=\frac{\psi\{m(\mathrm{Y}+\Delta\mathrm{Y})\}}{\mathrm{F}\{m(\mathrm{X}+\Delta\mathrm{X})\}}. \quad \text{(III)}$$

§ 10. The implications of these equations, regarded as general equations, are, of course, highly complex. It is legitimate, however, for an approximate result, to postulate that the functions involved are linear. The implications then are very simple, namely, that $\frac{\phi'}{f'}=\frac{\psi'}{\mathrm{F}'}$. By an extension of the argument it can be shown that $\frac{\mathrm{X}+\Delta\mathrm{X}+\mathrm{R}}{\mathrm{Y}+\Delta\mathrm{Y}}$ is less or greater than $\frac{\mathrm{X}}{\mathrm{Y}}$, that is, that in consequence of reparations, the real ratio of interchange is turned against or in favour of Germany, according as $\frac{\phi'}{f'}$ is $<$ or $>$ $\frac{\psi'}{\mathrm{F}'}$. It must be remembered that, since ϕ' and F' are obviously negative and ψ' and f' positive, both these quantities are negative. Hence, if we disregard sign, the above conditions are reversed. In order that the real ratio of interchange may be turned against Germany, $\frac{\phi'}{f'}$ must be numerically greater than $\frac{\psi'}{F'}$: in order that the real ratio may be turned in her favour, it must be numeri cally less. If the functions are not linear, but do not diverge seriously from linearity, the real ratio will be turned against Germany if both $\frac{\phi'(nY)}{f'(nX)}$ is numerically greater than $\frac{\psi'(mY)}{F'(mX)}$ and $\frac{\phi' n(Y+\Delta Y)}{f' n(X+\Delta X)}$ than $\frac{\psi' m(Y+\Delta Y)}{F' m(X+\Delta X)}$; and in her favour in the converse case. If one of the two quantities set out first above is greater than the corresponding quantity set out second and the other less, no solution in terms of first differentials only can be obtained.

§ 11. Let us now concentrate on the simple case of linear functions, and, for these functions, express our results in terms of elasticities of various sorts relevant to the quantities of goods that are traded in the absence of reparations. Write E_l, E_c for the elasticities of the American marginal utility function in respect of the pre-reparation quantity of German goods and of the marginal disutility function in respect of sacrificing the pre-reparation quantity of American goods ; and G_c, G_l for the elasticities of the corresponding German marginal utility and disutility functions. Then we have

$$E_l = \frac{\phi(nY)}{nY\phi'},$$

$$E_c = \frac{f(nX)}{nXf'},$$

$$G_c = \frac{F(mX)}{mXF'},$$

$$G_l = \frac{\psi(mY)}{mY\psi'}.$$

Hence
$$\frac{\phi'}{f'} = \frac{E_c}{E_l} \cdot \frac{X}{Y} \cdot \frac{\phi(nY)}{f(nX)} = \frac{E_c}{E_l} \cdot \frac{X^2}{Y^2},$$

and in like manner

$$\frac{\psi'}{F'} = \frac{G_c}{G_l} \cdot \frac{X}{Y} \cdot \frac{\psi(mY)}{F(nX)} = \frac{G_c}{G_l} \cdot \frac{X^2}{Y^2}.$$

Hence the condition for the price of linen in terms of cloth being reduced, *i.e.* for the real ration of interchange being turned against Germany, on account of her being compelled to pay reparations, is that $\frac{E_c}{E_l}$ is numerically greater than $\frac{G_c}{G_l}$: in other words, that $E_cG_l > E_lG_c$. That is to say, the condition for the real ratio of interchange being turned against Germany is that the product of the elasticities of the representative American's and the representative German's marginal aversions from surrendering domestic goods is greater than the product of the elasticities of their marginal desires for foreign goods. Thus the ratio of interchange is more likely to be turned against the reparations-paying country, (1) the more elastic is the marginal aversion to surrendering its own goods *either* in the reparations-paying *or* in the reparations-receiving country, and (2) the less elastic is the marginal desire for foreign goods in *either* the reparations-paying *or* the reparations-receiving country.

§ 12. A very important implication from our formula is that, if both E_c and G_c or both E_l and G_l are infinite, that is to say, if the marginal utility *either* of cloth *or* of linen is constant to *both* America and Germany, the imposition of a reparation levy leaves the ratio of interchange between them unaffected. This is in line with the well-known domestic trade proposition that, if a lump-sum tax in money is imposed on the sellers of any commodity and transferred to the buyers, provided that the marginal utility of money is unaffected (constant) to both sellers and buyers, the price of the commodity will not be changed.

§ 13. The following further implications from our formula in four limiting cases can be demonstrated in ordinary language as follows :

First, if the elasticity of the representative American's marginal aversion from surrendering American goods, E_c, is infinite and none of the other elasticities are infinite, the ratio of interchange must be turned *against* Germany. For the marginal utility of American goods to Americans is not diminished at all when, on account of reparations, they have to surrender less American goods abroad in order to procure the original quantity of German goods. Therefore, if the original terms of interchange are maintained, they will continue to procure that original quantity, partly by reparations and partly by purchase. But in these circumstances Germans are obtaining less American goods while sacrificing the same amount of German goods. Therefore to Germans the marginal utility of American goods is increased while that of German goods is left unchanged. For equilibrium, therefore, the total sendings of German goods must be increased and the terms of interchange moved against them.

Secondly, our formula shows that, if the elasticity of the German marginal aversion from surrendering German goods, G_l, is infinite, and none of the other elasticities are infinite, the real ratio of interchange must be turned *against* Germany. For the marginal disutility to Germans of surrendering German goods is not increased at all when more of them are surrendered. Consequently, the fact of having to send out some German goods to buy reparation receipts does not cause Germans to require any better terms than before as an inducement to purchase for import to Germany the original quantity of American goods. Therefore, if the original terms of interchange are maintained, they will continue to import the original quantity of American goods while sending out the original quantity of German goods plus a further quantity for the purchase of reparation receipts. But in these circumstances Americans are obtaining more German goods while surrendering the same amount of American goods. Therefore to Americans the marginal utility of German goods is decreased while that of American goods is left unchanged. For equilibrium, therefore, the sendings of American goods must be diminished, and, consequently, Germans will be prepared to pay more per unit for them.

Thirdly, our formula shows that, if the elasticity of the marginal utility of German goods to Americans, E_l, is infinite and none of the other elasticities are infinite, the real ratio of interchange must be turned *in favour* of Germany. For the marginal utility of German goods to Americans is not diminished at all when, on account of reparations, more are received. Consequently, if the original terms of interchange are maintained, Americans will continue to export the original quantity of American goods. But in these circumstances Germans are obtaining the original quantity of American goods while surrendering more German goods. Therefore to

Germans the marginal utility of American goods is unchanged while the marginal utility of German goods is increased. For equilibrium, therefore, the total sendings of German goods must be cut down below what they would have been had there been no reparations. This can only be done if the terms of interchange are moved in Germany's favour.

Fourthly, our formula shows that if the elasticity of the marginal utility of American goods to Germans, G_c, is infinite and none of the other elasticities are infinite, the real ratio of interchange must be turned *in favour of* Germany. For the marginal utility of American goods to Germans is not increased at all when fewer of them are obtained. Consequently, if the original terms of interchange are maintained, Germans will continue to export the original quantity of German goods, bringing back such reduced quantity of American goods as can be purchased with the surplus of German goods above what are required to buy reparation receipts. But in these circumstances Americans are obtaining the original quantity of German goods while surrendering fewer American goods. Therefore to Americans the marginal utility of German goods is unchanged while the marginal utility of American goods is diminished. For equilibrium, therefore, the sendings of American goods must be increased above what they would have been in these circumstances. This can only be done if the terms of interchange are moved in Germany's favour.

§ 14. On the basis of the foregoing abstract analysis we have next to inquire what sort of situation we may normally look to be confronted with in actual life. A vital consideration is as follows. Whereas the marginal disutility to anybody of surrendering so much of anything is necessarily equal to the marginal utility to him of the quantity he retains, so that in respect of given quantities we may speak indifferently of the marginal desire for (or, more accurately, for using) the commodity and the marginal aversion from surrendering it, the *elasticities* of marginal utilities and disutilities are *not* equivalent. Thus suppose that a representative American is parting with nX units of cloth and retaining $n(A-X)$ units. Call the former of the two above elasticities E_c— as before— and the latter P_c. Let the utility derived from retaining the $n(A-X)^{th}$ unit, which is necessarily equal to the disutility incurred in surrendering the nX^{th} unit, be written U. Then

$$E_c = \frac{\Delta X}{X} \div \frac{\Delta U}{U},$$

$$P_c = \frac{\Delta X}{A - X} \div -\frac{\Delta U}{U}.$$

$$\therefore \quad E_c = -\frac{A - X}{X} \cdot P_c.$$

In like manner, Q_l being written for the representative German's elasticity of marginal desire for using linen, we have

$$G_l = -\frac{B - Y}{Y} \cdot Q_l.$$

Now in the absence of special knowledge it is proper to presume that the elasticities of a man's marginal desire for using respectively such quantity of home-produced goods and such quantity of imported goods as are available to him are equal. Hence we may presume P_c to be about equal to E_l and Q_l to G_c. This implies that

$$E_c = -\frac{A - X}{X} E_l \quad \text{and} \quad G_l = -\frac{B - Y}{Y} G_c.$$

$$\therefore \quad E_c G_l = E_l G_c \frac{A - X}{X} \cdot \frac{B - Y}{Y}.$$

For the rest of the world, which is economically much larger than any one country trading with it, the proportion of home output consumed at home to exports must evidently be much greater than the corresponding proportion for the one country. Thus, if we suppose Germany normally to export one-sixth of her output and the rest of the world to be seven times as large economically as Germany, while $\frac{B - Y}{Y}$ will be equal to about 5, $\frac{A - X}{X}$ will be equal to about 35. Thus, in the absence of special knowledge, it is to be expected that $E_c G_l$ will be much larger than $E_l G_c$. It is in a high degree probable that the ratio of interchange will be turned against the reparations-paying country. Contrary to what might perhaps be expected, it is immaterial to this conclusion whether the reparations-paying or the reparations-receiving country is the larger of the two.

§ 15. The probability just asserted owes its strength to the presumption that, in the absence of special knowledge, the elasticities of the desire of a representative man to use home-produced goods and imported goods in either country are about equal to one another. If we have special knowledge of a kind to suggest that the marginal desire for the particular goods which are imported is abnormally elastic in comparison with that for home-produced goods, either in the reparations-paying country or in the other, or *a fortiori* in both, the probability is weakened and may conceivably even be reversed.

§ 16. It is possible to go a step further and express approximately, in terms of our several elasticities, the *extent* to which the ratio of interchange will be turned in various circumstances against, or in favour of, Germany. The approximation is obtained by assuming that R, ΔX and ΔY are small relatively to X and Y, so that their squares and products may be ignored. It cannot safely be extended to reparations that exceed, say, one-tenth of the value of the pre-reparation exports of either the reparations-receiving or the reparations-paying country. Writing, as before, $\frac{X}{Y}$ for the pre-reparation rate of interchange between American cloth and German linen, *i.e.* for the quantity of cloth required to buy a unit of linen, and $\frac{X+\Delta X+R}{Y+\Delta Y}$ for the post-reparation ratio, putting $\Delta\frac{X}{Y}$ for the excess of the latter over the former and choosing units so that $X=Y$, we obtain $\Delta\frac{X}{Y}=\frac{\Delta X-\Delta Y+R}{X}$. By a laborious algebraic manipulation this is found to signify approximately

$$\Delta\frac{X}{Y}=\frac{R}{X}\left\{\frac{E_lG_c-E_cG_l}{E_lG_c(1+E_c+G_l)-E_cG_l(1+E_l+G_c)}\right\}.$$

Obviously for $\Delta\frac{X}{Y}$ to be negative means that the ratio of interchange is turned by reparations against Germany; for it to be positive, that this ratio is turned in her favour. Reflection shows that, constant returns being postulated,[1] E_c and G_l are by nature positive and E_l and G_c by nature negative. Hence, the denominator of the expression for $\Delta\frac{X}{Y}$ must be

[1] Cf. *ante*, p. 175.

positive, and the whole expression negative or positive, according as E_cG_l is > or < E_lG_c. This, of course, agrees with the result reached in § 11. The ratio of interchange is turned against, or in favour of, Germany according as E_cG_l > or < E_lG_c.

Note to Chapter XIX

At first sight it might be thought that the effects of the annual transfer of loans of constant annual amount from Germany to America must, apart from subsequent interest payments, be identical with that of reparation transfers. But this is not so. If the reason for the loans is that America has come to offer improved opportunities for investment, so that Germany is induced to send to it goods in purchase of securities, the situation is, indeed, parallel to that created by reparation payments ; the security scrip that is purchased corresponding precisely with reparation quittances. In this case the ratio of interchange *may be* turned in favour of Germany, though it is very much more likely to be turned against her. If, however, the reason for the loan is that America has come to have an enhanced desire for German goods, the real ratio of interchange is *necessarily* turned in favour of Germany. It is not turned so far in her favour as it would be if America were unable to offer securities alongside of American goods in part payment of its extra purchases. But it must be turned in her favour to some extent. On the same principle, if European countries, on account of bad harvests, have to buy more in America, the real ratio of interchange, *i.e.* the terms of trade, are necessarily turned in favour of America, even though America accepts as part payment of what is due to her some new investments in Europe.

CHAPTER XX

THE IMPLICATIONS OF REPARATION PAYMENTS FOR PRICES UNDER AN INTERNATIONAL GOLD STANDARD

§ 1. The purpose of this chapter is not constructive, but to clear up a difficulty about prices that came under discussion when the problem of German reparations was prominent in the public mind. We suppose that Germany and the rest of the world, as represented by America, are linked together by an international gold standard. The cost of transport being ignored, alike before and after reparation payments from Germany to America have been undertaken, the gold price of American goods is equal in the two countries, and so also is the gold price of German goods. If, in consequence of reparation payments, the real ratio of interchange is turned against Germany, the gold price of German goods falls relatively to the gold price of American goods : in the converse case the opposite of this happens. So much is plain. But what will befall the general price levels in the two countries cannot be fully determined until the meaning of the term general price level has been precisely defined.

§ 2. Let us first mean by it for each country the price level in that country of the goods produced there — the index number problem being evaded by the assumption that only one sort of goods is being so produced, or, if there are many sorts, that they are all always produced in the same proportions. It follows that, should the price level in America remain unchanged, the price level in Germany, when reparations have to be paid, will be lowered or raised in the same proportion as that in which the real ratio of interchange is turned against Germany or in her favour. Since, as we have seen, this real ratio is extremely unlikely to be turned in Germany's favour, it is extremely unlikely that the general price level there will rise ; but it is not *impossible* for this to happen.

§ 3. If the general price level in each country means the price of the collection of goods (composite commodity) consumed there before reparations began, or if it means the price of the collection consumed there when reparations are being paid, or if it means the price of any defined composite commodity intermediate between these two collections, the issue is more complex. Provided, however, that each country's imports are small in value relatively to its consumption of home produce, a measure of general price level in Germany calculated on any of these plans will move in nearly the same way as the measure postulated in the preceding section. It will probably, though not certainly, be effected by reparation payments in the same way. It is extremely improbable, but not impossible, that, the American measure remaining unchanged, the German measure, after the payments have been imposed, will rise.

§ 4. The implication that, the American price level remaining unchanged, it is theoretically conceivable for the German price level to rise, presents itself to some persons, when looked at from the money side, as a violent paradox, which *must* be false. It is *impossible*, they hold, for the reparation goods to get out of Germany into America unless the price level in Germany falls relatively to the American price level. A consideration of the money mechanism involved renders this, as they hold, obvious. As a corollary, the conclusion reached in the last chapter to the effect that in certain conceivable circumstances the imposition of a reparations obligation will turn the real ratio of interchange in favour of Germany must be wrong. It would thus seem that monetary and non-monetary analysis lead to inconsistent results. There is thus something to be explained.

§ 5. The explanation, I suggest, is that the monetary analysis, if such it can be called, set out in the last paragraph involves a misunderstanding of the way in which the monetary mechanism works, and is incorrect. To show this, let us postulate a state of things in which reparation payments leave the real ratio of interchange exactly what it was before : and in which, therefore, all the trade transactions that used to go on still go on, with the reparation payments superimposed on them. The price levels in both countries will then be unaltered. There is no difficulty about the monetary mechanism. Both countries produce the same quantity of goods for the same aggregate money cost of production as before. Therefore they have the same aggregate money incomes. But every year out of the money income of the reparations-paying country, Germany, there is transferred gratuitously to the reparations-receiving country, America, £50 million, say, in gold. This gold does not stay in America, but is immediately on receipt handed back to Germany in purchase of her reparation goods. There is nothing in the monetary mechanism to prevent this state of affairs from arising and continuing indefinitely. Nor is it any harder to envisage a monetary arrangement that would allow of the German price level actually rising. As before, the £50 million handed over annually to America in gold is handed back to Germany in purchase of reparation goods. But in this case equilibrium in respect of traded goods has been disturbed to the disadvantage of America. To restore equilibrium other gold moves from America to Germany *and stays there*. On the basis of this, aggregate money income and the price level in Germany are both raised above what they were before. I am not, of course, suggesting that this is likely to happen. On the contrary, I have argued explicitly in the last chapter that it is exceedingly unlikely to happen. I am merely concerned to show that a consideration of the monetary mechanism of an international gold standard yields nothing incompatible with the results of the non-monetary analysis.

CHAPTER XXI

THE NET CONTRIBUTION RECEIVED BY THE REPARATIONS-RECEIVING COUNTRY FROM THE REPARATIONS-PAYING COUNTRY

§ 1. As in Chapter XIX we suppose that full adjustment has been made in the reparation-receiving country to the fact of reparations, so that the level of employment there is not affected and there is no question of balancing the advantage of receiving goods gratis from abroad against the disadvantage of wage-earners at home being thereby thrown out of work.

§ 2. If, in consequence of a reparation levy, the rate of interchange is turned against the reparations-paying, and so in favour of the reparations-receiving country, it is evident that the foreign contribution received by the latter exceeds the amount of the reparations; for, the reparations receiver being, as before, thought of as producing cloth and the reparations payer linen, the contribution consists in an amount of linen of the value of the reparations as assessed in cloth, plus a cheapening, in terms of cloth, of such linen as the reparation receivers continue to buy in excess of what they get as reparations. But, since in effect what happens is that the reparation receivers get more linen in consequence of reparations and have to pay away less cloth, two items are involved in the foreign contribution; and the relative values of these two items are different in post-reparation from what they were in pre-reparation days. Consequently, for anyone seeking to add together the part of the contribution which consists in increased linen imports and the part which consists in decreased cloth exports, there is not a single clear-cut price of linen in terms of cloth, by means of which he can combine the two parts, so as to express the whole in terms of so much cloth. Thus any definition of the foreign contribution, with a view to measuring its amount, must involve some degree of ambiguity. Fortunately, however, on the assumption—an assumption on which the validity of the formula given on page 185 depends — that R, and therewith also ΔX and ΔY, are small relatively to X and Y, the ambiguity is negligible. The value in terms of cloth of the contribution ΔY linen minus ΔX cloth $= (\Delta Y - \Delta X)$ cloth. But from the page just cited we know that, units being so chosen as to make $X = Y$, $\Delta\frac{X}{Y} = \frac{\Delta X - \Delta Y + R}{X}$. Therefore the contribution

$$C = (\Delta Y - \Delta X) = R\left(1 - \frac{X}{R} \cdot \Delta\frac{X}{Y}\right);$$

that is to say, the amount of the reparation levy plus the proportionate shift in the ratio of interchange in favour of the reparation receivers multiplied by the pre-reparation quantity of that country's exports. In the formulation of Chapter XIX this can be expressed as

$$C = R\frac{E_l G_c(E_c + G_l) - E_c G_l(E_l + G_c)}{E_l G_c(1 + E_c + G_l) - E_c G_l(1 + E_l + G_c)}.$$

§ 3. Since, as we have seen, E_c and G_l are by nature positive, and E_l and G_c by nature negative, C cannot be negative or nil. Thus the reparation receivers *must* obtain *some* net contribution from the reparation payer. Seeing that the ratio of interchange is in general turned in favour of the reparations-receiving country, C must in general be not merely positive, but greater than R. It is easy to see that in conditions where the marginal utility either of cloth or of linen is constant in both countries (*i.e.* where either both E_c and G_c or both E_l and G_l are infinite), no matter what the values of the other elasticities may be, $C = R$. Further, since our expression is completely symmetrical, it is clear that, contrary to what might be expected at first sight, the amount of the contribution yielded to the reparations receiver by a reparation levy on a given scale will be the same whether the reparations receiver is the rest of the world, America, or the single small country, Germany.

§ 4. The analysis can be carried a little further in more particular conditions thus. On the assumption set out in Chapter XIX, § 14, our formula reduces to

$$C = R \cdot \frac{-210E_l - 180G_c}{-210E_l - 180G_c - 174}.$$

In this case it is obvious at sight, not only that C must be $> R$, but also that it is larger the larger is either $-E_l$ or $-G_c$, that is to say, the more elastic is the marginal desire of either the reparations receiver or the reparations payer for imports. If we make the further assumption that $E_l = G_c$, *i.e.* that the elasticities of America's and Germany's desires for imports are equal, $C = R\frac{-390E_l}{-390E_l - 174}$. Should it be the case that either country's marginal desire for imports, instead of being equally elastic with its marginal desire for home produce, is more elastic than that, it is easy to see, on the lines of Chapter XIX, § 15, that C is made *pro tanto* smaller ; in converse conditions larger.

CHAPTER XXII

GENERAL UNIFORM *AD VALOREM* TAXES UPON IMPORTS OR EXPORTS

§ 1. For the purposes of this chapter we disregard the fact that international dealings embrace the granting and receipt of current loans and the payment of interest on past loans. We picture to ourselves one country confronting the rest of the world and simply trading its exports, represented by cloth, against imports, represented by linen. As in Chapter XIX, we postulate that the aggregate amount of productive effort engaged alike in the one country and in the rest of the world is unaffected by the imposition of general uniform taxes, and that complications connected with increasing and decreasing returns, which are important as regards duties confined to particular imports or exports, do not come into account.

§ 2. Provided, of course, that the government spends the proceeds in the same way in either case, it makes no difference on which side of the exchange transaction a general *ad valorem* tax is imposed. Marshall once put the matter thus: "For purposes of general analysis the all-round merchant is the only one that need be considered. It is true that the exporter prefers to sell bills drawn against his produce to an importer, each specialising his knowledge on one-half of the trade. But that is only because there is such keen competition between importers that, if one importer offers such bad terms for the bill as to keep an undue share of the profit for himself, the bill will be sold to some other importer. The difference to the export merchant doing all-round business of £200,000 arising from the change from a tax of £10,000 upon his export trade to a tax of £10,000 on his import trade, the date at which the tax is levied being the same, is nothing at all. In either case the tax would put out of the trade just those exports with which foreign markets are relatively saturated and just those imports with which English markets are relatively saturated."[1] When a country's imports consist in part of

[1] The citation is from a private note. The same point is made in other words in *Money, Credit and Commerce*, pp. 180-82.

goods received in payment of interest on past loans or of new investments by foreigners, or when its exports embrace similar elements, Marshall's simple statement requires some modification. If, indeed, we were to reckon receipts for interest payment and scrip issued in return for new investments as articles entering into trade, we could extend it to cover all international trade relations and assert generally that a given tax of so much per cent on the money value of the whole of a country's imports comes to the same thing as an equal percentage tax on the money value of the whole of its exports. But I shall not here make use of this extension.

§ 3. New loans and interest on old loans being then disregarded, taxes on imports in general and on exports in general are, in effect, taxes on resources devoted to "producing" imported goods by the indirect process of making exports to exchange against them. Thus, except in so far as they enable the taxing country to secure a contribution from foreigners, such taxes fall into the general class of taxes considered in Chapter IX. The part to be assigned to them among other taxes should be determined in accordance with the considerations set out in that chapter, and there is nothing further to be said about them. In so far, however, as a contribution from foreigners can be exacted, *from a purely national point of view* there is clearly a case for extending these taxes further than the analysis of Chapter IX suggests. It is, therefore, pertinent to ask — and that is the main purpose of this chapter — how far and in what circumstances a significant contribution from foreigners can in fact be obtained.

§ 4. We may begin by noting that, while for any country it is immaterial whether a 10 per cent money tax is levied on imports or exports, provided that the proceeds of the tax are in either event expended on cloth and linen in the same proportions, it is not immaterial what these proportions are. If the whole proceeds are expended on cloth the tax is, in effect, a tax in kind collected in cloth; in the contrary case a tax in kind collected in linen. These two sorts of tax do *not* come to the same thing. It follows that, in order to obtain an exact solution of the problem of tax incidence, as between cloth makers and linen makers, we must specify in what proportion the proceeds of the tax are to be expended on cloth and linen respectively. Until this is done the problem is not a determinate one. It is not, however, difficult to do this. The great bulk of every government's normal expenditure is, apart from foreign war debt, on services rendered by its own citizens. If, therefore, we put the cloth makers as the taxing country, it is reasonable to presume that the bulk of any foreign trade revenue that is collected will be expended on cloth. Following Marshall,[1] I shall confine attention to the problem as presented by a tax the proceeds of which are wholly so expended.

§ 5. Assuming the rate of tax to be small, the foreigner's contribution can be defined in the same way as in Chapter XXI. Writing ΔY for the increase of linen imports and ΔX for the increase in cloth exports — either of which may be negative — and choosing units such that $X = Y$, we express this contribution in terms of cloth as ΔY multiplied by the pre-tax price of linen in terms of cloth minus ΔX, that is by $(\Delta Y - \Delta X)$. Writing t for the rate of tax and Δp for the consequential rise in the price of linen in terms of cloth inclusive of tax, so that $(t - \Delta p)$ is the fall in price exclusive of tax (*i.e.* in bond),

we have $$t = \frac{R}{Y + \Delta Y} : \Delta p = \frac{\Delta X - \Delta Y + R}{Y + \Delta Y};$$

so that $$(t - \Delta p) = \frac{\Delta Y - \Delta X}{Y + \Delta Y}.$$

Hence $$\Delta Y - \Delta X = \frac{t - \Delta p}{t} R.$$

Our problem is to study the elements upon which the magnitude of this expression, when R is given, depends.

§ 6. In Chapter XIX, § 9, the fundamental equations determining the corresponding expression when a reparation levy is imposed by America upon Germany, the two together being conceived to embrace the whole world, was set out. Using the same notation and supposing an import tax at rate *t ad valorem* in cloth to be imposed by America on imports from Germany, we obtain in this case the following equations:

$$\frac{\phi(nY)}{f(nX)} = \frac{X}{Y} \quad \text{(I)};$$

$$\frac{\psi(mY)}{F(mX)} = \frac{X}{Y} \quad \text{(II)}.$$

[1] *Money, Credit and Commerce*, p. 181.

These are the same as before, but the two remaining equations are different. They are

$$\frac{\phi\{n(Y+\Delta Y)\}}{f\{n(X+\Delta X)\}}=\frac{(X+\Delta X)}{(Y+\Delta Y)} \quad \text{(III)};$$

$$\frac{\psi\{m(Y+\Delta Y)}{F\{m(X+\Delta X)}=\frac{X+\Delta X}{Y+\Delta Y}-t\frac{X}{Y}. \quad \text{(IV)}.$$

As before, we choose units such that $X=Y$: and we ignore squares and products of ΔX, ΔY and t (which is, of course, approximately equal to $\frac{R}{X}$).[1] On this basis, by an algebraic manipulation of the same type as that worked out in Chapter XIX, § 16, we find

$$\Delta p=\Delta\frac{X}{Y}=t\frac{G_cG_l(E_c-E_l)}{E_lG_c(1+E_c+G_l)-E_cG_l(1+E_l+G_c)}.$$

In view of the known signs of E_c, E_l, G_c and G_l, as found previously, this — apart from a freak case — is necessarily positive. That is, the ratio of interchange, when the price of linen is reckoned cum-tax, is turned *against* the taxing country; though, when the price is reckoned ex-tax, it is turned in its favour.

§ 7. Further, the net contribution, which we may call C′, made to America by Germany and represented by $\frac{t-\Delta p}{t}R$ works out at

$$C'=R\frac{E_lG_c(E_c+1)-E_cG_l(E_l+1)}{E_lG_c(1+E_c+G_l)-E_cG_l(1+E_l+G_c)}.$$

Apart from the freak cases, this is necessarily positive. That is to say, the taxing country necessarily exacts *some* net contribution from the other. On the assumptions set out in Chapter XIX, § 14, the above formula reduces to

$$C'=R\cdot\frac{-210E_l-174}{-210E_l-180G_c-174}.$$

Evidently then, since E_l and G_c are by nature negative, it must be $<R$. Further, whereas C, the contribution under a reparations levy of equal scale, is larger the larger (numerically) is

[1] It is also necessary to assume that ϕ' and f' are not extremely large, *i.e.* that the elasticities E_l and E_c are not very small. If they are, we are not entitled to ignore their products when they appear as multiplied by ϕ' or f'.

either E_l or G_c, C' is larger the larger is E_l or the smaller is G_c; that is to say, the more elastic is the marginal desire of the taxing country (America) for imports and the *less* elastic the corresponding marginal desire of the taxed country (Germany). It will be noticed that, as $-E_l$ approaches infinity, C' approaches R, while, as $-G_c$ approaches infinity, C' approaches nothing. If E_l and G_c are equal, our formula reduces further to

$$C' = R \cdot \frac{-210E_l - 174}{-390E_l - 174}.$$

§ 8. The above formulae are, of course, based on the fundamental assumption, stated in Chapter XIX, § 14, that P_c is equal to E_l and Q_l to G_c; namely, that in each of our two countries the elasticity of marginal desire for imports is equal to the corresponding elasticity in respect of home produce. If America's marginal desire for imports is more elastic than her marginal desire for home produce, which entails that $E_c < -35E_l$, this has the same effect on the value of C' as if $-E_l$ were larger; that is to say, it makes C' larger. In like manner, if Germany's desire for imports is *less* elastic than her marginal desire for home produce, this makes C' larger.

§ 9. These considerations are relevant to the question how far England is in a position to " tax the foreigner " by means of import duties. A century ago, as Marshall insisted, this country was practically the only place where foreigners could purchase manufactures made by steam machinery, not then in general use elsewhere, and tropical products, for obtaining which England had special facilities.[1] A large part of our exports consisted of these things, and the foreign desire for our sendings of them was naturally highly inelastic. Hence the foreign desire for English goods was abnormally inelastic; while no corresponding influences were at work to make the English desire for foreign sendings abnormally inelastic. At the present time, on the other hand, many countries besides ourselves produce steam-manufactured goods, so that, war conditions apart, foreigners are no longer compelled to come to us: whereas our own imports from abroad consist in the main of food and raw materials for our industries — classes of goods for which our marginal desire is probably a good deal less elastic than our marginal desire for home produce. These facts make it probable that England is

[1] *Money, Credit and Commerce*, p. 192.

now in a weak position for "taxing the foreigner"—in a much weaker one than she was a century ago.

§ 10. The analysis conducted in the foregoing paragraphs is different from that given in former editions of this book. There, following Marshall, I conceived of country A as wielding a demand function expressing various quantities of B goods demanded at various prices in terms of A goods; and of B as wielding a reciprocal demand function expressing various quantities of A goods demanded at various prices of A goods in terms of B goods, together with a supply function, with a definite mathematical relation to this, expressing the various quantities of B goods offered at various prices of B goods in terms of A goods. Writing η, γ and e for the elasticities of A's demand, B's reciprocal demand and B's supply in respect of the quantities traded in the absence of taxation, we found that, when A imposes import or export taxes yielding revenue R, the net contribution obtained from B is equal to $\frac{\eta}{\eta - e}$R, or, since e is easily shown to be equal to $-(\gamma+1)$,[1] to

[1] This matter may be developed as follows. The elasticity e is the quotient obtained by dividing a small proportionate change in the aggregate quantity of linen supplied by the associated proportionate change in the quantity of cloth offered per unit of linen. The elasticity of the foreign demand for cloth in terms of linen, γ, is not simply this fraction with the sign reversed. It is the quotient obtained by dividing a small proportionate change in the aggregate quantity of cloth demanded by the associated proportionate change in the quantity of linen offered per unit of cloth: which is quite a different thing. The difference, which is, of course, a consequence of the essential asymmetry in the concept of elasticity, can be made clear in symbols. Let b units of linen be offered against a units of cloth and let $(b+\Delta b)$ units of linen be offered against $(a+\Delta a)$ units of cloth. Then, the value of γ (negatively defined), when some specified quantity, say b units of linen, are being offered, is given by the equation:

$$\gamma\left[\left\{\frac{b+\Delta b}{a+\Delta a}-\frac{b}{a}\right\}\div\frac{b}{a}\right]=\frac{\Delta a}{a},$$

$$\therefore \quad \gamma=\frac{\Delta a}{a}\div\left\{\frac{a(b+\Delta b)}{b(a+\Delta a)}-1\right\}=\frac{b\Delta a\{a+\Delta a\}}{a\{a\Delta b-b\Delta a\}}$$

$$=(\text{approximately})\ \frac{b\Delta a}{a\Delta b-b\Delta a}.$$

Analogously, the elasticity of the supply of linen in terms of cloth (when b units of linen are being transferred), namely e, is given by the equation

$$e\left[\left\{\frac{a+\Delta a}{b+\Delta b}-\frac{a}{b}\right\}\div\frac{a}{b}\right]=\frac{\Delta b}{b},$$

$$\therefore \quad e=\frac{\Delta b}{b}\div\left\{\frac{b(a+\Delta a)}{a(b+\Delta b)}-1\right\}=\frac{a\Delta b\{b+\Delta b\}}{b\{b\Delta a-a\Delta b\}}$$

$$=(\text{approximately})\ -\frac{a\Delta b}{a\Delta b-b\Delta a}.$$

$\frac{\eta}{\eta+\gamma+1}$R. This was held to be exact if the demand and supply curves are straight lines, whether the tax is imposed at so much cloth on each unit of linen sold (*i.e.* a specific tax) or at so much per cent of the aggregate cloth value of the linen sold (*i.e.* an *ad valorem* tax). For taxes sufficiently small to make it probable that, over the relevant range, the curves of demand and supply, as conceived in Marshall's ordinary domestic trade analysis, do not diverge significantly from straight lines it was held to be an adequate approximation.

§ 11. If the marginal utility of cloth could properly be treated as constant for both America and Germany, if in fact we could treat it as we treat the marginal utility of money in problems about the effect of a tax on the output of a single commodity in domestic trade, the foregoing procedure would be fully warranted. In the formula for C′ developed in § 7, E_c and G_c would both be infinite, and the formula would reduce to $C' = R \cdot \frac{E_l}{E_l - G_l}$. Further, since in these conditions elasticity of demand in cloth for linen is obviously equivalent to elasticity of desire for linen and elasticity of supply of linen in cloth to elasticity of aversion from surrendering linen, E_l will be identical with η and G_c with e. Hence on this special assumption the value of C′ *is* $R\frac{\eta}{\eta - e}$, as the argument of § 10 suggests. But closer consideration shows that the marginal utility of cloth *cannot* properly be regarded as constant in this manner for the type of problem with which we are dealing here. This fact destroys the logical basis of the method

Thus, e is not equal to $-\gamma$, but is related to it by the equation $\gamma + e = -1$. The appended results follow immediately.

First, if the value of either γ or e lies between 0 and -1, the value of the other also must lie between these values, so that both are negative. If either has a value $-\frac{1}{2}$, the other also has this value, so that, in that case, $\gamma = e$.

Secondly, if either γ or $e = 0$, the other $= -1$. Thus, if the demand for cloth in terms of linen is represented by a rectangular hyperbola, the supply of linen in terms of cloth will be absolutely inelastic. A little reflection on the significance of the terms employed will show, without any mathematical technique, that this is necessarily so.

Thirdly, if γ is negative and greater than unity, e must be positive. If γ is only slightly greater than unity, say $1\frac{1}{10}$, it will be proportionately (disregarding signs) very much greater than e. But, as γ becomes a large negative quantity, e becomes a large positive quantity, approaching numerically to γ. Thus, if $\gamma = -2$, $e = 1$, but, if $\gamma = -10$, $e = 9$.

of attack described in the preceding paragraph. For that method is based on the assumption that there exists a demand function and a corresponding supply function, connecting two variables, which can be represented by curves; these curves "staying put", so to speak, when import or export taxes are imposed. This they do not do. On the contrary, in so far as a contribution is made from the tax-paying to the tax-collecting country, both curves are liable to be distorted, just as they are with reparation payments.[1] This entails that the elasticity of demand and supply in respect of given quantities of exports and imports, when reparations or taxation are imposed, are not the same as they were for those given quantities in the absence of reparations or taxation, and so cannot be used for determining the consequences of these imposts. In any conditions that can reasonably be postulated for real life the more complicated type of analysis developed in § 7 is, therefore, necessary.

§ 12. In our study of reparations we saw that, in view of the symmetrical form of the expression for C, in given conditions a single country, Germany, imposing a reparations levy of given scale on the rest of the world would secure for herself the same contribution that the rest would secure by imposing an equivalent reparation levy on Germany. With a levy made by means of import duties this is not so: for the expression for C′ is not symmetrical. On the assumptions of Chapter XIX, § 14, if America imposes a tax on Germany, assessed in cloth, to yield a revenue of R cloth

$$C' = R \cdot \frac{-210E_l - 174}{-210E_l - 180G_c - 174}.$$

But if Germany imposes a tax on America, assessed in linen, to yield a revenue of R linen — equivalent at pre-tax values to R cloth:

$$C' = R \cdot \frac{-180G_c - 174}{-210E_l - 180G_c - 174}.$$

If we further assume that $E_l = G_c$ the above expressions become respectively:

$$R \cdot \frac{-210E_l - 174}{-390E_l - 174} \quad \text{and} \quad R \cdot \frac{-180E_l - 174}{-390E_l - 174};$$

[1] Cf. Pigou and Robertson, *Essays and Addresses*; essay by Robertson, "The Transfer by Problem", p. 180.

so that, with America as the taxing country, the contribution from the foreigner is $\frac{-210E_l - 174}{-180E_l - 174}$ times what it is with Germany as the taxing country. If, purely for illustration, we put $E_l = -3$, this works out at $\frac{5}{4}$.

§ 13. It is evident to common sense that levies through import duties yielding a given revenue cannot enable a country, whether a single country or the rest of the world, to " tax the foreigner " so severely as equivalent reparation levies can do. A formal proof of this is provided by our formulae. For with America as the taxing country — a case more favourable than the other to the import duty plan —

$$\frac{C'}{C} = \frac{E_l G_c(E_c + 1) - E_c G_l(E_l + 1)}{E_l G_c(E_c + G_l) - E_c G_l(E_l + G_c)}.$$

The second term of the denominator of this expression must be substantially larger than the corresponding term in the numerator because G_c is negative ; and so also must the first term except in the highly improbable event that G_l, which is positive, < 1. Hence $\frac{C'}{C}$ must be < 1. On the assumptions of Chapter XIX, § 14, it reduces to $\frac{-210E_l - 174}{-210E_l - 180G_c}$, which, if we suppose E_l and G_c to be equal and to have, let us say, the value -3, becomes $\frac{39}{100}$.

§ 14. The ethical issue still remains. Granted that it is possible for the government of one country to benefit its citizens by " taxing the foreigner " through import and export duties, ought it to make use of this power ? This issue is evidently of the same general character as that discussed in Chapter XVIII, § 6. It cannot be settled for ourselves alone without reference to the conduct of others. *Pro tanto* what we ought to do depends on what foreigners do : if they make our people contribute towards their revenue, we are justified, other things equal, in making their people contribute towards ours. To this extent those popular controversialists are in the right who maintain that the case for free imports for England is not so strong in the actual world as it would be in a world where all other countries also leave imports free.

But, plainly, a tariff policy deliberately aimed at making petty gains at the cost of foreigners — which they can always, if they choose, counter by reprisals — would be at once impolitic and unworthy. Except as a means of tariff war, into which aggressive action on the part of others may have forced us, import and export duties should never, I suggest, be used with the intention of taxing foreigners. If such taxes are held to be desirable on other grounds, the fact that they will, as an unintended incident, tax foreigners to a small extent, is not, of course, a sufficient argument against imposing them. But, as a broad matter of principle, we may lay it down that, even if it were practicable for a country situated as England is to tax foreigners by import or export duties to a substantial extent, it would not be desirable to do this

CHAPTER XXIII

PROTECTIVE DUTIES

§ 1. The subject of protective duties is an awkward one to handle on account of the twofold character of the effects to which these duties lead. On the one hand, they are instruments for raising revenue ; on the other, instruments for excluding foreign products which compete with home-made goods. A single clear-cut issue is presented when it is proposed to institute duties so high that they would exclude the taxed product altogether and become, in effect, prohibitions against imports, thus yielding no revenue ; and also when a choice has to be made between a high rate and a low rate of duty, both calculated to yield the same revenue, but the one cutting down importation much more largely than the other. In general, however, the issue is not clear-cut, and it becomes necessary to weigh up and, perhaps, balance against one another the merits of so-called protective duties as revenue yielders and their merits (or demerits) as barriers against foreign competition.

§ 2. From the analysis of the preceding chapter it is easy to see that, other things being equal, an import tax on an import which competes with a home product is likely to exact a somewhat larger proportionate contribution from foreigners than an import tax on one which, like tea or coffee, does not so compete. The reason is that the presence of a rival home product tends to make our desire for the foreign product relatively elastic. From this point of view, therefore, protective import duties are likely to be better revenue raisers — I am taking a national standpoint here — than import duties on non-competing goods ; though, as was indicated in § 9 of the preceding chapter, the contribution of foreigners to our revenue is not likely in any event to be large. On the other hand, it was shown in Chapter IX, § 18 that, apart from the possibility of exacting a contribution from foreigners, import duties alone are likely, in general, to be worse revenue raisers than import duties *plus* equivalent excise duties, and even than excise duties alone. It is fair, I think, to set off these conflicting considerations against one another, and to conclude that, so far as revenue raising goes, it does not, as a rule, greatly matter whether we employ import duties on non-competing goods, or import duties on competing goods accompanied by an equivalent excise, or protective duties proper, *i.e.* import duties on competing goods not accompanied by an equivalent excise. If this be granted, our problem becomes much simplified. We may ignore revenue aspects altogether and assess proposals to impose protective duties by reference simply to their effects in excluding competitive imports.

§ 3. In this chapter we are concerned with the protectionist system conceived as permanent, protection versus free trade, so to speak, *sub specie aeternitatis*.[1] From this point of view it is reasonable to assume that wage rates will so adjust themselves to the general situation that the average percentage of unemployment will be substantially the same under either system. Nobody supposes or ever has supposed — as the classical economists are sometimes accused of implying — that there would be *no* unemployment under either system. All that we require is that *no difference to unemployment* is made by our choice between the systems. Granted this assumption, the entry of competitive imports cannot be responsible for bringing about unemployment in any country; and a reduction in the average volume of these imports cannot lead to any significant (lasting) increase of employment there. Rather, to restrict them simply means to prevent people from obtaining certain goods by the process of national production *plus* international exchange, and to force them to obtain them — or others — by that of national production alone. Presumably, however, if people prefer the roundabout process, they expect, by resort to it, to obtain more of the goods they want for a given expenditure of productive power. No doubt, they may make mistakes or find themselves defrauded. But, in general, what a person chooses as his immediate material interest is more likely really to be so than anything that a distant official manipulating tariffs can hope to press upon

[1] Interferences with foreign trade by means of import duties, whether protective or other, designed to counteract monetary difficulties that may be engendered by an adverse foreign balance, are referred to in Part III, Chapter V, § 16, but are not studied in detail in this volume.

him. There is thus a strong *prima facie* presumption against government interference with the natural flow of competitive imports.

§ 4. This presumption is not, however, decisive. Obviously it is not decisive when protective duties are advocated on military or social grounds ; the military advantage of not having to rely on importation, which might be interrupted in time of war, of certain key products ; the social advantage of life on the land. But it is not decisive even when economic considerations alone are relevant. The reasoning behind it does, indeed, warrant the inference that the direct and immediate effects of leaving those imports unrestricted are economically beneficial to the importing community. But, as List urged long ago, direct and immediate effects are not the sole effects. " The power of producing wealth ", he wrote, " is infinitely more important than wealth itself." [1] Consequently : " The nation must sacrifice and give up a measure of material prosperity in order to gain culture, skill and powers of united production ; it must sacrifice some present advantage in order to insure to itself future ones. . . . It is true that protective duties at first increase the price of manufactured goods ; but it is just as true, and, moreover, acknowledged by the prevailing economical school, that in the course of time, by the nation being enabled to build up a completely developed manufacturing power of its own, those goods are produced more cheaply at home than the prices at which they can be imported from foreign parts." [2] When List wrote, England had established herself as the dominant manufacturing Power. He did not deny that, for the moment, continental nations would obtain the largest return to their capital and labour by confining themselves to agriculture and buying manufactured goods from her. But he perceived that the commodities which a country can now produce most easily are not necessarily identical with those which it has the greatest natural advantages for producing. For natural advantages require for their development time and exercise. The building-up of manufacturing power, involving, as it does, the training of workmen, the perfecting of machinery, of transport, of credit and of market organisation, may take years to accomplish.[3]

[1] *A National System of Political Economy*, p. 133.

[2] Cf. *Ibid.* pp. 144-5.

[3] *Ibid.* p. 300.

Till it is completed, the old-established manufacturing State has "a thousand advantages over the newly born or half-grown manufactories of other nations".[1] This line of reasoning is particularly strong as regards an agricultural country wishful to develop manufactures. In such a country, since, *ex hypothesi*, it has no important class of artisans or factory workers, the skill required for starting any particular kind of mill will be very difficult to get. "Masters, foremen and workmen must first be either trained up at home or procured from abroad, and the profitableness of the business has not been sufficiently tested to give capitalists confidence in its success."[2] For a long time, therefore, it is improbable that any works which may be started will be able to compete on equal terms with established foreign rivals — and that in spite of the fact that the industry in question may be one for which the country has great natural advantages. In a country which is already largely industrial List's argument has less force. The initial difficulty involved in starting a new industry is likely to be much slighter, because it is comparatively easy to obtain from among a people already accustomed to many varieties of factory work hands capable of carrying on a new variety of it. Further, in an industrial community, those other important elements of productive power, organised systems of transport and of credit, which, in an agricultural country, may need themselves to be built up before manufactures can be profitably established, will be already in existence. Still the argument for protecting particular infant industries in a developed industrial community, no less than that for protecting infant industrial communities, is formally quite valid. The same thing is true of the analogous argument for defending particular established industries, for which a country is well suited, against deliberate attack. It is conceivable that foreign combinations might adopt a policy of killing British rivals in order to establish an exclusive control over our markets. They might sell in England at low prices — prices so low as to involve a positive loss — until their rivals were destroyed, and then, no longer having any competitors to fear, might gather in the fruit of their labours by raising prices to a very high level. In the face of action of that kind, to check the import of their cheap goods, though

[1] *A National System of Political Economy*, p. 300. [2] *Ibid*. p. 294.

still involving a direct loss, might, nevertheless, be sound policy, as tending to save us from monopolistic exactions afterwards. Of course, it would not necessarily be sound policy even in that case ; for, very often, the threatened firms would be rich and strong enough to defend themselves without direct or indirect government aid. Thus List, after he has argued that, in consequence of foreign aggression, " in a short time a complex combination of productive powers and of property becomes lost, which has been created only by the exertions and endeavours of several generations ", points out on the same page that, " when the government is unable to provide any remedy for its (*i.e.* an export trade's) interruption, we often see manufacturers continuing to produce at an actual loss. They want to avert, in expectation of better times, the irrecoverable injury which they would suffer from a stoppage of their works."[1] Still, the formal validity of the above extension of List's argument is not in doubt.[2]

§ 5. Up to this point nothing has been said about the effects which the cutting down of particular competitive imports may have upon distribution. The most obvious of these effects is produced as between the buyers of the commodity, imports of which are cut down, and the domestic producers of that commodity. In general these persons will find themselves able to charge higher prices, and so will, *prima facie*, make a gain at the expense of their customers. For most ordinary commodities this gain is transitory in its nature. The fact that the producers of a particular commodity are making an exceptional profit causes other people to come into their industry and to go on coming till the rate of returns is brought down again to the common level ; whatever addition to price remains being a consequence of greater real costs of production per unit, and not carrying with it any addition to average producers' gains. As a rule, the comparative earning power of the several factors of production regarded as wholes will not be appreciably altered. If, however, the competitive imports consist of a large class of goods in the making of which some one factor of production plays a predominant part, things may work out otherwise. Thus, suppose that, in an industrial country, heavy duties are imposed upon the generality of agricultural imports. As a result, farming

[1] *Ibid.* p. 298. [2] Cf. *ante*, Chapter VIII, § 3.

will become more profitable, farmers will be ready to pay higher rents, and, in the end, the consuming public will be mulcted in a lasting manner for the benefit of owners of agricultural land. In a country of peasant proprietors — provided that the products concerned are of a kind that can conveniently be grown on small farms — it may be that the beneficiaries of this distributional change are not appreciably better off than those who are injured by it. But in a country where land is owned in large blocks the beneficiaries are much better off; and though, no doubt, it is theoretically possible to cancel the distributional change by imposing special taxes on land ownership and paying bounties to consumers of agricultural produce out of the proceeds, no such plan has ever yet been tried in practice. It is a fair presumption, I think, that, in a country such as England, any large-scale restriction of competitive agricultural imports must involve an uncancelled, or imperfectly cancelled, shift of distribution from the general body of relatively poor consumers to a small number of relatively rich proprietors of agricultural land. *Per contra*, if imports, in the manufacture of which labour, as contrasted with capital and land, plays an exceptionally large part, were selected for restriction, and, in consequence, commodities of that class came to be more largely manufactured here, labour might obtain a larger proportionate share of the nation's real income, and, in specially favourable conditions, even a larger absolute share. If this were to happen, it would imply a shift in distribution favourable to relatively poor persons, and so would be, *pro tanto*, socially advantageous. This possibility is of some academic interest, though there is, I think, little chance that it could be exploited effectively in practice.

§ 6. From the foregoing discussion it is clear that conditions may easily arise in which — apart altogether from difficulties about foreign exchange, not considered here — a country would benefit economically by cutting the importation of particular competitive goods. There is thus from a national point of view, and in a less degree from a cosmopolitan point of view also, a clear theoretical case for certain applications of protectionist policy. It does not follow, however, that governments can with advantage attempt to make use of these theoretical openings. First, it has to be considered whether the desired results could be obtained more satisfactorily in some other way — for example, by means of bounties. Secondly, it has to be considered whether governments, as constituted in real life, can be trusted, or can trust themselves, with these difficult matters. Upon this aspect of the problem Sidgwick long ago wrote with great weight as follows: "I agree, as a conclusion of abstract economic theory, that protection in certain cases and within certain limits, would probably be advantageous to the protecting country — and even, perhaps, to the world — if only it could be strictly confined to these cases and kept within these limits: but I am, nevertheless, strongly of opinion that it is practically best for a government to adhere to the broad rule of 'taxation for revenue only' — at any rate in a free community where habits of commercial enterprise are fully developed. My ground for this opinion is that I do not think we can reasonably expect our actual governments to be wise and strong enough to keep their protective interference within due limits; owing to the great difficulty and delicacy of the task of constructing a system of import duties with the double aim of raising revenue equitably and protecting native industry usefully, and the pressure that is certain to be put upon the government to extend its application of the principle of protection if it is once introduced. I think, therefore, that the gain protection might bring in particular cases is always likely to be more than counterbalanced by the general bad effects of encouraging producers and traders to look to government for aid in industrial crises and dangers, instead of relying on their own foresight, ingenuity and energy; especially since the wisest protection in any one country would tend in various ways to encourage unwise protection elsewhere."[1] It does not fall within the scope of this volume to enter further into that debate; nor, as might easily be done, to point the moral by reference to British experience from the first planting of the McKenna duties till the full flowering of the new protectionist garden.

[1] *Principles of Political Economy*, p. 487.

PART III

PUBLIC FINANCE AND EMPLOYMENT

CHAPTER I

INTRODUCTORY

§ 1. Down to the beginning of this century the problems of public finance were regarded as so far self-contained that in discussions of them their relevance to the state of and fluctuations in the volume of employment were practically never mentioned. In this country the Majority and Minority reports of the Royal Commission on the Poor Laws published in 1909 first seriously examined the question whether central and local authorities might not be able, by a careful timing of their expenditures, to make the volume of employment steadier, and, maybe, even larger on the average, than it tended to be in existing conditions. Since that time the relation between the raising and spending of revenue by public authorities on the one hand, and the employment situation on the other, has been widely discussed. A number of separate issues have to be distinguished. The purpose of this Part is to disentangle and examine them. The problem is posed, not in general, so as to include economies such as that of Soviet Russia, where the great bulk of industrial activity is at the order of public authorities, but more particularly with regard to economies like our own, where, while the public authorities, central and local, engage for productive ends a substantial part of the national labour force, production for profit by private enterprise is, nevertheless, predominant.

§ 2. The volume of employment in any period must be equal to the money wages bill of that period divided by the mean rate of money wages. It is not among the prerogatives of public finance to exercise any authority over rates of money wages. The only way, therefore, in which it can affect the volume of employment is by acting on the size of the money wages bill. *Prima facie* it can do this in part through its own hirings of labour in part through its expenditures in purchasing goods the making of which requires labour to be hired, in part by stimulating the expenditures of industrialists and private persons through grants or subsidies. These processes may operate on the money wages bill either by affecting the proportion which that bill constitutes of aggregate money income or by affecting the size of aggregate money income itself. In any event a central place in our discussion must be occupied by this concept of aggregate money income; and it is important to be clear about the definition of it.

§ 3. By aggregate money income is meant, in accordance with common usage, the sum of money payments received by agents of production, including, of course, material agents such as farms or factories owned by government, in return for their services. This is sometimes called national money income at factor cost. It is obviously not equal to aggregate money outlay if that is taken to include any of the following items: (i) transfers against the sale of stocks and shares or other capital assets; (ii) transfers against movements of goods between successive middlemen on their way to the final buyer; (iii) transfers among private persons or from the government to private persons, that are not made against services rendered by these persons or their equipment; (iv) transfers from private persons to the government through taxes, whether direct or indirect, or through loans; (v) any net balance that there may be in outlays upon purchases or investment abroad over corresponding outlays by foreigners here. If we ignore the last item, and use net outlay to signify aggregate outlay minus the other four, this becomes simply income looked at in reverse — from the standpoint of those who make, as contrasted with those who receive, the payments that constitute income. There is a certain convenience in using the term net outlay — more loosely, outlay — in this sense; as equivalent to income-producing expenditure or what is sometimes called effective demand. In what follows, subject to a comment on the foreign balance at the end of Chapter V, I shall do that.

§ 4. One further preliminary observation is called for. The fact that the volume of employment is necessarily equal to the money wages bill divided by the money rate of wage implies, with a constant rate of money wages, that any given percentage shift in the money wages bill will carry with it an equal percentage shift in employment. If the number of would-be wage-earners is fixed, the sum of employment plus unemployment is, of course, also fixed, so that any given change in the quantity of employment implies a numerically equal inverse change in the quantity of unemployment. If, however, the number of would-be wage-earners is liable to change, employment and unemployment are not bound together in this way. Thus, if originally there were 100 men available and 90 employed, should the number available increase from 100 to 110 while employment stood constant at 90, unemployment would rise from 10 to 20 and the unemployment percentage from 10 to 18·2. In fact the number of would-be wage-earners is highly liable to change. If we take it that these persons constitute a sensibly constant proportion of the population of working age, what is happening to their number is determined in the main by what is happening to that. But the population of working age is very unlikely to be stationary even though the population as a whole is stationary. On the contrary, if the birth rate has recently undergone a substantial fall, the population of working age may well be growing at the same time that the population as a whole is declining. In this country in recent decades, while the population as a whole has only been rising slowly, the population of working age and, therefore, the number of would-be wage-earners has been rising rapidly. These variations in the number of would-be wage-earners complicate exposition somewhat in spite of the fact that, the quantity of employment being given, any change in the number of would-be wage-earners must modify the employment and the unemployment percentages in equal (and opposite) degrees.[1] But the *effects* on employment and

[1] Thus write K for the original number of would-be wage-earners and E for the original number employed. Then the employment proportion is $\frac{E}{K}$; the unemployment proportion $\frac{K-E}{K}$. Let the number of would-be wage-earners be increased by k. Then the employment proportion becomes $\frac{E}{K+k}$; the unemployment proportion $\frac{K+k-E}{K+k}$. The decrease in the employment proportion, namely $\left(\frac{E}{K}-\frac{E}{K+k}\right)$, and the increase in the unemployment proportion, namely $\frac{K+k-E}{K+k}-\frac{K-E}{K}$, are both equal to $\frac{kE}{K(K+k)}$. But this is, of course, obvious without the formal proof.

on unemployment of happenings to the money wages bill or to the rate of money wages are not different with a changing number of would-be wage-earners from what they would have been with a stationary one. Moreover, when the money wages bill and the numbers of would-be wage-earners both vary, the joint effect of the two sorts of change together on the employment (and unemployment) percentage is the same as would have resulted with a constant number of would-be wage-earners, if the total money wages bill had then varied in the proportion in which the money wages bill per head does in fact vary.

CHAPTER II

EMPLOYMENT AND UNEMPLOYMENT IN RELATION TO THE MONEY WAGES BILL APART FROM REFLEX EFFECTS OF CHANGES IN MONEY WAGE RATES ON THE MONEY WAGES BILL

§ 1. WITH these preliminaries we have now to study the way in which the size of the money wages bill per would-be wage-earner and variations in it are liable in different circumstances to effect the scale of employment and unemployment. To avoid continual repetition of the words " per would-be wage-earner " I shall phrase my discussion in the language that would be appropriate if the number of would-be wage-earners were fixed. Every proposition announced for that case in terms of the money wages bill is true also for the more general case, provided that we substitute for money wages bill money wages bill per would-be wage-earner. In this chapter reflex effects of changes in the money rate of wages on the money wages bill will be ignored, the discussion of these being reserved for the chapter that follows.

§ 2. Four situations have to be distinguished, in which respectively the money wages bill is supposed, first, to be stationary ; secondly, to fluctuate about a stationary centre ; thirdly, to trend progressively upwards ; fourthly, to trend upwards with fluctuations about the trend. In this discussion I shall ignore the fact that labour embraces work-people of many different kinds and qualities, split up among occupations between which movement is obstructed ; thus assuming, in effect, that it is homogeneous and perfectly mobile. For my present purpose the complications which would be introduced if these assumptions were removed are of secondary importance.

§ 3. Let us consider first a stationary wages bill. If work-people competed against one another for jobs in a thorough-going way money wage rates would so adjust themselves to the money demand in each several occupation that everybody seeking work would be able to obtain it. For, so long as anybody was out of work, his presence would exercise a downward pressure upon wage rates. In these conditions the size of the aggregate money wages bill would have no significance for employment. Whatever it was, everybody would be fully employed. In actual life, however, work-people do not compete with one another in so thoroughgoing a way as this. Where collective bargaining prevails, and where any form of provision is made for the financial support of unemployed persons, it is to be expected that, with a stationary wages bill, money wage rates will be set somewhat above the level at which full employment in the literal sense would be maintained. The percentage of unemployment — call it h — instead of being nil, will thus be something positive.

§ 4. There will, moreover, be a tendency, so long as psychological and other relevant conditions are unchanged, for this percentage to be the same whatever the money wages bill may be. This is not, of course, to deny that on occasions situations may exist, particularly, for example, after some large disturbance, in which h is in actual fact larger than it tends to be. In such a case a lifting of the money wages bill would reduce h permanently below what it was in the abnormal situation. But, if we start from a normal situation and if then the wages bill is permanently enlarged, or, with a varying bill, if its average amount is enlarged, wage rates will tend to be pushed higher, in such wise as to offset the extra wages bill — unless, of course, we imagine ourselves facing an authoritarian government, which, acting outside the sphere of public finance altogether, is able to prevent increases in the average rate of wages ; or, what is hoped for by some but to others seems very unlikely, a similar result is achieved by voluntary action on the part of trade unions.

§ 5. Considerable support for this thesis may be derived from a study of the long sequence of employment cycles as recorded by trade unions between 1852 and 1912. The average percentages of unemployment in the several cycles were extremely close together. Reckoning each cycle to start with the year of minimum and to end in the year before the next minimum, we get the following table of mean unemployment percentages.

1853–9	1860–64	1865–71	1872–81	1882–9	1890–98	1899–1905	1906–12	Whole Period of 60 Years
5·2	4·8	4·7	4·2	5·9	4·6	3·9	4·8	4·7

Reckoning each cycle to start with a year of maximum and to end in the year before the next maximum, we get

1852–7	1858–61	1862–7	1868–78	1879–85	1886–92	1893–1903	1904–8	Whole Period of 57 Years
4·4	5·7	5·0	3·8	6·1	5·2	4·2	4·6	4·7

Thus in the whole of the first set of cycles the maximum deviation from the general average was 25 per cent; for six out of the eight cycles it was less than 11 per cent and for four there were practically no deviations at all. In the whole of the second set the maximum deviation was 30 per cent, but for the five best cycles the deviations were all less than 11 per cent. These percentages are not large. The absolute deviations are, of course, very small. If we express the facts in terms of employment, instead of unemployment, they are still more — much more — impressive. The average percentage of work-people seeking employment who were actually employed was never appreciably less than 94 per cent or more than 96 per cent over the whole series of waves from 1852 to 1912; so that the average amount of employment and the available labour force must have stood throughout in very nearly the same proportion to one another; and that in spite of the fact that the available labour force had probably grown by something like 45 per cent. Broadly speaking, the volume of employment over the average of good and bad times together was a constant proportion of the available labour force.

§ 6. Of course, psychological or other relevant conditions may change for outside reasons, with the result that the normal percentage of unemployment is larger in one period than in another. For example, it may well be that a substantial part of the large excess of average unemployment in the inter-war period over what it was in the pre-1914 period — it was probably two and a half times as large — was due to the fact that a general system of State-aided unemployment insurance had been established, with the result that the restraint which the cost to trade unions and the individual suffering associated with unemployment had previously exerted on demands for higher wages was greatly weakened.

But that is really beside the point. Provided that the money wages bill stands constant, we may fairly say that, in general, from a long-run standpoint, it is immaterial how large that bill is.

§ 7. It must be understood, however, that in this statement the phrase " in general, from a long-run standpoint " is not otiose. For, should a very high level of unemployment have become established, it may well be that the attention of wage-earners and their leaders is focussed wholly on that; that any improvement in employment is welcomed as a gift of the gods and does *not* stimulate any serious pressure towards higher wage rates. If we will, we may explain this by saying that large differences in the normal employment percentage carry with them differences in the psychological atmosphere, which prevent them from leading to the same reactions as they would have done had the psychological atmosphere been constant. Moreover even apart from this, the reaction of the money wages bill upon money wage rates is not instantaneous, but subject to a time-lag, in some circumstances a considerable time-lag. Hence, even though the effect of pushing up the aggregate money wages bill from one stationary level to a higher one is transitory in character, it may nevertheless, on occasions, from the standpoint of practice, be well worth securing.

§ 8. Turn secondly to a situation in which the wages bill of successive periods, *e.g.* trade cycles, is of constant average amount, but fluctuates round the average. We are concerned to decide how the average percentage of unemployment would be affected if, instead of being allowed to fluctuate, the wages bill were held constant at its mean level — or, more generally, waiving the ambiguity involved in the phrase, if the extent of its fluctuation were reduced.[1] We have already seen that, with a constant wages bill, money wage rates will so adjust themselves that *some* constant percentage of unemployment tends in general to prevail. So much being premised, what will the situation be if the wages bill fluctuates? It *might* happen that money wage rates moved up and down in response

[1] When more than two quantities are concerned there are a variety of ways in which the extent of their variability about the average can be measured; and in certain cases one test would report system A more variable, while another reported it less variable, than system B.

to changes in the wages bill in such wise that, in good and bad times alike, unemployment stood constant at the percentage *h*, the percentage which is proper to a stable demand. In actual fact, however, the processes of collective bargaining render money wage rates sticky — considerably resistant to movements in either direction. This entails that they do not vary sufficiently between good and bad times to keep the percentage of unemployment constant at the level *h*. This entails, in turn, that in bad times the unemployment percentage is larger than *h*. If *h* were nil, it would follow that, on the average of good and bad times, unemployment *must* be larger with a fluctuating than with a stable wages bill; for, obviously, in the best of times unemployment cannot be less than nil. Since, however, we have allowed that in fact *h* is not nil, but has a positive value, this does not follow. For the stickiness of money wage rates against upward movements of the wages bill in good times might cause the unemployment percentage to fall as far below *h* then as it rises above *h* in bad times. Is this possibility likely to be realised in fact? The answer, I think, is clearly no; for the reason that, while there is no *ceiling* to upward movements in money wage rates, the fact that an unemployed man, in such a country as England, can look to unemployment benefit, or assistance, or, at the worst, relief through the Poor Law, fixes a definite *bottom*, below which they cannot be driven down. If the wages bill (*i.e.* aggregate demand for labour) fluctuated only slightly, this might not matter; for the bottom might never, so to speak, come into action. But with the sort of fluctuations experienced in practice, particularly if the scale of unemployment benefit is liberal, it is practically certain to do this sometimes. We may conclude, therefore, in a broad way, that, the aggregate wages bill over good and bad times together being given, if the amount of it fluctuates, the average level of money wage rates over the two sets of times will be higher, and the average percentage of unemployment larger, than if it is stable. That is to say, to steady the wages bill, while keeping its average amount unchanged, will diminish unemployment. There is, moreover, a further consideration which supports this conclusion. Attempts on the part of workpeople to force wages up in good times and on the part of employers to force them down in bad times often lead to strikes and lock-outs, which inflict injury, both directly [1] and indirectly, upon the volume of employment. With steadier demand there is good reason to believe that stoppages of work consequent upon industrial disputes would be less frequent and less extensive than they are in present conditions.

§ 9. From the above results an important practical inference may be drawn. Suppose that, apart from State intervention, the wages bill would have oscillated between A in good times and $(A - a)$ in bad times. The public authorities may make it stable either by causing it to expand in bad times and contract in good times to $(A - \frac{1}{2}a)$, or by causing it to expand in bad times to A, while leaving it unchanged in good times. Subject to the qualifications set out in § 6, provided that no progressive upward or downward trend is imposed on the wages bill, it makes no difference to the average volume of unemployment over good and bad times together which of these two contrasted lines of policy the public authorities elect to follow. Both of them reduce the average percentage of unemployment over good and bad times together to the same extent.

§ 10. In the third situation, distinguished in § 2, the money wages bill moves progressively upward. Once more it is evident that, if competition among wage-earners were thoroughgoing, so that, with a stationary wages bill, there would be full employment, a progressively rising wages bill could do nothing to better it. But, with a tendency in wage rates to adjust themselves so as to establish a positive unemployment percentage h, if the wages bill is constant, a continuously rising wages bill will almost certainly be associated with a percentage that is less than h. For the apparatus of wage adjustment is subject to a time-lag ; the pursuer never catches up with the pursued. This consideration goes far to explain the extremely low level of unemployment that usually exists, after the preliminary period of adjustment, in great wars. Demand for labour manifested through the wages bill is continually rising, while money wage rates, partly held back by patriotic reluctance on the part of wage-earners to press their claims to the limit, lag behind. At the same time, it must be remembered, labour is apt to be rendered abnormally

[1] Persons directly involved in industrial disputes are not counted as unemployed in British statistics.

mobile by official persuasion or even direction into the channels where it is most needed.

§ 11. There remains the fourth situation. It is easy to see, by reasoning similar to the above, that, if the wages bill fluctuates in a given degree about a centre which is moving continuously upwards, the unemployment percentage will be smaller than it would be if the centre was stationary. But, if the rate of upward trend were maintained and fluctuations about it removed, the unemployment percentage would be smaller still.

CHAPTER III

THE IMPLICATIONS OF REFLEX INFLUENCES UPON CHANGES IN MONEY RATES OF WAGES ON THE MONEY WAGES BILL

§ 1. We now come to a matter of crucial importance. When aggregate money income, and, through it, the money wages bill, is raised by public finance operations, it is *prima facie* to be expected that there will be a responsive rise in the rate of money wages. In the last chapter the character of this tendency and the implications to which it leads were worked out on the assumption that the induced movements in money wage rates do not themselves in turn set up any reflex movements in aggregate money income, and so in the money wages bill. But this assumption does not, in general, conform to the facts. Reflex movements *are* set up. We have now, therefore, to study the nature of these movements and to inquire how far their existence makes it necessary to modify the results reached in the last chapter.

§ 2. If money wage rates rise and the money wages bill does not rise, employment and real income must be contracted. This entails that the amount of resources which the public as a whole are willing to offer for investment in response to a given prospect of returns is contracted. The prospect of returns (demand schedule for investment) being given, this entails, *with a normal banking and monetary system*, namely one under which higher rates of interest and larger money incomes are associated together,[1] an upward movement in the rate of interest. This in turn, in the manner to be described in Chapter V, evokes a transfer of money from passive to active balances accompanied by an increase in bank loans, with the result that aggregate money income and the wages bill are increased. Thus the supposition set out at the beginning of this paragraph, that money wage rates rise and the money wage bill does not, turns out, when its implications are examined, to be self-contradictory. Granted, however, that the proportionate part of aggregate money income constituted by the money wages bill is not sensibly altered, the

[1] Cf. *post*, Chapter V, § 9.

money wages bill cannot be expanded *in as large a ratio* as the money rate of wages. For, if it were, there would be the same real income as there was originally, the same readiness to supply resources for investment in response to given prospects of return, and the same prospects of return from, *i.e.* demand schedule for, resources for investment. But in these circumstances there would be no reason for the rate of interest to be higher than before and, therefore, no reason for aggregate money income to be larger than before. It follows that, though aggregate money income and the money wages bill will be pushed up in consequence of a rise in the money rate of wages, they will not be pushed up in so large a ratio. Thus, when an initial upward movement (brought about, maybe, by public investment policy) in the money wages bill from 100 to $(100 + X)$ evokes an upward movement in the money rate of wages from 100 to $(100 + Y)$, this in turn evokes a further upward movement in the money wages bill to $(100 + X + kY)$, where $k > 0$ but < 1.

§ 3. In these conditions it is not difficult to see how the consequences of the tendency of money wage rates, on which we insisted in the last chapter, to push themselves up in such wise as ultimately, in *steady conditions*, to secure an unchanged unemployment percentage, will be affected. The money wages bill is raised at a first step from 100 to $(100 + X)$ and the money rate of wage also from 100 to $(100 + X)$; that is to say, the Y of the last paragraph is equal to X. At the next step the money wages bill rises to $(100 + X + kX)$. But thereupon the money rate of wages again follows suit; and so on. Hence, money wages bill and money rate of wages being alike represented initially by 100, after the various reactions have taken place, both ultimately stand at $\left\{100 + X(1 + k + k^2 \ldots)\right\}$, *i.e.* at $\left\{100 + \frac{X}{(1-k)}\right\}$. Thus, if $k = \frac{1}{4}$, they both stand at $(100 + \frac{4}{3}X)$; if $k = \frac{1}{2}$, at $(100 + 2X)$; if $k = \frac{3}{4}$, at $(100 + 4X)$; and so on. We do not know what in actual conditions the value of k is. But, whatever its value, so long as it is < 1, the reflex action of increases in the money rate of wages on the money wages bill does not prevent the tendency, described in the last chapter, for money wage rates to move up to match upward movements in the money wages bill from realising itself. All the results reached in that chapter thus remain intact in spite of the existence of this reflex action.

§ 4. So far we have had in mind a normal monetary and banking system. If we suppose, instead of this, that the stock of money is so controlled by or on behalf of the government that the money rate of interest is held constant no matter what happens, the situation will develop differently. For now, when the money rate of wages is raised, an equi-proportionate rise in the money wages bill is no longer incompatible with an unchanged rate of interest. Such a rise may then be expected to take place. Consequently, real income, and so employment, will be the same as before.[1] The analysis of the last paragraph has, therefore, in this case to be modified. The tendency for money wage rates to move up to match upward movements in the money wages bill no longer leads, when an upward impulse is given to the wages bill, to it and the money rate of wages both rising in some equal finite proportion. Rather, it leads — for now k in the series summed in the last paragraph is not less than, but is equal to, unity— to an unending upward procession, in divergent series, on the part of both of them. In this jungle of infinities it is difficult to move with confidence. In view, however, of the fact that the several reactions are not instantaneous but are subject to time-lags, I conclude, though confessedly with diffidence, that the money wages bill in its upward flight will maintain its initial lead over the pursuing money rate of wages.

§ 5. As regards fluctuating movements set up in the money wages bill, the consequence for our analysis that follows when, instead of the monetary and banking rates operating in a normal manner, the rate of interest is held constant, are less serious than they might seem to be at first sight. The reason is that the reactions we have been describing do not work themselves out at a single blow, but gradually over a number of months or even years. In spite, therefore, of the fact that in the conditions now supposed the offsetting effects of expansions due to associated rises in the money rate of wages are ultimately themselves offset by further expansions induced

[1] It must be borne in mind that a policy under which the rate of interest is held constant, while it thus prevents changes in wage rates from affecting employment as they do under a normal banking policy, does not prevent changes in the demand function for investment from doing that. This asymmetry is exhibited in detail in the mathematical appendices to my *Employment and Equilibrium*.

by them in the money wages bill, it is nevertheless true that, the larger these offsetting effects are, the less employment will be altered through given initial movements in the money wages bill. The fact that wage rates are more sticky against downward than against upward pressures still, therefore, leads to the consequences described in the last chapter. It is still true that steadying the wages bill, if it is originally unsteady in a sufficient degree, leads to a reduction in the average percentage of unemployment over good and bad times together. Reasoning on the same lines shows that what was said in the last chapter about the consequences of upward (or downward) trend movements in the money wages bill is also still true. Such movements entail the average percentage of unemployment being permanently higher (or lower) by some absolute amount than it would have been had there been no trend.

§ 6. In the case, however, of policies designed to push up the money wages bill from a lower to a higher fixed level the conclusion implied in §§ 4-6 of the last chapter, that *in general and in the long run* consequential parallel increases in the money rate of wages will prevent any effect from being produced on employment, is not now valid. As we have seen, it would be valid, in spite of the reflex effect of rises in the money rate of wages upon the money wages bill, with a normal monetary and banking system. But, with a system under which the rate of interest is held rigid, the conjoint effect of the original movement and the successive secondary reactions must be to keep the money wages bill permanently higher relatively to the money rate of wages than it would have been had no movement taken place. This is accomplished at the cost of a never-ending process of expansion, alike in money income, money wages bill and money rate of wages, being set in motion; for the intention to raise the money wages bill to a new *fixed* level does not, of course, succeed.

CHAPTER IV

THE MONEY WAGES BILL IN RELATION TO AGGREGATE MONEY OUTLAY IF MONEY WAGE RATES ARE FIXED

§ 1. THE most obvious way in which public finance operations can affect the money wages bill is by affecting aggregate money outlay, — *i.e.* aggregate money income looked at in reverse — to which the money wages bill is closely related and whose movements may be expected *prima facie* to set up in it sympathetic movements in the same sense. But the connection between aggregate money outlay and the money wages bill is not a rigid one. Our next step, therefore, is to inquire in detail how the behaviour of aggregate money outlay would affect that of the money wages bill apart from any reaction that it might set up in rates of money wages — if we will, on the assumption that these rates are fixed.

§ 2. It is evident that if money wage rates are fixed, upward or downward *trends* in aggregate outlay or income will be associated, so long, of course, as sufficient men are available to be called into work, with similar trends in the money wages bill. It is not necessary for my purpose to go further into that; and this chapter will be confined to the problems presented by fluctuations about a fixed centre.

§ 3. Let us begin by supposing that labour is perfectly homogeneous and absolutely mobile between different places and occupations. How in these conditions will the behaviour of the money wages bill differ if money outlay or income fluctuates between $(A+a)$ and $(A-a)$ from what it would be if money income stood constantly at A?

§ 4. We have to distinguish four cases: (1) some available labour (with appropriate co-operative factors) is unemployed when money income is $(A+a)$ and, therefore, of course, also when it is smaller than this; (2) some available labour is unemployed when money income is $(A-a)$, but all is employed when it is A or $(A+a)$; (3) some is unemployed when money income is $(A-a)$ or A, but all is employed when it is $(A+a)$; (4) no labour is unemployed but there are unfilled vacancies even when money income is $(A-a)$ and, therefore, *a fortiori* when it is larger than this.

§ 5. The different ways in which in these four cases the money wages bill is affected when aggregate money outlay is respectively steady or fluctuating are most easily understood with the help of a diagram :

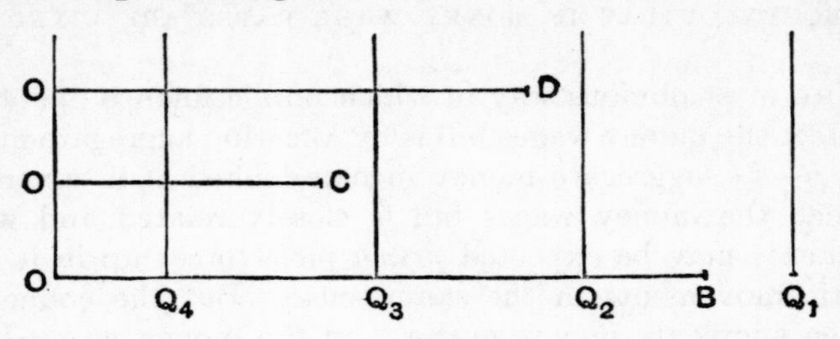

Let OB be the quantity of labour (and appurtenances) wanted with income $(A+a)$ in period 1 ; OC that wanted with income $(A-a)$ in period 2, and OD the intermediate quantity wanted in each period with income A. The quantities available in the four cases distinguished above may be represented by OQ_1, OQ_2, OQ_3, and OQ_4. With OQ_1 the quantity of labour engaged if incomes are $(A-a)$ and $(A+a)$ is OC in the one period and OB in the other ; if incomes are A and A it is OD, *i.e.* $\left(\frac{OC+OB}{2}\right)$ in each ; so that, the money rate of wages being fixed, the average size of the wages bill is the same in both cases. With OQ_2 the quantity engaged over the two periods if incomes are $(A-a)$ and $(A+a)$ is $(OC+OQ_2)$, if incomes are A and A, it is 2OD, which, since it is equal to $(OC+OB)$, is necessarily larger than $(OC+OQ_3)$; therefore the wages bill is greater in the latter case. With OQ_3, if incomes are $(A-a)$ and $(A+a)$ the quantity of labour engaged is $(OC+OQ_3)$; if incomes are A and A it is $2OQ_3$; therefore the wages bill is again larger in the latter case. With OQ_4 employment is obviously equal to OQ_4 in each period with both sets of incomes, so that the size of the wages bill is the same with both. Thus in case 1 the steadying of aggregate money income steadies the money wages bill without altering its average size ; in cases 2 and 3 it both steadies the money wages bill and increases its average size ; in case 4 — which is certain never to arise in actual life — it does not affect its steadiness or its average size.

§ 6. Our argument so far has proceeded on the assumption

that labour is perfectly mobile among places and occupations. If this is forgotten a mistaken inference may easily be drawn. Since in actual life there is always some unemployment even in the best of times, it may be supposed that case 1 above is the only one relevant to practise, so that, if the money rate of wage is fixed, fluctuations in aggregate money outlay, while promoting fluctuations in the money wages bill, never affect its average amount. This is not so, because, in view of the obstacles that actually exist in the way of labour movement, it may easily happen that a swing-up of money outlay leaves considerable unemployment in some places and occupations and at the same time creates a number of unfilled vacancies in others. Thus the fact that there is always some unemployment in good times does not prove in actual life, as it would prove in a régime of perfect mobility, that there are no unfilled vacancies.

§ 7. The analysis of § 5 can be extended without change to the more general case in which a set of money outlays oscillating between $(A - a)$ and $(A + a)$ is modified not into a set constant at A, but, by a transfer of b (supposed to be less than a) from good times to bad, into one oscillating between $(A - a + b)$ and $(A + a - b)$. It is easy to see that, in circumstances in which the stabilisation of outlays at A will make the money wages bill steadier, this kind of adjustment will also do that, but in a less degree ; the degree being, of course, smaller, the smaller is b. The conditions in which it will also make the average wages bill larger are also the same as before. If b is greater than a, the result may, of course, be different.[1] But this case is not of practical interest.

§ 8. Let us next, still, for simplicity, supposing that labour is perfectly homogeneous, imagine that it is divided up into two sectors, one serving the demand of the public authorities

[1] Thus, if $b > a$, it may happen that, even though initially there was some unemployment in both good times and bad, after the change the transfer creates, not only employment, but also some unfilled vacancies in what used to be bad times ; in which case, of course, the average size of the wages bill is diminished. If there were one hundred men unemployed in good times and two hundred in bad, which implies that $a = 50$, a transfer in excess of 50 would increase unemployment in what used to be good times without increasing employment in what used to be bad times by so large an amount. But, if unemployment in good times was 300 and in bad times 400, which also implies that $a = 50$, a transfer substantially larger than 50 might be made without the average size of the money wages bill being affected.

and the other that of private persons. Initially public outlay and private outlay together oscillate between $(A+a)$ and $(A-a)$. The public authorities decide to reduce their own outlay in period 1 when total outlay is $(A+a)$ by c, and to increase it by an equal amount when total outlay is $(A-a)$. For the present, we suppose that an alteration in public outlay in either period does not affect at all private outlay in that period.[1] It is really enough for our argument that it should not affect it to an equivalent extent. On that assumption, and the money rate of wages being taken as fixed, how would the steadiness of the money wages bill be affected? To answer that question we need to bring into account a new and important element, the state of labour mobility.

§ 9. If labour is absolutely immobile between the two sectors, it is plain that the behaviour of money outlay in the public sector cannot, on our assumption, influence at all that of the wages bill in the private sector. The aggregate wages bill can only be affected through that part of it which is attached to the public sector. The behaviour of this part of the wages bill is related to the behaviour of the aggregate outlay of the public sector in the manner described in § 5. But two cases have to be distinguished. For the public sector to transfer outlay from times when public and private outlay together are larger to times when they are smaller in some conditions entails transferring it from times when outlay in the public sector is larger to times when it is smaller; in other conditions, transferring it from times when outlay in that sector is smaller to times when it is larger. Thus it may entail, according to circumstances, either stabilising or destabilising outlay in the public sector.[2] In the former event, unless in the absence of transfers there would be some unfilled vacancies even at the low level of the public sector's outlay, the transfers must make that sector's wages bill, and, consequently, the aggregate wages bill, steadier; and this to a larger extent the larger are the transfers — subject, of course,

[1] Cf. *post*, Chapter V, §§ 5-7.

[2] The fact that action by the public sector directed towards stabilising aggregate outlay may entail destabilising its own outlay, of course, implies that action directed towards stabilising its own outlay may destabilise aggregate outlay. When it does in fact do this, the aggregate wages bill is likely to be steadied if labour is perfectly immobile, but to be unsteadied if it is perfectly mobile.

to c being less than a. In the latter event opposite consequences will follow, and the aggregate wages bill will be rendered less steady. Since in practice, as we shall see presently, the outlays of the public and the private sectors usually vary in the same sense, the former event is the more likely.

§ 10. If labour is perfectly mobile between the two sectors it is impossible for unfilled vacancies to exist in one at the same time that unemployment exists in the other ; for, if there were any unfilled vacancies, unemployed men would at once occupy them. We are thus in effect concerned with a single unified sector. Unless over this field even at the low point of aggregate outlay there are some unfilled vacancies — a situation which we may regard for all practical purposes as impossible — transfers of outlay by the controllers of the public sector from good times (in respect of the field as a whole) to bad are bound to render the aggregate wages bill steadier — irrespective of whether the wages bill of the public sector is rendered steadier or less steady.

§ 11. If labour is neither perfectly immobile nor perfectly mobile, it is evidently more likely to have this effect the more mobile labour is. Hence anything, such as the development of a national system of employment exchanges or a growth in the number of jobs common to many industries, which makes in a general way for improved mobility, whether between places or between trades, increases the likelihood that transfers of outlay by public authorities designed to make aggregate outlay steadier will also make the aggregate money wages bill steadier ; and so strengthens the case for such transfers. This can be further strengthened if the authorities entrusted with the management of national and local spending do not merely take account of the general percentage of unemployment, but also, in allocating such transfers as they decide to make, have regard to the detailed figures of individual industries and places.

§ 12. There is, however, a complication. So far we have supposed labour to be homogeneous, so that there can be no question of different parts of it enjoying different degrees of mobility. In fact it is not homogeneous. It may be more mobile between some pairs of centres affected by the public and the private sectors of demand respectively than it is between other pairs. Thus the public sector may demand labour for building roads or schools. Labour may be highly mobile between the centres affected by that demand and neighbouring centres engaged in building and navvying work for private industry, but not at all mobile between these centres and others, whether neighbouring or remote, devoted to coal-mining or engineering. Again, labour may be highly mobile between forestry work for private persons and for the State, and not at all between State forests and businesses employing artisans and mechanics.[1] All this does not, however, invalidate the broad conclusion reached in the last section.

§ 13. On the lines of § 5 it can be shown that transfers in the public sector from times that in both the public and private sectors together are good to times that are bad, of a sort that steady the aggregate wages bill, in some circumstances leave the average size of that bill unaffected ; in others increase it : they do not in any case decrease it. Since, however, as we saw in Chapter II, the average level of the wages bill is, in general, without long-run significance for employment, because money wage rates adjust themselves to it, this distinction is not important for our purpose.

[1] The experience of Belgium seems to show that forest work is well adapted to give winter employment to *unskilled* workmen engaged in the building trade during the rest of the year. (Cf. Rowntree, *Land and Labour*, p. 507.)

CHAPTER V

AGGREGATE MONEY OUTLAY IN RELATION TO PUBLIC FINANCE OPERATIONS

§ 1. In the course of the three preceding chapters we have studied the relations of employment and unemployment to movements in the money wages bill; the relation of movements in that bill to movements in aggregate money outlay on the assumption that money wage rates are held steady; and the implications of the fact that in actual life, when movements in the money wages bill induce responsive movements in the average rate of money wages, this in turn sets up a reflex effect on the money wages bill itself. The next step is to inquire whether and how operations of public finance — the raising and spending of tax or loan revenue — can modify aggregate money outlay in the first instance; prior, that is to say, to any reflex influences set up in it by induced changes in the money rate of wages.

§ 2. This inquiry is best approached by way of negating a negation. That it is possible for public authorities to affect the size of aggregate money outlay in any period by Public Finance operations will seem to many too plain for argument. None the less, it has sometimes been maintained that it is beyond their power to do this, that money income will be what it will be irrespective of them, and that not merely on the average of a long period, but even from day to day. A very clear-cut expression of this thesis may be found in the report of the Transvaal Indigency Commission of 1908: "Wealth is the only source from which wages are paid, and the State must levy taxation (or raise loans) in order to pay wages to its workmen. When, therefore, a government gives work to the unemployed it is simply transferring wage-giving power from the individual to itself. It is diminishing employment with one hand, while it increases it with the other. It takes work from people employed by private individuals and gives it to people selected by the state." [1] Similar sentiments

[1] *Report of the Transvaal Indigency Commission*, p. 129.

have often been expressed in this country in discussions about the effect on employment of policies of public works designed to alleviate industrial depressions. During the great slump of 1930 the opinion that for public authorities to increase their money outlay always and necessarily entails other people decreasing theirs to a corresponding degree even came to be labelled "The Treasury View", though it is inconceivable that in this extreme form that opinion was ever in fact entertained by the highly competent civil servants at Whitehall. The whole matter is, however, less simple than it seems to be at first sight.

§ 3. It is possible to imagine an arrangement under which the banking system, working through the discount rate and open market operations, holds aggregate money outlay rigidly fixed; though, in order to accomplish that, it would need on occasion to establish substantial *negative* rates of interest! With an arrangement of this kind no operations of public finance, and equally no operations undertaken by private industrialists, could affect the size of aggregate money income at any time in any degree. That is to say, the so-called Treasury View in its extremest form would be valid. But, of course, no actual monetary and banking system is of this kind. In this country, for example, it is well known that, when private industrialists think prospects are good, they tend at once to turn over their existing balances more rapidly — or, if we prefer it, to move their money out of passive or savings deposits into active deposits — and also to provide themselves with more balances by borrowing from the banks. They thus bring into play two influences, both of which promote an increase in aggregate money income. Similarly, when private industrialists think that prospects are black, they so act as to promote a decrease in aggregate money income. On the face of things it seems plain that public authorities, through operations of a like kind in respect of their own balances, must be able to influence aggregate money income in a like manner. No doubt, when private persons enjoying given incomes decide to expand their outlays above what they have been hitherto, they do so for different reasons from those that influence governments. They act, in general, from the profit motive, whereas the motives of governments may be of other and much larger scope. There is nothing to prevent them from undertaking, in the interests of employment, investments whose yield is expected to be nil or even negative. But the fact that the motives behind decisions may be different is immaterial to the mechanism through which decisions, once taken, work themselves out and the consequences to which they lead. This is a sufficient answer to the so-called Treasury View. But the problem to which that view offers a crude and incorrect answer calls for further analysis. To that end I shall distinguish and discuss separately five principal types of public finance operation.

§ 4. Suppose first that the public authorities borrow money and so are enabled to expand their expenditure in securing the production of investment goods — durable additions to the stock of capital. The following six paragraphs are concerned with that case.

§ 5. A consideration that immediately presents itself has to do with the character of the public authorities' investment. In so far as they devote their additional outlays to types of investment whose future output will compete with the output of instrumental goods in which private persons are accustomed to invest, a direct check will be imposed on private investment. For example, in a country where house-building is predominantly undertaken by private enterprise, public authorities cannot build houses without checking that type of private investment; the extent of the check being greater, the less elastic is the general demand for new houses to hire. This is a chief reason why "public works" undertaken to help employment are usually restricted to occupations such as road-making, in which private persons do not normally engage, and not extended to the building of steel mills or cotton mills. Of course, in a fully socialist community, in which no investment was made by private persons, there would be no point in this distinction: for the whole of the additional investment made at any time by public authorities would be net additional investment. For this country, however, the point is an important one. An expansion of S in the public authorities' investments, even if the rate of interest is not affected at all, does not entail an expansion of the same size in aggregate investment except when it is entirely non-competitive. Otherwise it entails one of, say, mS; where m is less than unity and approaches to nothing as the elasticity of demand for the things which the investment produces approaches to nothing.

§ 6. Next we must take account of possible reactions on private investment that may take place even though the addition to public investment is wholly non-competitive. Such reactions may take place by way of the rate of interest. Thus, if ordinary economic motives and processes are allowed free play, an expansion of investment by public authorities, requiring, as it does, the use of money, will be associated, except in periods of extreme depression, with a tendency for the rate of interest to rise ; and this will check borrowing for investment, and so investment itself, by private persons, not indeed to an equivalent, but to some extent. In a country tied to the rest of the world by a rigid international gold standard the tendency of interest to rise might — not necessarily would — be further stimulated through the enlarged money incomes pushing up prices, with the result that imports expanded relatively to exports and either gold was drained away or the Central Bank took action, via discount and open market dealing, to prevent that from happening. On the other hand, in a country whose money is autonomous the government is free to maintain a policy of cheap money, creating whatever amount of new currency for under-pinning bank credits is required for that purpose. In that case the rate of interest is not affected and no reaction on private investment is set up by way of it.

§ 7. There is a further important consideration bearing on the relation between expansions in public investment financed by borrowing and in total investment. In certain circumstances when public investment is expanded psychological reactions may be set up among private industrialists in such wise that, in the common phrase, " confidence is undermined ". On occasions the risk of this may be very serious. Thus in the great depression of 1930–31 there was widespread alarm about the state of British Government finance, wild talk of national bankruptcy, and, after the gold standard had been abandoned, widespread uncertainty about the future status and purchasing power of the pound sterling. In these conditions it may well have been that any attempt on the part of the public authorities to expand public expenditure with a view to offsetting the contraction of private expenditure would have made things worse; and, paradoxical though this may sound, that the most effective action open to the State for stimulating aggregate money demand was rigorously to cut its own demand down, and generally to promote, as it did, a strict economy campaign among all public authorities. It is fashionable nowadays to condemn that campaign out of hand as a mere stupidity. There is no warrant for this; though there is, in my opinion, strong ground for holding that, after the shock to confidence associated with the abandonment of the gold standard had been absorbed, this campaign, having done its work, should have been closed down and the engines reversed much sooner than in fact they were. In contrast with these negative psychological reactions, in other circumstances there may result from expansions in public investment positive psychological reactions. Instead of affecting business confidence adversely, such expansions may have the opposite effect, stimulate business confidence and act as an effective pump primer. To discriminate between these two sorts of circumstance, though easy in the abstract, must often, in the varied and varying situations of actual life, be a very difficult task.

§ 8. But this is not the end of the story. Let us suppose that the processes we have been considering have worked themselves out and there has emerged from them a certain net expansion in investment expenditure, the primary effect on aggregate money income of the action taken by the public authorities. There are still to be considered possible reactions on the outlay of private persons on consumption goods. This is obviously a very important matter; for, if these were negative and sufficiently great, the Treasury View would be right after all. In § 3 we have already seen reason to believe that, with a normal type of banking and monetary system, they will not at all events be negative enough for that. For a part of the extra investment expenditure will be financed, not by transfers from consumption expenditure, but by shifting money from passive to active balances and the creation, for use in active balances, of new money. If the government prevents the rate of interest from rising in the manner described in § 6, there is no reason for *any* check in expenditure on consumption, and the whole will be so financed.

§ 9. We need not, however stop here. Not only is it

extremely unlikely that there will be a negative reaction on consumers' expenditure large enough to offset a *once-for-all* expansion in investment expenditure. It is, moreover, to be expected that, with a *continuing* higher level of investment expenditure, there will be associated a secondary continuing higher level of consumers' expenditure. This cannot, indeed, be demonstrated, as is sometimes attempted, by saying that the extra men called into work in the investment industries will want to spend their income and, by doing so, will generate employment for other people. For, if at the same time that a thousand men are called into employment in the investment industries a thousand are thrown out of work in the consumption industries, the damage done to employment elsewhere by that will offset the benefit resulting from the expenditure of the new men in the investment industries. It is necessary to assume that men will not be thrown out of work in the consumption industries in order that the argument may be legitimately employed. In other words, we have to use our conclusion as a premise for the proof of it! There is, however, a different method of attack, which is not thus circular. When, through a decision of the public authorities, a net increase in the rate of investment is brought about, this entails that more funds for it have to be supplied. But this will only be done if the rate of interest rises, or if aggregate real income, and so aggregate employment, increases, or if both these things happen. With a normal banking and monetary system the rate of interest will rise to some (probably) slight extent. This entails that people will find advantage in having less money in passive as compared with active balances, which entails that aggregate money income rises. With a banking and monetary policy hinged on cheap money and so regulated that, in order to prevent interest from rising, the banks will always create whatever new money is required for that purpose, real income has to be enlarged; since otherwise the funds for additional investment which we have supposed to take place would not be forthcoming. But extra real income implies more employment and so, with money wage rates fixed, in general a larger money income. Thus in any event aggregate money income is not only increased, but is increased by more than the addition made to the part of it derived from investment. In the language which is now fashionable among some economists, not only is the relevant multiplier positive, but it is greater than unity.[1]

§ 10. The broad conclusion to which the analysis of the preceding five paragraphs points is clearly that, in general, investments by public authorities financed by loans carry with them increases in aggregate money outlay.

§ 11. Let us now suppose, secondly, that money borrowed by public authorities is transferred by them to poor persons, for example the beneficiaries of State-aided unemployment insurance. The bulk of this money is pretty sure to be expended on the purchase of consumption goods, and so indirectly in creating money income for the producers of those goods. Though some of the borrowed money may have come out of what would have been private investment and some out of what would have been outlay by private persons (other than the recipients of the State grants) on consumption goods, the primary effect of this public finance operation is bound, for the reasons given in § 3, namely that a part of the loans to government will be made by shifts of money from passive to active balances and the creation of new bank money, to be an increase in aggregate money outlay. All we have to determine, therefore, is the character of the secondary effects that follow from a larger proportion of aggregate purchasing power [2] coming to be held by relatively poor persons. It is sometimes argued in very crude terms that this secondary effect must entail an expansion in aggregate money outlay, because poor people may be expected to spend a larger proportion of their income than rich people, and spending generates income whereas saving does not. This will not do. Nothing is gained for aggregate money income if a poor man spends £100 on food and clothes instead of a rich man saving and investing it in building a garage. But, though this reasoning fails, the conclusion to which it points is, nevertheless, correct. The larger the proportion of any given real income that is in the hands of poor persons, the less, in all probability, will be offered against a given prospective return from investment. But, if the supply schedule of resources for investment is

[1] For a more adequate discussion of these matters compare my *Employment and Equilibrium*, part iii.

[2] I use this term to avoid an awkwardness arising from the fact that the receipts of poor persons from government transfers are not technically income.

raised while the openings for them are unchanged, a tendency must be set up towards a rise either in the rate of interest or in aggregate real income or in both. This means, in the manner indicated in § 9, that aggregate money income tends to be pushed up. Thus, as with public borrowing for investment, not only is the primary effect favourable to aggregate money income, but it is reinforced and strengthened by a secondary effect.

§ 12. It will be observed that all the proceedings described so far entail that the public authorities borrow money. In so far as they are operated by the Central Government under the aegis of the Budget, they thus involve also "budgeting for deficits": so that it is incorrect to speak, as is sometimes done, of public works outlay and deficit budgeting as *alternative* policies. There is in this country a traditional objection to budgeting for deficits in normal peace-time conditions except when some special enterprise for which loan finance is obviously appropriate, such as the rebuilding of the fleet, has to be undertaken. But this tradition does not affect expenditure by local authorities; and, as regards the central authority, it is easily got round by operating on funds held outside the Budget, *e.g.* by reducing the employers' contribution to the Unemployment Insurance Fund or allowing that Fund itself to borrow. Even import taxes can be kept outside the Budget if politicians so choose; witness the pre-war levy — it was not, of course, a tax! — on imported wheat. These are politicians' devices and make no difference to the essential facts.

§ 13. Next and thirdly we come to public finance operations in which the authorities raise money, not by loans, but by taxes, and, having done so, expend that money on public works of a sort that do not compete with private investment. Two limiting situations suggest themselves. At the one extreme we might suppose that the money raised in taxes and invested by the public authority is exactly equal to the cut in expenditure on investment and consumption together which the persons paying the taxes are led by them to make. At the other extreme we might suppose that these persons raise the money for taxes by reducing personal outlay, by drawing money out of passive deposits and by calling upon new creations of bank money in exactly the same degree in which these sources would have been drawn upon had the public authorities raised an equal amount of money by borrowing instead of by taxation. That the former limiting situation will not manifest itself can be shown as follows. It is certain that not all the money collected for the government's public investment will come out of what would have been private investment. This being so, aggregate investment must be increased. But, as was shown in § 3, when investment is increased (by influences on the demand side) aggregate money outlay will also be increased. This rules out the former limiting situation. The other limiting situation is equally certain in practice not to manifest itself. For, while the government has full freedom to borrow new money from the banks, and private persons desiring to lend to the government can also do this to some extent by offering as collateral the government securities purchased with the loans, they will often be unwilling and more often still unable to borrow from banks to meet tax demands. The inference is that under the tax method aggregate money income will be increased to some extent, but, to a substantially less extent than it would be for equivalent government expenditures under the loan method.

§ 14. Very similar consequences will follow — this is my fourth head — should public authorities raise money by taxation and transfer it to relatively poor people.

If the people to whom transfers are made are not relatively poor, but of substantially equal wealth with those from whom they are made, no significant reaction on aggregate money outlay can be looked for in a general way.[1] No doubt, if the people *to* whom transfers are made are accustomed to hold larger real balances in the form of money relatively to their real incomes than the people *from* whom they are made, the transfers will have the effect of reducing active and increasing passive deposits, or, in other words, of reducing the income velocity of money; so that aggregate money outlay is contracted. If, on the other hand, the people from whom the transfers are made are more attached to real balances in the form of money, aggregate money outlay will be expanded. But, if the two sets of people are initially of similar wealth,

[1] It will be understood that money outlay here is equivalent to money income as defined in Chapter I, § 3. The transfer payments themselves, *e.g.* pensions or unemployment pay, are not money income. If they were counted the enlargement would appear much bigger; but to count them would be inconsistent with the usage here followed.

neither group is likely to be more attached to real balances in the form of money than the other ; so that neither type of reaction is more likely than the other ; and neither on any substantial scale is likely at all.

But when the transfer is from richer to poorer people things work out differently. Such a transfer tends to augment aggregate money income for the reasons given in § 11 in connection with the secondary reaction there discussed. Nor is this all. Even if poor people were prepared to save the same proportion of their incomes as rich, transfers to them would still tend to make aggregate money income larger. For, partly because for the most part their incomes are paid out to them at shorter intervals, they normally hold smaller real balances in the form of money relatively to their incomes (plus any Government grants they may receive) than richer people. It follows that a redistribution of income favouring the poor at the expense of the rich would lead, apart altogether from the reaction described a moment ago, to a lowering of the average amount of real balances held in the form of money, that is, to an increase in the income velocity of money ; with the result that aggregate money outlay will be made larger. For reasons similar to those set out in § 13, with a given volume of transfer to poor persons the effect on aggregate money income will be smaller when the money for the transfers is raised by taxes than when it is raised by loans.

§ 15. Next, as our fifth main problem, we have to consider the policy of taking government expenditures of all kinds as given, but financing them out of loans instead of out of taxes, thus budgeting for a deficit. It is obvious that the difference made to aggregate money income by the choice between financing so much *existing* expenditure out of loans or out of taxes must be similar in character to that made by the choice between financing so much *additional* expenditure in the one or the other of these ways. Thus what is relevant has already been said in §§ 13-14, where the comparative effects of financing additional expenditure for investment and for transfers to poor persons out of taxes and out of loans were commented on. In accordance with what was there said we conclude that the above policy must, in general, make for an enlargement in aggregate money income. Our previous discussion shows further that this tendency will be stronger the more the tax relief benefits poor persons as compared with rich.

§ 16. Attention has now to be called to a very important consideration of a general character. Where one country has trading relations with the rest of the world expenditure in it does not necessarily generate, as in an isolated community it must do, equivalent incomes *at home*. If the one country undertakes an expansionist policy leading to improved employment, its people are sure to want to buy more imported goods. This reaction is likely to be specially important for England, whose dependence on foreign trade is exceptionally large. If foreign countries are also undertaking expansionist policies at the same time, this will lead to their wanting to buy more imported goods also ; so that the relation between imports and exports of the one country — say England — need not be disturbed. But, if England undertakes an expansionist policy and other countries do not, the stimulus to our imports will not be offset by a corresponding stimulus to our exports. If and for so long as foreigners are prepared to buy securities from us to fill the gap, this does not, for the time being, matter. But it is not likely that the whole of the gap can, or at all events will, be filled in this way. Consequently, some expenditure which would otherwise have constituted home outlay will be absorbed in creating passive balances held here by foreigners ; and a continuing downward drag on our home outlay income is set up. This tendency may be offset, if no overt action is taken, by a fall in the exchange rate between our money and foreign money, which will encourage exports and discourage imports ; or it may be corrected by State action designed to increase exports, *e.g.* through export bounties, or to check imports, *e.g.* through tariffs or quotas. But, so far as it is not offset or corrected, its existence entails that, in order to bring about a given expansion in aggregate money outlay, the expansion in government outlay on investment or on transfers to poor persons, whether financed out of loans or out of taxes, will have to be larger than would have been necessary otherwise. Indeed, if the offsetting influence of a drop in the exchange rate is barred by the rules of an international gold standard, it may in some circumstances be beyond the power of a government, by any practicable expansion of its expenditure, to secure a significant increase in aggregate money outlay at home.

§ 17. Finally, there is a no less important consideration of opposite tendency. In all the various cases discussed in this chapter, if and in so far as the action of public authorities does lead, in spite of the foreign balance difficulty, to an increase in aggregate money income, substantial cumulative reactions of a positive kind are set up. To begin with, the increase in money income entails that, with any given set of tax rates, the government's own money revenue is expanded. Consequently, in order to accomplish a given amount of public investment or of transfer, it does not need to borrow or to raise by new taxes an equivalent amount, but a smaller amount of new money. This is true even if money wage rates are contemporaneously expanded to such an extent that employment is not improved. But, further, if, as is practically certain to happen, employment is improved and if, as in this country, there exists a system of unemployment insurance to which the State contributes, a second favourable reaction is brought about. Unemployment being reduced, the government does not need to contribute so much toward unemployment benefit, and *pro tanto* the amount of loans or of taxes that it has to raise is lessened. Thus a public finance operation that succeeds in any degree in increasing aggregate money income and alleviating unemployment, so to speak, feeds upon itself. Each man thrown against the enemy comes back with a prisoner or part of a prisoner, who thereupon joins him in the attack. This means that, if the command desires the attack to be delivered by a thousand men, it need not to that end itself throw in so large a number. How large a number will be needed depends on the detailed character of the situation. Any estimate of it would be largely guesswork. Nevertheless, in the existing circumstances of this country, we may be fairly sure that, to enable the public authorities to disburse any assigned sum for purposes of the kind we are contemplating, loans or new taxes to an amount *substantially* less than that sum will suffice.

CHAPTER VI

THE PRINCIPAL WAYS IN WHICH PUBLIC AUTHORITIES MAY AFFECT AGGREGATE MONEY OUTLAY IN THE INTEREST OF EMPLOYMENT

§ 1. HAVING established in the last chapter that public authorities have the power to modify the size of aggregate money income, not merely through one but through several alternative types of public finance operation, we have now to distinguish the principal ways in which they may engage this power in the interest of employment. As we have seen, modifying aggregate money outlay in general entails — apart from obstacles to labour mobility and possible reactions on the foreign balance — modifying the money wages bill in the same sense. Public authorities, therefore, will presumably seek to operate on aggregate money income so as to impress upon it conditions and movements such that the parallel states and movements induced in the money wages bill will be of a kind favourable to employment.

§ 2. In theory two main types of operation may be distinguished : (1) operations that in the first instance simply steady money income, and (2) operations that lift it to a level higher than that at which it would have stood apart from intervention by the public authorities. While, however, certain sorts of public operations affect only the stability of the money wages bill, it is unlikely that any will affect only its average level, since there is a natural tendency for public authorities to take more emphatic ameliorative action in bad times than in good. Consequently, in practice the convenient distinction is not between steadying operations and lifting operations, but between operations that are only steadying and operations that are both steadying and lifting.

§ 3. It is evident that operations directed simply to switch the expenditure of public authorities from good times to bad without affecting their aggregate amount, and also operations which consist in the authorities purchasing goods for stock in bad times and selling them out of stock in good, fall within the former of these two divisions. So also do the policy adumbrated in the White Paper on Employment for varying the contributions of employers and employed towards the Unemployment Insurance Fund between good times and bad, and the policy of budgeting for deficits on given government expenditures in bad times and for equivalent surpluses in good times. The two latter policies, as has already been hinted,[1] are identical in principle and would be identical in form if the contributions of employers and employed, instead of being called contributions and paid into the insurance fund, were called taxes and paid into the revenue account. In the three following chapters brief descriptions will be given of these policies.

§ 4. On the other hand such operations as expansions in public expenditure, whether financed out of loans or out of taxes, in bad times above what would have been undertaken if the public authorities had had no regard for employment, unaccompanied by contractions below what would in that case have been undertaken in good times, must, besides steadying aggregate money income, also raise its average level. Operations of this type were presumably in the mind of the authors of the White Paper on Employment Policy (1944) when they envisaged public opinion being "brought to the view that periods of recession provide an opportunity to improve the permanent equipment of society by the provision of better housing, public buildings, means of communication, power and water supply, etc.".[2] I shall not illustrate this type of policy in detail; for everything relevant to it can be gathered from what was said in Chapter V. I shall, however, devote Chapter X to a brief account of another policy similar in general effect, namely the granting of subsidies on wages in bad times unaccompanied by any countervailing action in good times.

[1] Compare *ante*, Chapter V, § 12. [2] *Loc. cit.* para. 66.

CHAPTER VII

THE TIMING OF OUTLAYS BY PUBLIC AUTHORITIES[1]

§ 1. In this chapter we are concerned with a stabilising device which has a considerable history. This consists in switching elements of public capital expenditure, sometimes expenditures financed by taxes, more usually expenditures financed by loans, but in any case financed in the same way whether switched or not, which would normally have been undertaken in good times, to bad times. Public authorities are accustomed on occasions to give large orders for goods, which imply large orders on the part of the manufacturers of these goods for labour wherewith to make them. From the present point of view it does not matter whether the orders are given to private concerns or to productive establishments belonging to the government departments that need the goods. In either case equally there is scope for a transfer of orders from good times to bad, and a consequential corresponding transfer of demand for labour as manifested in the money wages bill. Boards of Guardians order so much stores, the Board of Admiralty so many ships, municipalities so many school and other buildings and so much repair work on roads; and there is no rigid compulsion on them to order these things at a particular instant. In actual fact it usually happens that, when industry in general is depressed — and at such times most individual industries are depressed too — the demand of public authorities is low, and in converse circumstances high. "The reasons for this are easy to tell. Public revenue faithfully follows the fluctuations in the economic activity of the country; in times of crisis it tends to diminish. In order to meet the resultant deficit, the Administration, for prudential reasons, cuts down expenditure as far as possible, and, consequently, postpones all work that does not seem absolutely indispensable. With the resumption of business, the execution of many orders, which it had been thought could be postponed without inconvenience, becomes urgent.

[1] Portions of this chapter are taken from my *Industrial Fluctuations*, part ii, chap. xiv.

Economic equipment, which had seemed sufficient for the needs of commerce and industry in a period of calm, proves inadequate, and the deficiency must be remedied with all speed. On the other hand, the surplus values obtained at the same time in receipts encourage the administrative authorities to set going less urgent works."[1] It is not necessary, however, that the orders of public authorities should be operated in this way. A policy designed in the interest of stability can, if desired, be adopted.

§ 2. Such a policy was embodied in a circular concerning the Organisation of the Provision of Employment, issued by the Prussian Minister of Commerce in 1904, and quoted in Schloss's Report on foreign methods of dealing with the unemployed. The circular runs: "We further request you to have the goodness to direct your attention to those measures which are calculated to prevent the occurrence of want of work on a wide scale or to mitigate its effects when it is unavoidable. Not only the State, but also the provinces, districts and communes, in their capacity as employers, are bound to do their utmost to counteract the evil in question by paying general and methodical attention to the suitable distribution and regulation of the works to be carried out for their account. In almost every industrial establishment of importance there are tasks which do not absolutely need to be performed at a fixed time; just so in every state and communal administration there are works for the allotment of which the time may, within certain limits, be freely chosen according to circumstances. If all public administrations, in making their arrangements, would take timely care to choose for such works times in which want of employment is to be expected — if, especially, works in which unemployed people of all kinds, including, in particular, unskilled labourers, can be made use of, were reserved for such times of threatening want of employment as have almost regularly recurred of late in winter in the larger towns and industrial centres — the real occurrence of widespread want of employment could certainly be prevented in many cases and serious distress warded off."[2] The same policy in a more restricted form, was

[1] R. Viviani, quoted in the *Report of the International Labour Office on Remedies for Unemployment*, 1922, p. 117.

[2] *Report on Agencies and Methods for Dealing with Unemployment in Foreign Countries*, p. 108.

embodied in the proposal of the Majority of the Poor Law Commission concerning irregular municipal work. They wrote: "So far as it may be inevitable to employ occasionally other than their own regular workers, or to place contracts, we think that it may be desirable for public authorities to arrange such irregular work so that, if possible, it comes upon the labour market at a time when ordinary regular work is slack. This point was well put by Professor Chapman, who suggested that, so far as the public authorities' demand for labour fluctuates, it is desirable to liberate such demand from the influences of good and bad trade and seasonality, and then deliberately to attempt to make it vary inversely with the demand in the open market."[1] A policy on similar lines won the approval of the Royal Commissioners on Afforestation. They were concerned to satisfy themselves that "that part of sylvicultural work which requires most labour, namely, the establishment of the forest, is of a sufficiently flexible character to be capable of being pushed on when labour is abundant, and suspended when labour is scarce";[2] and they advised that it should in fact be pushed on, and suspended, on these principles.

§ 3. The same point of view, in respect of a much more extended field, was adopted by the Minority of the Royal Commission on the Poor Law. They wrote: "We think that there can be no doubt that, out of the 150 millions sterling annually expended by the National and Local Authorities on works and services, it would be possible to earmark at least four millions a year as not to be undertaken equally, year by year, as a matter of course; but to be undertaken, out of loans, on a ten years' programme, at unequal annual rates, to the extent even of ten or fifteen millions in a single year, at those periods when the National Labour Exchange reported that the number of able-bodied applicants, for whom no places could be found anywhere within the United Kingdom, was rising above the normal level. When this report was made by the Minister responsible for the National Labour Exchange — whenever, for instance, the Percentage Unemployment Index, as now calculated, rose above four — the various

[1] *Report of the Royal Commission on the Poor Law*, p. 41.
[2] *Report of Royal Commission on Coast Erosion and Afforestation*, vol. ii, p. 13.

Government departments would recur to their ten years' programme of capital outlay ; the Admiralty would put in hand a special battleship and augment its stock of guns and projectiles ; the War Office would give orders for some of the additional barracks that are always being needed, and would further replenish its multifarious stores ; the Office of Works would get on more quickly with its perpetual task of erecting new post offices and other Government buildings and of renewing the worn-out furniture ; the Post Office would proceed at three or four times its accustomed rate with the extension of the telegraph and telephone to every village in the kingdom ; even the Stationery Office would get on two or three times as fast as usual with the printing of the volumes of the Historical Manuscripts Commission and the publication of the national archives. But much more could be done. It is plain that many millions have to be spent in the next few decades in rebuilding the worst of the elementary schools, greatly adding to the number of the secondary schools, multiplying the technical institutes and training colleges, and doubling and trebling the accommodation and equipment of our fifteen universities. All this building and furnishing work, on which alone we might usefully spend the forty millions per decade that are in question, is not in fact, and need not be for efficiency, done in equal annual instalments. There might well be a ten years' programme of capital grants-in-aid of the local expenditure on educational buildings and equipment. It requires only the stimulus of these grants-in-aid, made at the periods when the Minister in charge of the National Labour Exchange reports that the index number of unemployment has reached the warning point, for these works to be put in hand by the local Education Authorities all over the kingdom to exactly the extent that the situation demands. At the same time the Local Authorities could be incited to undertake their ordinary municipal undertakings of a capital nature, whether tramways or waterworks, public baths or electric power stations, artisans' dwellings or town halls, drainage works or street improvements, to a greater extent in the years of slackness than in the years of good trade. This, indeed, they are already tending to do ; and to the great development of municipal enterprise in this direction, setting up a small ebb and flow of its own to some extent counteracting the flow and ebb of private industry, we are inclined to attribute the fact that the cyclical depressions of the last twenty years have been less severely felt in the United Kingdom than were those of 1878–9 and of 1839–42." [1] Twenty years ago an estimate of the scale of adjustment then needed *on the assumption that the rates of aggregate money income and aggregate money wages bill remain fixed*, was made by Dr. Bowley as follows : " The wage bill for 1911 was computed to be about £800 million. A typical cycle may be thus represented, the first year being one of maximum employment :

	Ten Successive Years									
Unemployed (per cent) . .	$2\frac{1}{2}$	$3\frac{1}{2}$	$4\frac{1}{2}$	$5\frac{1}{2}$	$6\frac{1}{2}$	$7\frac{1}{2}$	$6\frac{1}{2}$	$5\frac{1}{2}$	$4\frac{1}{2}$	$3\frac{1}{2}$
Relation to average (per cent) .	$-2\frac{1}{2}$	$-1\frac{1}{2}$	$-\frac{1}{2}$	$+\frac{1}{2}$	$+1\frac{1}{2}$	$+2\frac{1}{2}$	$+1\frac{1}{2}$	$+\frac{1}{2}$	$-\frac{1}{2}$	$-1\frac{1}{2}$
Variation of wage bill (million sterling) .	+20	+12	+4	−4	−12	−20	−12	−4	+4	+12

In public expenditure we may perhaps take wages to be 80 per cent of the whole cost. On these figures the wave of unemployment would be levelled to a uniform 5 per cent if a total of £36 million wages (£45 million expenditure) were held over during the first three years, the average period of postponement being four years ; and if a total of £16 million wages (£20 million expenditure) were advanced in the seventh and eighth years ; the average period of advancement being two and a half years. . . . At present the employable population is about 8 per cent more than in 1911 and weekly wage rates about 70 per cent more. The expenditure to be postponed in the first three years would now be 81 million pounds and that advanced in the seventh and eighth years 37 million pounds." [2] Obviously, with the higher levels of money incomes and of prices that are current now and may be looked for henceforward, higher figures would have to be substituted for these. But the principle remains the same.

§ 4. In a country organised as England is, the dominant part of those sorts of public expenditure that might be made available for transfer from good times to bad is in the hands of *local* authorities. Such authorities, with their system of

[1] *Royal Commission on the Poor Laws*, Minority Report, p. 1196.

[2] *Is Unemployment Inevitable ?* 1924, pp. 367-8.

committees in control of different departments of work, with their frequent changes and the constant fear of the ratepayers before them — all of which things make a well-thought-out general financial policy very difficult — have seldom of themselves the power or the will to undertake a compensating policy in employment. Hence we may conclude, with Dr. Bowley, "that the only possible way of influencing the amount of employment provided by local authorities, without whose co-operation the policy of regularisation can only be partly successful, is by exercise by the Central Government of its powers of compulsion, of making or withholding grants, of granting or refusing power to borrow and, above all, of providing capital on easy terms at times when it is desirable on national grounds that public works should be set in hand ".[1] During the difficult period of the 1920–21 post-war slump the Central Government exercised its power of stimulus through grants-in-aid in very considerable measure.[2] An arrangement looking to regular and continuous action on these lines had already, in 1909, been embodied in the Development and Road Fund Act, where it is provided that parliamentary grants to local authorities "must be expended, bearing in mind the general state and prospects of employment ". When, therefore, the 1944 White Paper urges that "public investment, both in timing and in volume, must be carefully planned to offset unavoidable fluctuations in private investment ",[3] it is treading, at all events as regards timing, upon ground that was prepared long ago.

§ 5. This policy cannot, indeed, be pressed without limit. For the time incidence of a large part of public capital expenditure can only be adjusted on these lines at a prohibitive cost in inconvenience or in risk. A particular town, for example, may be quite uncertain now whether it will want more school buildings ten years hence ; and ten years hence, when it does want them, it cannot without grave dereliction of duty further postpone the satisfaction of its needs. The central government again cannot foresee exactly its future requirement of ships and guns : it will not care to anticipate

[1] *Is Unemployment Inevitable?* 1924, p. 376.

[2] For a summary of what was done, cf. Morley, *Unemployment Relief in Great Britain*, pp. 189-91.

[3] White Paper on Unemployment Policy, p. 18, § 48(c).

these for fear of finding itself saddled with obsolete types; and when the requirement becomes urgent it will not dare to delay. Yet again when a war threatens there can be no question of allowing care for steadiness of industry to affect the time at which the fighting services order necessary materials. There are, however, other parts of public capital expenditure in regard to which it makes very little difference either to convenience or to cost at what time within a year or two the requirements of government authorities are satisfied, and in these conditions the obstacles to transferring investment expenditure from good times to bad are easily overcome. Moreover, it must be borne in mind, transfers of outlay aimed at stabilisation need not be transfers *backwards*. It is also open to public authorities to *put forward* the construction of capital works that would normally be undertaken at a later date.

CHAPTER VIII

GOVERNMENT PURCHASES FOR STOCK IN BAD TIMES AND SALES OUT OF STOCK IN GOOD TIMES

THE policy whose nature is roughly indicated by the title of this chapter, is of the same general character as that discussed in the last. By means of it a government, if it so desires, can do something towards equalising aggregate money outlay and the aggregate wages bill over time. I shall not analyse this type of policy elaborately, for most of what is relevant has already been said. A few comments may, however, be made on it from the standpoint of practice. The policy is clearly out of the question as regards goods which are perishable or subject to sudden changes of fashion, but it is *prima facie* defensible as regards other sorts of goods. Owing to the long period covered by cyclical industrial fluctuations, it must, however, always prove very expensive. Apart from anything else, with interest at 5 per cent, to hold anything for four years involves a cost of 21½ per cent — is equivalent, that is to say, to selling immediately at a reduction of that amount. Moreover, in a period of that length " styles will change and specifications alter, so that few goods are durable in the sense of holding their economic value through the changing phases of boom and depression ".[1] This is, of course, especially true in a period of rapid mechanical improvement and invention. Nor do these considerations exhaust the case. There is a further very important practical consideration. For public authorities to regulate the time at which they give orders for things which they *must* order at some time, all that is needed is a decision as to method in a field they already occupy. But for these authorities to buy commodities in bad times and to sell them to the public in subsequent good times involves their entering into an entirely new field — the field of commercial speculation. To any such action on their part violent objection would be taken by all the dealers who already occupy part of that field. This would make successful action difficult. But, apart from this, even those

[1] J. M. Clark, *The Economics of Overhead Costs*, p. 164.

who agree that public authorities are adequately equipped to operate productive enterprises may well hesitate about the fitness of the central government — and no public authority except the central government could act here — for speculative commerce. The achievements of the various official purchasing authorities during the two wars do not throw much light upon this matter ; for the conditions prevailing then were entirely different from those that rule in normal times. This kind of action by public authorities is thus subject to greater difficulties than the more orthodox kinds sketched out in earlier sections. That, however, is a reason for studying such projects carefully, not for rejecting them out of hand.

CHAPTER IX

THE ADJUSTMENT OF INSURANCE CONTRIBUTIONS BETWEEN BAD TIMES AND GOOD

As was mentioned in Chapter VI, the White Paper on Employment Policy, 1944, contains a proposal calculated to make aggregate money income steadier without affecting its trend. The proposal, set out in paragraphs 68-9 of the White Paper, is as follows. The government " after examining a number of methods, favour the adoption, when settled conditions return, of a scheme for varying in sympathy with the state of employment the contribution to be paid by employers and employed under the proposed new system of social insurance. The standard rate of contribution would be assessed on the basis of a forecast of the average level of unemployment in such a way as to keep the social insurance fund in balance for a number of years. But the rate of contribution actually levied would exceed the standard rate at times when unemployment fell below the estimated average level and would be less than the standard rate when unemployment exceeded this average. . . . The effect of this scheme would be that, above a certain level of unemployment, a rise of two points in the unemployment percentage would decrease by an average of £500,000 a week the total of the social insurance contributions paid by workers in employment — apart from the corresponding reduction in the costs of employers. This would substantially augment the purchasing power in the hands of employed workers ; and the additional money thus left in the hands of many millions of people would help to maintain demand for consumers' goods, thereby offsetting at least in part the decline in the expenditure of those who had lost employment. This maintenance of purchasing power would reduce substantially the variations in total expenditure and employment." This plan, it should be observed in passing, does not *merely* enable the purchasing power available to private persons to be stepped up in bad times and stepped down to a corresponding degree in good. As regards the contributions of employers, it, in effect, accords to them in bad times a subsidy on wages and imposes on them in good times a corresponding tax on wages; with favourable consequences in steadying the wages bill and improving employment, over and above those claimed in the White Paper.[1] The principal feature of the plan is, however, to substitute in some measure borrowing for (virtual) taxation in bad times and (virtual) taxation for borrowing in good times. Since, as we saw in Chapter V, the substitution of borrowing for taxation tends to increase, and, by parity of reasoning, the converse substitution to decrease aggregate money outlay, these two processes together necessarily make aggregate money income steadier than it would otherwise be.

[1] Cf. *post*, p. 258.

CHAPTER X

SUBSIDIES TO EMPLOYERS IN RESPECT OF WAGES IN BAD TIMES

§ 1. SUBSIDIES paid to employers in bad times, whether in respect of output or in respect of wages, if financed out of taxes of the income tax type which do not directly differentiate against employment, and, *a fortiori*, if financed out of loans, must tend, like the policies described in the last three chapters, to steady aggregate money outlay and so the money wages bill. Granted, however, as is to be expected in practice, that no offsetting imposts are arranged in good times, it is plain, as was indicated in Chapter VI, that this type of policy must also make the average level of money outlay, and thus in general of the money wages bill, higher than it would otherwise be. Subsidies designed to stimulate particular sorts of output, such as those on beet sugar, milk, beef and so on, do not concern us here, nor do *ad hoc* subsidies introduced as a *deus ex machina* to preserve industrial peace, such as the coal subsidies of 1921 and 1926. A brief comment on the other kinds is offered in the present chapter.

§ 2. As a rule, subsidies payable to industrialists in bad times have been suggested, not all round, but in particular industries or groups of industries. Thus in 1923–4 the Unemployment Grants Committee made grants of government money to private enterprises willing to commence revenue-producing works of a public utility character, such as gas, water, electricity, tramways, docks, harbours and canals, which would otherwise have been postponed.[1] Similar grants were at one time advocated, *e.g.* by the late Earl Balfour, for certain export industries. Differential favours in the form of direct money payments by the government to particular industries are, however, likely to be resented very strongly by other industries not similarly favoured. When it is an export industry that receives a subsidy, there are the further objections: (1) that foreign purchasers receive, at least in part, what British taxpayers have provided; and (2) that foreign

[1] Cf. Morley, *Unemployment Relief in Great Britain*, p. 191.

governments are very likely to retort by imposing retaliatory import duties. Partly for these reasons the policy of subsidies in bad times to particular industries, *as a means of fostering employment*, has not hitherto played an important part in practice. Attention will be confined here to subsidies covering the main body of industry. Moreover, not subsidies in general, but only subsidies in respect of wages will be discussed.

§ 3. An ingenious plan falling under this head was suggested by the late Lord Melchett in a pamphlet published in 1925.[1] In substance the suggestion was that any four workmen who chose could hand over to the State their insurance benefit money (23s. a week each), that the State would then pay this money over to an employer on condition that he set to work at trade union rates, in addition to the existing staff, these four men together with one other. The root ideas here are, first, that the only money used for the bounty should be money which otherwise would have been paid in insurance benefits, so that no extra funds would have to be raised for it; secondly, that the bounty should be paid, not in respect of the whole of a firm's work, but only of additions made to its work. If we reckon the then standard wage at 40s., the plan, from the employer's point of view, amounted to an offer on the part of men out of employment to work at a wage of $21\frac{3}{5}$ shillings, the remainder of the standard wage being paid out of the insurance fund. There can be no doubt that an arrangement of this sort would lead to increased employment in bad times, if the bounty could be confined to the excess of staff that employers do engage over what they would have engaged apart from the bounty. Except, however, in conditions so bad that immediate improvement is despaired of, the staff that would be engaged apart from the bounty cannot be treated as equivalent to the staff that was engaged just before the bounty. When what is desired is a heroic remedy for a single emergency by means of a special *ad hoc* law, this difficulty need not be fatal. Plainly, however, any plan on Lord Melchett's lines could not be made a regular standard means of dealing with unemployment; for, if it were, individual employers, when they saw a depression coming, would be tempted to dismiss workpeople in the hope of re-engaging them immediately on terms

[1] *The Remedy for Unemployment.*

that would throw a large part of their wages bill upon the shoulders of other people.[1]

§ 4. Let us turn, therefore, to subsidies in respect of wages in bad times payable, not merely for additional wage-earners taken on in response to the subsidies, but for all wage-earners. In the way of such subsidies there is a serious practical difficulty. If all occupations were rigidly separated from one another, so that not only could nobody pass directly from one to another, but also the choice among them to be made by each new generation coming to industrial age was rigidly fixed, everything would be quite simple. Each occupation could be treated as a single problem. In real life, however, different occupations are not rigidly separated and account must, therefore, be taken of the possibility that subsidies may modify the proportions of work-people attached to different occupations. If exactly equal fiscal encouragement were given to all occupations, no effects of this kind would tend to come about. In practice, however, there might well be strong political pressure for larger subsidies in industries with low wage rates and large unemployment than in others. For example, at the time of the great 1931 slump the relatively distressed engineering and shipbuilding industries would certainly have demanded more favourable treatment than, say, the railway industry. Further, as the demand for the products of any industry fell off and distress became more pronounced, higher subsidies, not only absolutely, but relatively to those ruling in other industries, would be asked for. Such pleas might prove successful, and, if they did, too many people would be set to and kept at work in some industries and too few in others. Great strength and competence on the part of the government might be needed to prevent a policy of wage subsidies from acting in this way. The manipulations of the employers' contributions towards unemployment benefit suggested in the White Paper on Employment Policy (1944) and referred to in the last chapter, constitute, in effect, subsidies at equal rates to all employers in respect of wages in bad times, balanced by offsetting taxes in good times. This proposal, if adopted, would circumvent the difficulty referred to above.

[1] Cf. *Report of the Blanesburgh Committee on Unemployment Insurance*, 1927, pp. 79-80.

CHAPTER XI

AN ACADEMIC REFINEMENT

§ 1. The purpose of this Chapter is to work out the direct contemporaneous effects of wage subsidies, on the assumption that no reaction is set up in rates of wages, in a real economy where wages and everything else are paid in kind, where there is only one " kind " and where there is no foreign trade. It is postulated that the subsidies are financed by contemporaneous taxes on non-wage-earners, *e.g.* income tax, of a kind that do not differentiate significantly against employment. Our real economy may conveniently be represented by an agricultural community in which farmers own the land and employ labourers, all of whom are of equal skill. Let nothing else be produced except wheat and let wages be paid in wheat. Let the conditions be such that in bad times with wages at w_1 bushels of wheat per day, x labourers would find employment, but that when the rate is put at w_2 bushels (less than w_1), $(x+h)$ will be employed. In these conditions suppose that the public authority arranges to pay a subsidy s, equal to $(w_1 - w_2)$, to employers in respect of each labourer employed ; the funds for the subsidy being collected, as was postulated above, through an income tax on non-wage-earners, and the rates of wages paid to labourers not being altered.

§ 2. Employment being increased by h labourers, aggregate real income in wheat is increased by something between hw_1 and hw_2, which latter is equal to $h(w_1 - s)$. For an approximation we suppose the marginal productivity function of labour to be linear. The increase in aggregate real income is then $h(w_1 - \frac{1}{2}s)$, the real receipts of wage-earners being, of course, increased by hw_1. It follows that the real net receipts of non-wage-earners is decreased, through their subsidy payments, by $\frac{1}{2}hs$.

§ 3. It thus seems at first sight that the gain to employment and to real income is necessarily secured at the expense of a net injury to non-wage-earners. But this is not so. We have seen that the expression $\frac{1}{2}hs$ measures the decrease in the real receipts available to non-wage-earners after their payments to finance the subsidies have been made. Now, in modern communities men out of work are not allowed to starve; and, in one way or another, non-wage-earners have to provide at least a substantial part of what is required to maintain them. It follows that, when employment is increased, the amount that non-wage-earners have to contribute out of their income for this purpose is diminished. Hence under a subsidy plan of the type described above there is an offset to the loss of available income which non-wage-earners suffer. Write c for the rate of payment contributed by them in aid of every unemployed man. The net burden imposed on them on account of the subsidy plan, when allowance has been made for the reduction in what they have to pay in relief of the unemployed, is — as an approximation — $(\frac{1}{2}s - c)h$. This is positive if the rate of subsidy is more than twice the rate of contribution; but, if the rate of subsidy is less than this, it is negative, and the cost of the subsidy to non-wage-earners is more than made good by the reduction in their necessary out-goings.

CHAPTER XII

ONCE-FOR-ALL EXPANSIONS IN THE MONEY WAGES BILL

§ 1. In Chapter II it was argued that in any given set of physical and psychological conditions money wage rates in a country such as this tend to react to once-for-all increases in the average level of the wages bill in such a way as to keep the unemployment percentage sensibly constant. This conclusion, if pressed *à outrance,* would rule out once-for-all expansions altogether as effective remedies for unemployment. In the chapter cited it has already been indicated that it should not be pressed *à outrance.* In this chapter a little more will be said about that.

§ 2. First, as we saw in Chapter II, after a period of severe disturbance when employment has been greatly beaten down, the psychology of wage-earners may be so affected that an improvement in the wages bill, and so in employment, brought about by a once-for-all uplift in outlay, may be accepted as a gift of the gods and *not* stir up any wage reaction. Secondly, even if it does stir up such a reaction, since this is sure to be subject to a time-lag, for some while at all events the improvement in employment will be maintained. Transient it may be; but this does not imply that it is either unreal or unwelcome:

> I do but ask *good* things may pass
> I quarrel not with time.

These two considerations must not be regarded as mere minor palliatives and mitigations of austere doctrine. They may, both of them, well have substantial practical importance.

§ 3. There is, however, a more fundamental consideration. The tendency described in Chapter II is not something imposed upon us by an overmastering external fate. It results from the fact that in this country wage rates are settled over a wide field by negotiations conducted independently in separate industries without much regard for the economic situation of the country as a whole. But a tendency so originated is capable of being overcome, or at all events greatly softened, by deliberate policy on the part of Labour leaders.

The responsibility is theirs. In some measure better employment and higher money wage rates are alternatives to one another. There is also a third alternative : progressive monetary inflation. This will be considered in the chapter that follows. The practical issue is well set out by Sir William Beveridge in a short section of his book *Full Employment in a Free Society*.[1]

[1] *Loc. cit.* pp. 198-201.

CHAPTER XIII

TREND MOVEMENTS

§ 1. For the purpose of this chapter I shall call aggregate money income divided by the number of would-be wage-earners corrected money outlay. If then in any country corrected money outlay is subject to a downward trend, this, entailing as it is fairly sure to do, a downward trend in the money wages bill per would-be wage-earner, is bound to affect the percentage of unemployment adversely. It will do this whether or not there are fluctuations about the trend. The reason, as was made clear in Chapter II, is that, while money wage rates tend so to adjust themselves to the money wages bill per would-be wage-earner that, from a long-run standpoint, it is immaterial whether that bill is large or small, the process of adjustment is a lagging one. Conversely, if corrected money outlay is subject to an upward trend, the percentage of unemployment is bound to be affected favourably. Moreover, whether, apart from special action by public authorities, there is a downward trend or an upward trend or no trend at all, action by these authorities making for an upward trend must *affect* the percentage of unemployment favourably. There are, however, other associated consequences of action by public authorities devoted directly to promoting an upward trend which are different according as, apart from their action, the trend would have been on the one hand downward, on the other upward ; and it is, therefore, necessary to distinguish between these cases.

§ 2. Suppose first that, apart from intervention by public authorities, the trend would be downward. Then nobody suggests that action by public authorities making for an upward trend, *so long as it was not carried to the point of creating a net upward trend*, would entail any injurious consequences. The case for this type of public action is, therefore, especially strong when it can be shown that the independent trend, so to speak, is downward. During the inter-war period the belief that this was in fact so in Great Britain gave zest to much of the argument in favour of public action. It may, therefore, be of interest, though it is aside from the main argument, to inquire whether this belief was justified.

§ 3. The reasoning behind it was twofold. On the one hand the mechanism described in Chapter V, § 16, by which a downward trend might be generated, was appealed to. On the other hand, attention was directed to the fact that in the inter-war period the average percentage of unemployment was much higher than it had been before 1914, and the inference was drawn that, *therefore*, this mechanism must have been in action. Plainly this is slipshod reasoning. For there were, beyond doubt, other causes tending to make unemployment high. The dislocations that took place in consequence of the first world war and in connection with the great 1930 slump, coupled with the natural unwillingness of work-people to leave their homes for a doubtful chance elsewhere, led to the establishment of a hard core of unemployed persons in places and occupations where demand had decayed. Further, the greatly eased position of persons out of work and the relief to trade union funds, consequent upon the development of insurance against unemployment, substantially strengthened work-people in pressing for increases and resisting decreases in wage rates. This may well have made the level of unemployment, to which money wage rates tend to adjust themselves, considerably higher than it used to be. These are, of course, merely pleas for a verdict of not proven. The issue still remains open.

§ 4. To settle it, the obvious procedure is to study directly such statistical evidence as is available. Dr. Bowley estimates for the years 1924–38 the aggregate money income of the United Kingdom as follows[1]:

£ Million

1924	1925	1926	1927	1928
3900	3800	3750	3900	3925
1929	**1930**	**1931**	**1932**	**1933**
3925	3800	3450	3325	3550
1934	**1935**	**1936**	**1937**	**1938**
3700	3900	4150	4350	4350

[1] *Studies in National Income*, p. 81.

There is no evidence here of a downward trend in the uncorrected aggregate income or outlay — rather the contrary. But of corrected income that cannot be said. On the strength of statistics given by Dr. Bowley,[1] together with the census figures for the male population of working age in England and Wales,[2] we may reasonably reckon that, between 1924 and 1938, the number of would-be wage-earners underwent an upward trend at about the rate of 1½ per cent per annum. Using this figure and combining it with Bowley's income estimates, we obtain the following index numbers: (1) for corrected money income, (2) for money wages bill per would-be wage-earner:

Year	Corrected Money Income	Money Wages Bill per Would-be Wage-earner
1924	102	100
1925	95	97
1926	93	93
1927	97	96
1928	96	94
1929	94	92
1930	90	87
1931	80	78
1932	78	76
1933	82	76
1934	83	80
1935	86	82
1936	90	86
1937	94	91
1938	93	91

This table suggests that there was in the inter-war period a slight downward trend in corrected money income, coupled with a slightly stronger one in money income per would-be wage-earner.

[1] *Studies in National Income*, p. 111.

[2] The number of males between 15 and 64 years of age in England and Wales in the census years, absolutely and expressed as percentages, were:

	1891	1901	1911	1921	1931
Numbers (000 omitted) .	9509	11,131	12,536	13,309	14,568
Percentages . .	100	117	132	140	153

§ 5. Returning from this digression, let us suppose conditions to be such that, in the absence of intervention, the independent trend would have been upward. Then for public authorities to exert an upward pressure making for an upward trend entails that the trend of intervention will be *a fortiori* upward. In these conditions the danger of injurious consequences being brought about outside the field of employment itself has to be seriously weighed. So long as the total upward trend in corrected money income is moderate, there is, indeed, no danger. On the contrary, there is a prospect of considerable social advantage. With continuing technical progress, real income per head may be expected to expand and, therefore, unless there is an upward trend in corrected money income, money prices will fall. This entails that the owners of War Loan stock (and other fixed interest securities) obtain an uncovenanted benefit and — which is the obverse side of the same fact — that the Chancellor of the Exchequer's technical Budget problem, which we might reasonably expect to be eased in consequence of improved productivity, will not be eased. Moderate progression in corrected money income is thus to be welcomed. This is, however, by no means so with rapid and violent trends. These, after a point, generate distrust of the currency and, as it were, grow mountainous by feeding on themselves. These "galloping inflations" gravely disorganise a country's economic life and inflict on its social and, maybe, its political structure heavy damage. The story of the post-1918 inflation in Germany leaves no doubt about that.

§ 6. Evidently the danger point is more likely to be reached if public authorities take action to promote an upward trend where the independent trend is already upward than where it is downward. Thus for the guidance of immediate practice it is of interest to know what manner of independent trend there is likely to be in this country in the near future. The fact that in the inter-war period there was probably a slight downward trend gives no ground for believing that this trend will continue then. In view of the enormous destruction of buildings and means of communication which has taken place, there can hardly fail to be large opportunities for profitable private investment for many years to come, that will exert a strong upward pull on money income. An upward trend in corrected money income is therefore, for some time at all events, more likely than a downward one.[1]

§ 7. One further point remains to be considered. Suppose that we start with a situation in which there is no independent trend either upwards or downwards. Public authorities set out to reduce the unemployment percentage (as averaged over good and bad times) in given measure by lifting corrected money income, and so the money wages bill per head. For the moment — apart from difficulties connected with labour mobility — they will achieve their purpose. If they can persuade or compel wage-earners to allow the old rates of wages to stand, they will achieve it permanently. But if, as in such a country as England is far more likely, money rates are pushed up in response in the manner described in earlier chapters, the unemployment percentage will worsen again, unless corrected money income is again pushed up. Thus, if the authorities continue to strive after the goal they originally set themselves, they must so act as to push aggregate money income always higher and higher. There is reason to believe that, apart from frictional unemployment associated with imperfect mobility, something not far from full employment could be secured and maintained, provided that public authorities were prepared, not merely to make corrected money income larger than it would have been without them, but to make it go on growing ever larger and larger in a geometrical progression. But with this type of policy a scale of inflation beyond safe limits may easily be induced. The only way in which that risk can be obviated is by restraint on the part of wage-earners in pressing for increases in money wage rates. Granted this, a "full employment policy" need not entail monetary inflation. But to secure at the same time a high average level of employment, rapidly expanding money wage rates (for work of given productivity) and a reasonable stability in the value of money passes the wit of man.

[1] During the war the death of large numbers of men of working age and the effective raising of the school-leaving age to be expected in the near future is bound to make the number of persons of working age, and so of would-be wage-earners, smaller in, say, 1948 than it would have been had the pre-war rate of increase continued; so that corrected money income will be larger relatively to uncorrected money income than it would have been. But this does not imply that from 1948 onwards a given scale of upward trend in uncorrected money income will carry with it a more rapid upward trend in corrected money income than it would have done in pre-war conditions. The conclusion of the text cannot be fortified in that way.

INDEX

THE END

PRINTED BY R. & R. CLARK, LTD., EDINBURGH